WISE Selling

The Art of Creating Remarkable Experiences - Every Customer Every Time

Matthew Hudson, PhD

Order other books by Matthew on Amazon.com

Culturrific!
Creating an experiential culture in your organization.
$19.95

The Retail Sales Bible
The G.R.E.A.T. Selling System for Retail. Written for retail sales professionals.
$19.95

Advisor Selling
The art and science of becoming a trusted sales advisor. Written for B2B sales reps.
$19.95

Signs Sell
Harnessing the Power of Your Interior Advertising
$25.95

Herd Mentality: Leadership Lessons from Rescue Horses
Proceeds Benefit the Layla Rose Ranch Equine Rescue
$20.00

GREAT Sales Coaching
A Framework for Coaching Retail Sales Professionals
$20.00

WISE Selling The Art of Creating Remarkable Experiences - Every Customer Every Time

Copyright © 2026 Matthew Hudson
All rights reserved. No part of this publication may be reproduced, distributed or transmitted in any form or by any means, including photocopying, recording, or other electronic or mechanical methods, without the prior written permission of the publisher, except in the case of brief quotations embodied in critical review and certain other noncommercial uses permitted by copyright law.

Request for permission should be sent to:
matt@hudsonhead.com
Annetta, Texas 76008

Printed in the United States of America
ISBN 978-0-9719731-9-0
Library of Congress Control Number 2026901433

Content Table

Introduction: The Evolution of Retail Selling

Chapter 1: The WISE Philosophy – Why Traditional Sales Methods Fail

Chapter 2: Welcome – The First 60 Seconds That Change Everything

Chapter 3: Interview – The Lost Art of Listening

Chapter 4: Solution – Becoming the Expert They Need

Chapter 5: Experience – Creating Moments That Matter

Chapter 6: The Four Sales Before the Sale

Chapter 7: Know Your Customer – The Three Tribes of Retail

Chapter 8: The Psychology of Trust – Fear, Compassion, and Confidence

Chapter 9: Benefit Statements – Speaking the Language of Value

Chapter 10: The Multiplication Effect – Crafting Complete Solutions

Chapter 11: Handling Objections – When "No" Means "Not Yet"

Chapter 12: Experience – Creating Moments That Are Remarkable

Chapter 13: Building Your Sales Culture – The Foundation for Remarkable Experiences

Your Journey Begins

Acknowledgements/ Sources and Further Development

Introduction: The Evolution of Retail Selling

The retail landscape has changed more in the last fifteen years than in the previous century combined. Walk into any store today, and you'll encounter a fundamentally different Customer than existed even a decade ago. They arrive armed with smartphone research, price comparisons from 17 competitors, YouTube tutorials, and a healthy skepticism developed from years of disappointing shopping experiences.

Yet despite this seismic shift in Customer behavior, most retail sales training remains stuck in 1985. I should know, I was selling at a RadioShack in 1985. The old "May I help you?" greeting that elicits the reflexive "Just looking" response. The feature-dump presentation where salespeople rattle off specifications that mean nothing to the Customer. The awkward closing techniques that make everyone uncomfortable. The transactional mentality that treats each Customer as a one-time opportunity rather than a potential lifetime relationship.

This book represents a different approach entirely. And in fact, a different approach to the teaching process as well. But more on that in a minute.

The WISE Selling system emerged from something remarkable – actual field research. Okay, maybe not so remarkable, but this was not the kind of research conducted in conference rooms by consultants who haven't worked a retail floor in twenty years. It was a genuine, ground-level observation of what works when retail sales professionals interact with real Customers in real stores. Over five years, researchers visited hundreds of retail locations across North America, interviewed top-performing retail sales professionals, surveyed thousands of Customers, and identified the patterns that separate the exceptional from the ordinary.

What they (and by they, I mean me) discovered challenges much of conventional sales wisdom. The best sales professionals weren't using clever closing techniques or memorizing feature lists. They weren't employing high-pressure tactics or treating every Customer the same. Instead, they had developed an intuitive understanding of something deeper: that selling is fundamentally about creating an **experience that makes people feel understood, valued, and confident in their decisions.**

This insight crystallized into the WISE framework: Welcome, Interview, Solution, Experience. Four deceptively simple phases that represent a complete reimagining of the retail sales process. But don't mistake simple for easy. Mastering WISE Selling requires understanding human psychology, developing genuine empathy, building extensive product knowledge, and practicing specific skills until they become second nature.

The acronym itself tells a story. To be WISE is to possess wisdom – that combination of knowledge, experience, and judgment that Customers desperately seek but rarely find. My favorite definition of wisdom is "the prudent use of knowledge." Not sure where I heard that - I didn't create it - but it sums it all up very well.

In an age where product information is abundant, but insight is scarce, where options are overwhelming, but guidance is absent, the WISE sales professional becomes an invaluable resource.

Consider the typical Customer journey today. Let's call her Cat. She needs a new piece of fitness equipment, appliance, or consumer electronics – the specific product doesn't matter. Cat has already spent three hours online reading reviews, watching comparison videos, and checking prices. She's visited two other stores where salespeople either ignored her or overwhelmed her with technical specifications she didn't understand. She's frustrated, confused, and increasingly tempted to just order something online and hope for the best.

Then Cat walks into your store. The next fifteen minutes will determine whether she becomes a loyal Customer who refers her friends, a one-time buyer who never returns, or another person who leaves empty-handed to continue their exhausting search elsewhere.

What makes the difference? Not your product selection, though that matters. Not your pricing, though that matters too. The difference is whether Cat experiences the WISE Selling approach – a sales interaction that feels less like being sold and more like being guided. An experience that reduces her anxiety rather than amplifying it. A conversation that makes her feel smart about her decision rather than manipulated into a purchase.

This is what WISE Selling delivers. Not through manipulation or coercion, but through an approach that aligns your interests with the Customer's interests. When executed properly, WISE Selling creates what business researchers call a "high-trust transaction" – where both parties feel they've received excellent value and look forward to future interactions.

The research underlying WISE Selling revealed several counterintuitive findings that challenge conventional retail wisdom:

The greeting matters far more than anyone realized. Those first 60 seconds don't just set the tone – they largely determine the outcome. Customers make unconscious decisions about whether to engage or disengage almost immediately, and most traditional greetings trigger disengagement.

Customers don't know what they want. And that's okay. Despite arriving with research and opinions, most Customers haven't accurately diagnosed their own needs. The Interview Phase of WISE Selling exists precisely to help them discover what they require, which is often different from what they thought they wanted.

Features don't sell; benefits do. But only specific benefits. Not all benefits are created equal. Customers only care about benefits that address their particular situation, which is why the Interview Phase must precede the Solution Phase.

There are actually four sales before the merchandise sale. Customers must buy you, your store, the experience, and only then the product. Most salespeople skip straight to product, wondering why Customers remain reluctant.

The transaction isn't the end; it's the beginning. The most valuable Customers aren't the big spenders on first visits – they're the repeat buyers who refer others. But creating these relationships requires specific techniques that too many retailers ignore.

This book will teach you the complete WISE Selling system, from the philosophy underlying each Phase to the specific language and techniques that make it work. You'll learn why certain approaches succeed while others fail, how to adapt WISE Selling to different Customer types and product categories, and how to practice and refine your skills.

More importantly, you'll understand that WISE Selling represents more than sales techniques – it's a philosophy about what retail should be. In an era of declining foot traffic and e-commerce competition, physical stores survive only by offering something online shopping cannot: genuine human connection, expert guidance, and memorable experiences. WISE Selling provides the framework for delivering exactly that.

Some sales training books promise secret shortcuts or magic words that will transform your results overnight. This isn't one of them. (Okay, maybe I do use the term "magic words" once in this book.) WISE Selling requires practice, reflection, and continuous improvement. It asks you to genuinely care about your Customers' success, not just your sales numbers. It demands that you develop real expertise, not just memorize scripts.

But here's what WISE Selling doesn't require: an extroverted personality, natural charisma, or the ability to "sell ice to Eskimos." Some of the best WISE practitioners are introverts who listen more than they talk. The system works because it's based on authentic human interaction, not performance or persuasion. In other words, use the WISE framework, but be authentically you.

Throughout this book, you'll encounter real examples from actual retail environments – mostly from various specialty retail categories. These examples are all from retailers I have worked with in my career.

While the specific products differ, the principles remain constant. WISE Selling works across categories because it's fundamentally about understanding and serving people, not about product-specific tactics.

Each chapter builds on the previous ones, so I recommend reading sequentially the first time through. Later, you can return to specific chapters as reference material when you want to refine particular aspects of your approach. At the end of each chapter, you'll find practice exercises designed to help you internalize and apply the concepts. Don't skip these – the difference between understanding WISE Selling intellectually and executing it effectively is practice.

In this book, I took a different approach from my normal tact. Typically, I would start at the beginning of the sale and move step-by-step through it with the teaching. This time, I am going to cover the four Phases of WISE Selling in the beginning chapters and then do some deep dive conversations on specific techniques in the WISE Selling process. I'm taking the approach for two reasons. First, it will give you more repetition with the information. This is to practice the Principle of Exercise. Second, My hope is that you work on the basics of the WISE Selling process first and then as time progresses, you go deeper and get more skilled. In fact, I will give you a sample timeline "agenda" to follow for your development.

One final note before we begin: WISE Selling asks you to view your role differently than traditional sales training does. You're not a salesperson trying to move merchandise. You're a professional consultant helping Customers solve problems and achieve goals. As Donald Miller would say, "You are not the hero. You are the guide." This reframing isn't semantic – it changes everything about how you approach your work and how Customers perceive you.

The retail professionals who embrace this identity shift consistently outperform their peers, experience less job stress, and report higher satisfaction with their careers. They also earn more, both because their sales increase and because they build valuable relationships that generate referrals and repeat business for years.

Ready to become WISE? Let's begin with understanding why traditional sales methods fail – and what makes WISE Selling different.

Chapter 1

The WISE Philosophy – Why Traditional Sales Methods Fail

American retail is experiencing an identity crisis. Despite technological advances, sophisticated inventory systems, and unprecedented access to Customer data, the actual human interactions that drive sales remain stuck in outdated paradigms from the 1970s and 1980s.I should know, my first retail sales role was at a RadioShack in 1984.

Traditional retail sales training has created an entire industry of counterproductive habits, ineffective techniques, and Customer-repelling behaviors. Walk into most retail establishments, and you'll witness the same tired script:

- The greeting that triggers automatic rejection
- The feature dump that overwhelms and confuses
- The pressure close that activates Customer defenses
- The transactional mindset that burns bridges

These methods persist not because they work, but because they're familiar. They're what everyone learns, what everyone teaches, what everyone expects. They've become the standard despite their spectacular failure rate.

Consider these statistics:

68% of Customers leave without buying specifically because they felt pressured (Meyer, 2019)

72% of salespeople admit they don't enjoy using traditional closing techniques (National Retail Federation, 2021)

Only **18%** of Customers trust salespeople—ranking them below politicians in trustworthiness (Edelman Trust Barometer, 2023)

Something is clearly broken. But what?

My "StoryBrand" Revelation

Donald Miller's StoryBrand framework revealed something for me that transforms how I think about sales: Every Customer is the hero of their own story, and they're looking for a guide to help them succeed (Miller, 2017).

Think about every great story you've ever experienced:

Luke Skywalker needed Obi-Wan Kenobi

Katniss Everdeen needed Haymitch Abernathy

Frodo Baggins needed Gandalf

Harry Potter needed Dumbledore

The hero doesn't succeed alone. They need a guide—someone who has walked the path before, who understands the challenges, who possesses wisdom and tools the hero lacks. The guide doesn't take over the hero's journey; they empower the hero to succeed on their own terms.

This is your role in every sales interaction. You're not the hero of the story; your Customer is. Your job isn't to be interesting or impressive or dominant. Your job is to be the guide the hero needs to overcome their challenges and achieve their goals.

When you position yourself as the guide rather than the hero, everything changes:

Instead of: "Look how great our product is!" (hero trying to impress)

You say: "I understand your challenge. Here's how this solves it." (guide offering wisdom)

Instead of: "Let me tell you about all our features." (hero dominating conversation)

You say: "Tell me about what you're trying to accomplish." (guide seeking understanding)

Instead of: "You should buy this today." (hero pushing their agenda)

You say: "Here's a clear path forward that addresses your needs." (guide providing direction)

See the difference? The guide doesn't need to impress. The guide needs to understand, empathize, and provide direction. This is the essence of WISE Selling.

I have always embraced this ideology throughout my retail career. You can find this idea sprinkled throughout my books. But let's be honest - Donald's way of framing this discussion is the best.

The 5 Traditional Retail Traps

Picture this: You walk into a store, and within seconds, a salesperson approaches with a forced smile and asks, "Can I help you find something today?"

Your automatic response? "No thanks, just looking."

This exchange happens millions of times daily in retail stores worldwide. It's so common that both parties have their lines memorized. The salesperson doesn't expect a different response. The Customer doesn't even think before answering. It's retail theater – a performance both actors have rehearsed so often they could do it in their sleep.

But here's the tragedy: that exchange just killed the sale before it started.

Our retail selling behaviors have created bad habits and ineffective techniques. To understand why WISE Selling works, we must first understand why traditional methods fail – and fail spectacularly in today's retail environment.

1. The "Can I Help You?" Disaster

Let's start with that greeting. "Can I help you?" or its cousin "May I help you?" seems like a polite, Customer-focused opening. It offers assistance. It's friendly. So why does it fail so consistently?

The problem lies in how our brains process language and make decisions. "Can I help you?" is what linguists call a "closed question" – one that can be answered with a simple yes or no. But it's worse than that. It's a closed question where the default answer has already been culturally established as "no thanks, just looking."

When Customers enter a store, they're often in what psychologists call a "high cognitive load" state. They're processing visual information, spatial awareness, potential threats (yes, unfamiliar environments trigger primitive threat-detection systems), and their own agenda. In this state, the brain defaults to autopilot responses for common situations.

"Can I help you?" triggers the autopilot response: "Just looking." The Customer says this even when they're *not* just looking, even when they came in specifically to buy something, even when they would genuinely benefit from assistance. The words come out before conscious thought engages. It has been this way for decades. And it's not getting any better.

Now you're stuck. The Customer has declared they don't need help. Persisting makes you pushy. Leaving them alone means you've failed to engage. You've created a lose-lose situation with your opening line.

Traditional sales training recognizes this problem but offers the wrong solution: "Different words that mean the same thing." Sales managers train their teams to say, "What brings you in today?" or "Are you looking for anything particular?" These alternatives, while better, fail for the same reason. They're still closed questions that activate the same autopilot response, just with slightly different wording. And please don't talk about the weather either as an opener. Sorry, was that too close to home?

The WISE Welcome Phase solves this entirely differently, but we'll get to that in Chapter 2. For now, understand that this seemingly small failure cascades into everything that follows. When the opening interaction feels scripted and triggers defensive responses, the entire relationship starts on the wrong foot.

2. The Feature Dump

Assume a Customer survives the greeting and indicates interest in a product. Traditional sales training now instructs the salesperson to present the product. And here's where the second major failure occurs: the feature dump.

A feature dump happens when a salesperson rattles off product specifications, technical details, and features without understanding what the Customer actually cares about. It sounds like this:

"This treadmill has a 3.5 horsepower motor, a 22-inch running surface, 15 incline levels, 12 preset programs, Bluetooth connectivity, heart rate monitoring, and a 350-pound weight capacity. It's our best seller."

The Customer's eyes glaze over. They nod politely. They say they'll "think about it" and leave. What happened?

The salesperson just played "tapper" in one of psychology's most revealing experiments. In 1990, Stanford psychologist Elizabeth Newton created a simple game. One person (the tapper) thinks of a well-known song and taps out the rhythm on a table. Another person (the listener) tries to guess the song.

Before each attempt, tappers predicted that listeners would guess correctly about 50% of the time. The actual success rate? A dismal 2.5%.

Why? When tappers tap, they hear the song in their heads – the melody, harmony, lyrics, everything. To them, the taps clearly represent the song. But listeners hear only disconnected taps. They have no melody, no context, just... tap tap tap.

Tappers are shocked when listeners can't identify songs that seem obvious. "How could you not get 'Happy Birthday'? It was so clear!" I have used this in many sales seminars, and I am always amazed at how hard it truly is. The participants always think they can beat the research, but they never do.

The "tapper game" is exactly what happens during a feature dump. The salesperson hears the song – they understand what "3.5 horsepower motor" means for workout quality, why "22-inch running surface" matters for comfort, and how "Bluetooth connectivity" enables workout tracking. Each feature connects to a benefit in *their* mind.

The Customer, on the other hand, hears taps. Random specifications without meaning or context. They don't know if 3.5 horsepower is good or bad. They can't visualize a 22-inch running surface. Bluetooth connectivity? They're not sure why that matters for a treadmill.

Traditional sales training creates tappers. Salespeople learn features and specifications, then recite them to Customers, baffled when this information fails to excite or persuade. The curse of knowledge – once you know something, it's nearly impossible to remember what it was like not to know it – turns product expertise into a sales liability.

3. The Pressure Close

Traditional sales training climaxes with "closing techniques" – a collection of psychological pressure tactics designed to force a buying decision. These have names that sound like wrestling moves: the Alternative Close, the Puppy Dog Close, the Ben Franklin Close.

The Alternative Close presents two buying options as if the purchase decision is already made: "Would you like this in blue or red?" The Assumptive Close acts as if the sale has already happened: "I'll get this written up for you." The Puppy Dog Close ("Try it for a week. I'm confident you'll love it") relies on loss aversion psychology.

These techniques share a common feature: They're manipulative. And Customers know it.

Modern consumers have been exposed to sales tactics since childhood. They've read articles about manipulation techniques. They've been warned about pushy salespeople. Heck, they might have just seen the latest TikTok trend on retail salespeople! When someone uses a closing technique, Customers recognize it instantly – and their defenses go up.

Psychological reactance is the term for what happens when people feel their freedom is being threatened. When Customers sense they're being pushed toward a decision, they push back, even if they were already inclined to buy. The pressure close creates resistance where none previously existed.

But traditional sales training doubles down on these techniques because, occasionally, they work. Some Customers do respond to pressure. Some people have difficulty saying no. Some are more susceptible to manipulation.

So traditional training teaches salespeople to use tactics that alienate most Customers while successfully manipulating a few. This is optimizing for the wrong outcome. You're selecting for Customers with poor boundaries while repelling Customers who know their own minds – exactly backward from building a sustainable business.

SIDEBAR: Every sales training methodology ever created works - some of the time. That's why the techniques I just dumped on are in existence - they do work. As you begin the process of introducing your people to WISE Selling, you are working with people who - in their minds - have succeeded. Customer came in looking for a shirt - Customer left with a shirt. They succeeded. WISE Selling is trying to take the success rate to a level where it can truly be called success.

4. The No Close

The opposite of the Pressure Close is the No Close. A sales professional knows they have to ask the Customer to buy at some point. The WISE sales professional knows that comes only after guiding the Customer to a Solution that best fits his or her needs.

I have seen literally thousands of sales presentations end in "silence". The salesperson has completed their feature dump and now just stands there and waits. They wait for the Customer to do something - either buy or leave. Either way, the salesperson gets to move on with his or her life.

WISE Selling uses a logical conclusion to the sale with the phrase, "Since We've agreed." Now to some this still may feel like pressure, but if you have followed all of the WISE Selling principles to this point in the sale, then it is nothing more than you continuing to guide the hero to the conclusion of their story.

The point here is that even online shopping sites do a better job than a lot of retail salespeople in the store. But I often feel like the interaction in the store is no different. The website doesn't say, "please click buy to purchase." It just waits with the cursor blinking endlessly on the monitor waiting for the Customer to make their next move. And that is exactly what I see happening in retail stores today.

The truth is, most Customers need you to ask them to buy. It helps them feel better - not all the pressure is on themselves. In some cases, it is a significant purchase and therefore a significant decision. They want and need the help of "Since We've agreed."

5. The Transaction Mindset

Perhaps the deepest failure of traditional sales training is its fundamental philosophy: viewing each Customer interaction as a discrete transaction to be maximized.

This mindset manifests in several ways:

Focusing on the sale, not the relationship. Traditional training measures success by immediate revenue. Did you close the sale? How much did they spend? This creates incentives to maximize short-term revenue even at the cost of long-term Customer value. Not very "guide-like".

Treating all Customers identically. When each interaction is a transaction, Customer differences don't matter much. You have a script, you follow it, you try to close. Whether the Customer is a first-timer or a regular, knowledgeable or confused, ready to buy or early in research – the approach remains the same.

Stopping after the purchase. Traditional training rarely addresses what happens after checkout. The sale is complete, time to move on to the next Customer. Building relationships, ensuring satisfaction, earning referrals – these happen accidentally, if at all.

Competing with coworkers. When sales are transactions, other salespeople are competitors for those transactions. Traditional retail culture often discourages collaboration and knowledge-sharing. Why help a coworker get better at your expense? It's what I like to call the "did anyone help you today with this purchase?" You know the questions you get asked when checking out?

This transactional mindset made some sense in previous retail eras. When Customers had limited options and information, when stores competed primarily on product selection and price, when loyalty was assumed rather than earned – treating each interaction as a one-time event was less damaging.

Those days are gone. The modern Customer has infinite options, abundant information, and zero assumed loyalty. The only sustainable competitive advantage is the relationship – the experience that makes Customers *want* to return, *choose* to pay slightly more, *and actively* refer others.

Traditional sales training optimizes for transactions while the market now rewards relationships. It's like training for a different sport than the one you're actually playing.

Why These Methods Persist

If traditional sales methods work so poorly, why do they persist? While we just talked about this a page or two ago, let's go deeper. Several factors contribute to their surprising durability:

They sometimes work. Bad techniques occasionally succeed, which provides just enough reinforcement to keep people using them. It's like a slot machine – variable rewards create the strongest behavioral conditioning.

They're easy to teach. Scripts and techniques can be taught quickly to new employees. Complex skills like reading Customers, adaptive communication, and genuine rapport-building take more time and effort to develop.

They feel like "selling." Traditional techniques feel professional and business-like. They give new salespeople something to do, a process to follow. The discomfort of not knowing what to say feels worse than following a mediocre script.

Management can measure them. Traditional techniques are observable: Did the employee greet within 30 seconds? Did they present three features? Did they attempt a close? Relationship-building is harder to quantify and therefore harder for management to monitor.

Inertia is powerful. Sales managers teach what they were taught. Training companies recycle old materials. No one wants to be the first to try something radically different when the current approach is "good enough."

But "good enough" isn't good enough anymore. Retail is changing too rapidly, Customer expectations are evolving too quickly, and competition is too fierce. The stores that thrive in the coming decade will be those that abandon traditional methods and embrace approaches like WISE Selling.

The 50/50 Principle

One of the most powerful research projects I ever did was the simplest. I would stand outside of a retail store and ask people three questions - not a survey of a bunch of questions - just three. The first one was:

How likely are you to return to this store if they did NOT meet your expectations?

And I found that the likelihood was about 12%. Now I have always thought that this was a little high, after all, I would not be that nice myself. But I have to realize that we are standing right outside the store (sometimes I do this survey standing inside the store), so I think people are trying to be polite and not be too harsh on the store.

Then I would ask them:

How likely are you to return to this store if they DID meet your expectations?

And the likelihood shot up to 49%. That's a big jump for sure

Finally, I would ask:

How likely are you to return to this store if they EXCEED your expectations?

And the response goes to 98%! A 98% chance you will see me again. Isn't that what every retailer is looking for? Of course it is.

But here is the real "eye-opener" of this survey - if your **MEET** expectations there is only a **50/50** chance you will see them again!

Wait, what? That's right 50/50. Now here is what keeps me up at night as a retailer - salespeople who MEET expectations think they are doing a great job! But can you run a business with a 50% chance of success?

You have to EXCEED Customer expectations every time. And that means a fundamental shift in the approach of measuring success in your retail store and that is what WISE Selling is based on. Here it is:

Success is not based on selling something to the Customer.

Success is based on HOW you sell something to the Customer.

What do I mean by that? Your salespeople feel like they did a good job because the Customer came in for new shoes and they left with new shoes. But the Customer is telling us that if you measure success this way - meaning sales metrics only - then there is only a 50/50 chance you will see them again. I don't know about you, but that scares me.

WISE Selling focuses on the HOW you sell. It focuses on you being the guide and not the hero. It took me a long time to realize that. I have an ego like every other man, and I loved being the hero. But heroes have a 50/50 chance. And that does not sound very heroic to me.

The WISE Alternative

WISE Selling, in its efforts to EXCEED Customer expectations every time, rejects every aspect of the traditional approach:

Instead of scripted greetings, WISE teaches genuine welcome that makes Customers feel valued without triggering defensive responses.

Instead of feature dumps, WISE builds understanding through careful interviewing, then presents benefits that specifically address each Customer's unique situation.

Instead of pressure closes, WISE develops trust and removes barriers until buying feels like the natural, obvious choice - the Customer's choice.

Instead of transaction focus, WISE builds relationships that generate Customer lifetime value through repeat business and referrals.

Instead of one-size-fits-all, WISE adapts to different Customer types, needs, and situations.

The philosophy underlying WISE Selling can be summarized in three principles:

1. Trust Over Tactics

Traditional sales training teaches tactics – what to say, when to say it, how to overcome objections. WISE Selling teaches trust-building. When Customers trust you, tactics become unnecessary. They believe your recommendations, accept your guidance, and give you the benefit of the doubt when questions arise.

Trust develops when the combination of two things come together: confidence and compassion. Customers must believe you know what you're talking about (confidence) and that you care about their success (compassion). Traditional training over-emphasizes product knowledge while neglecting the relationship skills that demonstrate genuine care. I have dedicated a whole chapter to this topic - Chapter 8.

WISE Selling balances both. The Interview Phase builds compassion – Customers feel heard, understood, valued. The Solution Phase demonstrates confidence – you provide expert guidance they couldn't find elsewhere. Together, these create a high-trust environment where sales happen naturally.

2. Discovery Over Presentation

Traditional selling is presentation-focused: Here's our product, here are its features, here's why you should buy it. The salesperson talks, the Customer listens (or pretends to listen).

WISE Selling is discovery-focused: What's your situation? What have you tried? What matters most to you? The Customer talks, the salesperson listens – really listens, not just waiting for their turn to present.

This inversion makes all the difference. When Customers talk about their needs, challenges, and goals, four things happen:

First, they feel valued. Everyone wants to be heard. In a world of talking heads and automated responses, someone genuinely interested in understanding you is refreshingly rare.

Second, they clarify their own thinking. Often Customers don't fully understand their own needs until they articulate them. The Interview phase helps them think through their situation, sometimes discovering considerations they hadn't recognized.

Third, you gather the information necessary to provide genuinely helpful recommendations. You can't solve a problem you don't understand. Discovery before presentation ensures your solutions actually address real needs.

Fourth, you have moved from salesperson to trusted guide. No one wants to be sold something; they want to buy. You have never heard anyone say, "look what that guy sold me!" Rather, you hear "look what *I* bought!"

3. Experience Over Transaction

Traditional sales training treats the sale as the endpoint. Once the Customer buys - the mission is accomplished. WISE Selling recognizes that the purchase is merely one moment in an ongoing relationship.

The Experience phase – the E in WISE – extends beyond the transaction. How does the Customer feel leaving your store? What happens when they use the product? Do they think of you as a resource for future needs? Will they tell friends about their experience?

These questions matter more than the immediate sale because they determine Customer lifetime value. A Customer who buys once but never returns generates far less value than one who becomes a regular and refers others.

Traditional training optimizes for transaction size. WISE Selling optimizes for relationship quality. In the long run, the latter approach generates far more revenue – and it's also more enjoyable for everyone involved.

The Research Foundation of WISE Selling

WISE Selling didn't emerge from theory or consultant speculation. It emerged from systematic research into what actually works in real retail environments.

Researchers, myself included, spent years studying high-performing salespeople across multiple retail categories. We observed thousands of Customer interactions, interviewed top performers, surveyed Customers, and analyzed sales data. Patterns emerged:

The best performers spent more time on discovery (Interview) than presentation. They asked more questions, listened more carefully, and customized their approach to each Customer.

The best performers created emotional connection. Customers described feeling "understood," "valued," and "comfortable" – words that never appeared in descriptions of average sales interactions.

The best performers thought long-term. They sacrificed immediate sales that didn't serve the Customer's interest, knowing this built trust that would pay dividends later.

The best performers treated selling as a helping profession. They viewed themselves as consultants, advisors, and problem-solvers rather than salespeople. A guide.

These patterns crystallized into the WISE framework. The phases weren't invented; they were discovered by observing what naturally occurred in the most successful sales interactions.

This matters because WISE Selling isn't asking you to behave unnaturally or adopt a fake persona. It's teaching you to do deliberately and systematically what the best salespeople already do instinctively. You're not learning tricks; you're developing genuine skills.

SIDEBAR: We also spent time studying the bottom 10% of retail salespeople. Again, looking for patterns. And what we found was that in almost every case, the habits and techniques that made the top 10% successful were the same habits and techniques the bottom 10% lacked.

Making the Transition

If you've been trained in traditional methods, transitioning to WISE Selling requires unlearning as much as learning. Several mindset shifts are necessary:

From script to adaptation. Traditional training provides scripts: say this, then say that. WISE Selling provides principles and frameworks, then asks you to adapt them to each unique situation. This is initially more difficult but ultimately more effective and more interesting.

From product to person. Traditional training focuses on product knowledge. WISE Selling focuses equally on understanding people – their psychology, their needs, their decision-making processes. Product knowledge matters, but people skills matter more.

From technique to authenticity. Traditional training teaches techniques that feel artificial because they *are* artificial – they're designed to manipulate behavior. WISE Selling teaches authentic interaction. When you genuinely try to understand and help someone, you don't need manipulation.

From performance to presence. Traditional salespeople are performing – playing a role, using a script, wearing a professional mask. WISE practitioners are present – genuinely engaged, listening actively, responding authentically to each moment.

These shifts feel uncomfortable at first. Scripts provide security; adaptation requires confidence. Techniques give you something to do; authenticity requires trusting yourself. Performance is familiar; presence is vulnerable.

But on the other side of this discomfort lies something remarkable: work that feels meaningful rather than manipulative, Customers who become relationships rather than transactions, and results that compound over time rather than requiring constant hustling.

What Success Looks Like

So, after having read all that, you are probably wondering - when WISE Selling is working, what does it look like? Several indicators:

Customers talk more than you do. In traditional sales interactions, the salesperson dominates conversation. In WISE interactions, Customers talk extensively during the Interview Phase because you're asking good questions and listening carefully.

Buying feels natural, not pressured. When you reach the Solution Phase, recommendations flow logically from what Customers told you. They recognize their own needs in your suggestions. In fact, you get to use the most powerful phrase in selling - "based on what you've told me!" Buying doesn't feel like being sold; it feels like being helped.

Objections are rare. Traditional selling generates frequent objections because solutions don't align with needs. WISE Selling prevents most objections through thorough interviewing and customized solutions.

Customers return. The ultimate measure: Do Customers come back? Do they ask for you specifically? Do they refer their friends? These behaviors indicate you've created a memorable experience, not just completed a transaction.

You enjoy your work. Perhaps surprisingly, WISE practitioners report higher job satisfaction than traditional salespeople. Helping people is more fulfilling than manipulating them. Building relationships is more interesting than executing transactions. And we all want a job where we can feel good about ourselves when we go home at night.

The Path Forward

We're living through the most dramatic transformation in retail since the invention of the shopping mall. E-commerce has eliminated the need for physical retail in many categories. If Customers just want products, they can click a button and have items delivered tomorrow.

Physical retail survives and thrives only when it provides something online shopping cannot: genuine human connection, personalized guidance, and expert consultation. In other words, physical retail succeeds when it provides guides for Customer heroes.

Amazon can deliver products. Amazon cannot deliver wisdom, understanding, empathy, or customized problem-solving from an expert who cares about your specific situation. That's your advantage. That's your purpose. That's your opportunity.

But only if you learn to be the guide Customers need.

Go back to our 50/50 Principle that says if you **MEET** Customer expectations there is only a 50/50 chance you will see them again. Let's be honest, can we have our expectations met online? Can Amazon meet our expectations? Of course they can. Can they **EXCEED** them, though - that is much harder to do. WISE Selling can do that. Every Customer. Every Time.

The remaining chapters will teach you each phase of WISE Selling in detail. You'll learn specific techniques, language patterns, and practice methods. You'll understand the psychology behind each phase and how to adapt the approach to different Customers and situations.

But before diving into techniques, internalize this chapter's core message: **Traditional sales methods fail not because salespeople execute them poorly, but because they're fundamentally misaligned with how humans make decisions, build trust, and form relationships.**

WISE Selling succeeds because it's aligned with human psychology, social dynamics, and the realities of modern retail. It respects Customers' intelligence, values their time, and genuinely serves their interests. In doing so, it also serves your interests – but indirectly, as a consequence of creating value rather than extracting it.

This is the WISE philosophy. Everything that follows builds on this foundation. Get this part right – understand why traditional methods fail and why WISE Selling succeeds at a deep level – and the specific techniques will make sense. Skip this foundation, and the techniques become just another collection of things to try, no different from what you've tried before.

Customers are the heroes of their own stories, and they're looking for guides. When you position yourself as that guide with empathy, authority, and authentic desire to help then remarkable things happen. Sales increase, relationships deepen, work becomes meaningful, and Customers achieve their goals.

Ready to build properly? Let's start with the first impression – the Welcome phase that determines everything that follows.

Chapter 2

Welcome – The First 60 Seconds That Change Everything

You have precisely 60 seconds.

That's how long research shows you have to make a first impression that determines whether a Customer will engage with you or spend the rest of their visit avoiding eye contact. Sixty seconds to signal whether you're helpful or pushy, knowledgeable or clueless, genuine or performing or if you even care they are in the store. Sixty seconds to either earn the opportunity for a real conversation or get relegated to "just another salesperson to dodge."

No pressure, right?

The Welcome phase is the W in WISE, and it's arguably the most critical component of the entire system. Everything else – the careful interviewing, the customized solutions, the remarkable experience – depends on successfully navigating these crucial opening moments. Mess up the Welcome, and you'll never get the chance to demonstrate your expertise or build a relationship.

Yet this is precisely where traditional retail training fails most spectacularly. As we discussed in Chapter 1, the standard "Can I help you?" greeting actively sabotages the sales process. But understanding what doesn't work is only half the battle. This chapter teaches you what does work – and why.

The Neuroscience of First Impressions

Before we discuss specific techniques, let's understand what's happening in your Customer's brain during those first 60 seconds. This isn't abstract theory; it's practical information that explains why certain approaches succeed while others fail.

When a Customer enters your store, their brain is processing multiple streams of information simultaneously - including some fears we will break down in Chapter 8. The visual cortex is mapping the space, identifying products, noting other people's locations. The auditory system is filtering background noise, potentially processing music or announcements. The proprioceptive system is managing movement through an unfamiliar environment.

Overlaying all this sensory processing is what neuroscientists call "threat detection." This sounds dramatic for a retail environment, but it's real. The amygdala – the brain's alarm system – constantly scans for potential threats. In our evolutionary past, entering an unfamiliar space populated by strangers was genuinely risky. Your ancient ancestors who carefully assessed new environments survived; those who blithely walked into danger did not.

This threat-detection system doesn't distinguish between physical danger and social discomfort. Being approached by a stranger triggers the same neural circuits that respond to a predator. I get it, that's almost not fair. The intensity is obviously different, but the same systems activate.

When you approach a Customer, you're registering as a potential threat. Not because you're actually dangerous, but because you're an unknown person entering their personal space with unclear intentions. The Customer's brain is asking: "Friend or foe? Safe or threatening? Helpful or bothersome?"

Your greeting, body language, and demeanor in those first moments answer these questions. Traditional greetings often fail because they trigger social threat responses. "Can I help you?" feels like an obligation being imposed. It activates the Customer's defenses rather than deactivating them.

Understanding this neuroscience explains why certain Welcome techniques work. You're not just being polite or following a script; you're actively working to signal safety, trigger social bonding circuits, and create the neurological conditions for trust and openness.

The Two Goals of Welcome

The Welcome phase serves two specific purposes, and it's important to keep both in mind:

Goal 1: Make Customers feel valued, not vulnerable.

Every Customer wants to feel that their decision to visit your store was wise. They want to feel welcomed in the genuine sense – not tolerated, not targeted, but genuinely glad they came. This feeling must be authentic, not performed. Customers instantly detect fake enthusiasm, and it triggers skepticism rather than trust.

Goal 2: Create an opening for conversation.

You need a pathway from initial greeting to substantive dialogue about the Customer's needs. This transition should feel natural, not forced. Traditional greetings often create a dead-end: "Can I help you?" "No thanks, just looking." Now what? You've engaged and been rejected, leaving both parties in an awkward situation.

A successful Welcome accomplishes both goals efficiently. Customers feel positive about the interaction, and you've established the foundation for moving into the Interview phase.

The WISE Welcome: A Better Way

The WISE Welcome consists of three components, each serving a specific purpose:

1. The Gratitude Opening
2. The Name Exchange
3. The Connection Question

Let's examine each in detail.

Component 1: The Gratitude Opening

Remember everything we discussed about threat detection and Customer psychology? The Gratitude Opening solves these problems elegantly with one simple phrase:

"Thanks for coming in!"

That's it. No question mark, no request, no implied obligation. Just genuine appreciation for their presence.

Why does this work so effectively? Several reasons:

It's unexpected. Customers enter stores braced for "Can I help you?" When they hear something different, it disrupts their autopilot response. They actually process what you said rather than triggering a pre-programmed reply.

It's compliment based. Psychologically, gratitude is a form of compliment. You're acknowledging that they made a choice to visit your store out of countless alternatives, and you appreciate that choice. Everyone likes being appreciated.

It creates no obligation. Unlike "Can I help you?" which implicitly asks the Customer to do something (accept help, state their needs), "Thanks for coming in!" requires no response. It's a complete statement. Paradoxically, this lack of pressure makes Customers more likely to engage.

It's authentic. You should genuinely be grateful when Customers visit. They could shop online, go to competitors, or spend their time elsewhere. Every Customer who walks through your door is giving you an opportunity. "Thanks for coming in!" expresses a truth, which is why it feels genuine rather than scripted.

The tone matters as much as the words. Deliver this line warmly but naturally, as you would greet a guest in your home. Not over-the-top enthusiasm (which feels fake), but genuine warmth. Smile, make eye contact, but don't stare. Your body language should be open and relaxed, not aggressive or hovering.

Some sales professionals worry this greeting is too casual or doesn't immediately offer help. This concern misses the point. You're not avoiding helpfulness; you're creating the conditions where offering help *will be welcomed* rather than rejected. Patience during Welcome pays dividends in every subsequent phase.

Component 2: The Name Exchange

After the gratitude opening, introduce yourself and get the Customer's name. This seems basic, but it's surprising how often salespeople skip this step or execute it poorly.

The name exchange serves multiple functions:

Personalization. Using someone's name throughout an interaction increases rapport and trust. Research consistently shows that people respond more positively when their name is used appropriately (though beware overuse, which feels manipulative).

Professional credibility. Introducing yourself establishes you as a professional rather than anonymous retail staff. It signals "I'm someone, not just a role."

Memory and accountability. Exchanging names makes the interaction memorable for both parties. It also creates a subtle accountability – you're no longer strangers; you're Sterling talking with Jessy. This increases the social stakes of the interaction in ways that encourage better behavior from both people.

Future relationship foundation. If this Customer becomes a regular, you'll already be on a first-name basis. You're building relationship infrastructure from the first moment.

The execution matters. Don't just announce your name; create an exchange. After "Thanks for coming in!" continue naturally:

"I'm Matthew. And you are?"

The phrasing "And you are?" is deliberate. It's gentler than "What's your name?" which can feel like an interrogation. It's also more likely to prompt a response than just stating your name and waiting.

If the Customer hesitates or seems uncomfortable, don't push. Some people are private about their names with strangers. Simply smile and continue. But most Customers will reciprocate. Humans are wired for social reciprocity; when you offer your name, they feel prompted to offer theirs.

Once you have their name, use it periodically throughout the interaction. Not constantly – that's the hallmark of manipulative sales tactics – but naturally, as you would in any conversation. "So, Christine, what brands have you tried in the past?" "That's a great question, Brayden."

A note on handshakes: In some retail environments, offering to shake hands is appropriate and professional. In others, it feels too formal or invasive. Read the situation. A handshake works well in higher-end specialty retail where consultative service is expected. In casual retail, it might feel overly aggressive. When in doubt, let the Customer's body language guide you. If they extend their hand, shake it. If they maintain distance, respect that boundary.

Component 3: The Connection Question

You've expressed gratitude and exchanged names. Now you need to transition from greeting to conversation. This is where the Connection Question comes in.

The traditional approach asks, "What can I help you with?" or "What brings you in today?" These are marginally better than "Can I help you?" but still problematic. They're direct questions about the Customer's needs, which can feel premature. You've barely met; now you're asking them to explain their problems?

The WISE approach uses a more subtle question: **"Is this your first time in our store?"**

This question is brilliant for several reasons:

It's low-stakes. Everyone can answer this easily. It's not asking them to articulate complex needs or make themselves vulnerable. It's a simple factual question.

It provides valuable information. Their answer tells you immediately whether you're dealing with a first timer who needs orientation or a returning Customer who already knows the store.

It opens different conversation paths. Each answer leads naturally to a different follow-up, both productive. We'll explore these paths in a moment.

It demonstrates curiosity about them. Rather than immediately focusing on products, you're showing interest in their relationship with the store. This subtle shift signals that you care about them as people, not just as transactions.

When asking this question, maintain the warm, conversational tone you've established. You're not interrogating; you're chatting. Make it feel natural, not scripted.

The First Timer Path

If the Customer answers "Yes, this is my first time here," you've received valuable information. This person knows nothing about your store. They don't understand your layout, your product selection, your specialty, or your differentiators. They're essentially in unknown territory.

Your response has two goals: orient them and establish credibility. Here's how:

"Great! Let me tell you a bit about us."

Then share what I call "Points of Pride" – the things that make your store special. This isn't a sales pitch; it's context. You're helping them understand what kind of store they're in and why it's worth their time.

Points of Pride might include:

- **Years in business:** "We've been serving this community for 25 years."
- **Specialization:** "We focus exclusively on backpacking, so we have the deepest selection in the region."
- **Exclusive products:** "We carry several brands you won't find anywhere else."
- **Expertise:** "Our team has over 100 combined years of experience."
- **Service:** "We provide free training workshops every Saturday."
- **Values:** "We're family-owned and committed to supporting local artisans."

Choose two or three Points of Pride that are genuinely distinctive and relevant to your Customer base. Don't create a laundry list; you're sharing highlights, not reading a corporate brochure.

The key is authentic pride. These should be things you genuinely value about your store, not marketing copy you're reciting. If you don't actually believe your store is special, the Customer won't either. But if you authentically love what makes your store unique, that enthusiasm comes through naturally.

After sharing Points of Pride, transition to the Interview phase with:

"So, what project are you working on?" or

"What part of your wardrobe are we working on today?" or

"Are you shopping for you or for a gift?"

Use what works for your retail scene. The first transition phrase example works great for DIY craft, hobby or Home improvement stores

The second example works great in apparel and footwear retail.

The third one works for specialty stores.

The key here is to transition into the Interview Phase without the obvious and tired "what are you looking for/shopping for" lines. It should feel natural like a guide taking you through the store and not coerced.

SIDEBAR: In all things WISE Selling the key is to be uniquely and authentically you. It is not about exact phrases or "scripts." It is about the principle. I am not trying to create an army of WISE robots. Craft your variation of every line, phrase or technique offered as we go. Stay focused on the principle and not the exact phrasing.

Now you've earned the right to ask about their needs. You've established credibility, provided context, and demonstrated that this interaction is consultative rather than transactional.

The Returning Customer Path

If the Customer answers "No, I've been here before," you also have valuable information. This person already knows your store. They've chosen to return, which suggests their first experience was at least acceptable. Your goal now is to acknowledge their return and build on the existing relationship. And then make today's experience remarkable.

Your response: *"Wonderful! It's great to see you back. What did you get last time?"*

This question accomplishes several things:

It shows you care about continuity. You're not treating them as a blank slate; you're acknowledging their history with the store.

It gathers intelligence. Learning what they purchased previously helps you understand their interests, budget level, and expertise. Someone who bought a premium router last time is likely a serious woodworker with different needs than someone who bought finishing supplies.

It creates conversation. Asking about their previous purchase gives them something easy to talk about. Most people enjoy discussing their purchases, especially if they're happy with them.

It provides project context. Often, today's visit relates to the previous purchase. "I got some of the night serum last month" immediately tells you they're investing in skin care and may need related supplies or accessories.

Listen carefully to their answer. Are they enthusiastic about the previous purchase? This suggests satisfaction and readiness to buy again. Are they hesitant or negative? This might indicate problems that need addressing before you can make progress.

Follow up with: *"How's that working out for you?"* or *"How did your project turn out?"*

These questions demonstrate genuine interest in their success, not just their spending. You're establishing that you care about outcomes, not just transactions. This differentiates you dramatically from most retail experiences.

Then, like discussed before, transition naturally to the Interview Phase with

"So, what are you working on now?" or

"What's your next event?" or

"What would you like to explore today?"

Or any of the previous examples work as well. You've reconnected with a returning Customer and created a foundation for today's sale by showing interest in their ongoing journey.

The Regular Customer Variation

Some Customers aren't just returning; they're regulars. You recognize them. Maybe you even remember their name from previous visits.

This situation requires a modified Welcome that acknowledges the relationship:

"Hey, Emery! Good to see you again. How did that dress work for your work dinner?"

Mentioning a specific previous project or purchase shows you remember them as an individual. This is relationship gold. Every Customer wants to feel remembered and valued. In an age of anonymous transactions, being recognized as an individual is increasingly rare and valuable.

If you don't remember specific details, don't fake it. Simply say: **"Good to see you again! What brings you back?"** I myself have found my mind going blank when a regular Customer walks in. I am awesome with faces, not so much with names. Showing genuine understanding that you know they are a regular is the important part. So don't freak out if you forgot their name. It's totally fine to say. "Remind me your name again?"

Building a system for remembering regular Customers pays enormous dividends. Some sales professionals keep notes on index cards or in a notebook. Others use their phone to jot quick reminders after interactions. In my stores, we kept the notes in the POS under the Customer record. However, you do it, capturing key details about regulars – their names, projects, preferences, work, interests – transforms occasional transactions into ongoing relationships.

Body Language and Nonverbal Communication

Everything discussed so far focuses on words, but body language matters just as much. Your nonverbal communication can reinforce your message or undermine it entirely.

Approach angle matters. Never approach a Customer head-on; this triggers unconscious threat responses. Instead, approach at a slight angle, stopping a comfortable distance away. This feels less confrontational and gives the Customer space.

Maintain open body language. Arms uncrossed, relaxed posture, weight evenly distributed. Crossed arms signal defensiveness or judgment. Hands in pockets can seem disengaged. Find a neutral, open stance that feels natural.

Eye contact but not staring. Make eye contact during the greeting to show attention and respect, but don't maintain unwavering eye contact throughout the conversation. That's unnatural and uncomfortable. Normal conversation involves eye contact mixed with glances away.

Smile genuinely. Fake smiles use only mouth muscles. Genuine smiles involve the eyes – what's called a Duchenne smile. You can't fake a Duchenne smile, so the only solution is genuine warmth. Actually, be glad the Customer is there. (And you can impress your friends that you know the term Duchenne!)

Match their energy level. If a Customer is energetic and enthusiastic, you can mirror that energy. If they're quiet and reserved, dial down your energy to match. This subconscious matching, called mirroring, builds rapport.

Respect personal space. Different cultures and individuals have different comfort zones. Americans typically need about three feet of personal space with strangers. Stay at or beyond this distance unless the Customer's body language invites closer proximity. I have three daughters. One is a hugger and one is not. But I definitely am. So, I have had to learn to adapt based on the daughter just like you have too based on the Customer.

Don't block exits. Position yourself so the Customer has clear paths to leave. Blocking exits triggers unconscious anxiety. Stand to the side, not in front of doorways or aisles.

These nonverbal elements seem small, but they profoundly affect how Customers perceive you. You can say perfect words with terrible body language and still fail. Conversely, appropriate body language makes even imperfect words more effective.

Handling the "Just Looking" Response

Despite your best efforts with the WISE Welcome, some Customers will still say "Just looking" or "I'm fine, thanks" and try to disengage. This happens *much less* frequently in WISE Selling than with traditional greetings, but it happens. Your goal in the Welcome is to make "Just looking" the rare response rather than the normal one. But let's be honest - some people are just wired to say it and there is nothing we can do about it.

Don't panic. Don't give up. Don't immediately leave them alone. You have tools for this situation. I call this tool the Bridge. You are working to build a *bridge* between the Welcome and the Interview phase of WISE Selling

The **Bridge** has two parts - **Soften** and **Ask**

When the Customer says they are just looking, we have to offer a response to initiate that we understand their desire to look. When the Customer says just looking, you might "Soften" their response by saying

"I understand how you feel. When you are trying to make a good decision, it's important to take your time." Or

"No problem. I can certainly appreciate your wanting to take your time and make the right decision; after all we have the largest selection in town."

The key to softening when someone says just looking is to let them know it's okay to be just looking. Express your understanding of their situation and how they feel. Once you Soften, then you Ask. When you "ask" a question, this poses the opportunity to engage the Customer in conversation - the purpose of the Interview - and determine whether the Customer really is "just looking." Remember, the key to success in the Welcome phase of WISE Selling is to engage in conversation with the Customer. If you simply soften and then leave them alone, you are not engaging them.

You might say something like

"Do you mind if I ask you a few questions to help you narrow down your choices?" or

"If you wouldn't mind, I'd like to ask you a couple of quick questions to point you in the right direction and save you some time today?"

Here are a couple more examples putting the Soften and Ask together:

"That's great, Jude. I can understand why you'd want to take your time and look around; we certainly have a lot to choose from, and you want to make the right choice, after all it is an investment! But if you wouldn't mind, I would like to ask you a few questions to help you narrow down some of the choices and maybe save you some time today. Would that be okay?"

or

"Hey, I completely understand! The holidays are coming up, and you want to make a wise decision when picking out gifts. But I'm sure you've got a really busy schedule, so if it would be okay, I'd love to ask you a few questions to help you narrow down your choices?"

If after you deliver the Bridge, the Customer responds with "Thanks, but I really am just looking" then validate their desire for space without surrendering the interaction entirely. Then, provide value without pushing:

"My pleasure. If you have any questions while you're looking around, I'm Michael. I'll be [location] if you need anything."

This does several things:

- Reiterates your name (relationship building)
- Gives specific location (reduces the "where did that person go?" frustration)
- Offers help without pressure
- Maintains connection without hovering

Then – and this is crucial – actually move away and give them space. Don't hover nearby. Don't circle back every thirty seconds. Give them genuine space to look.

But don't disappear entirely or become engrossed in other tasks. Stay visible and aware. Watch for buying signals: extended time looking at one product, picking items up, reading labels carefully, looking around as if searching for help.

When you see these signals, you have a second opportunity to engage. This time, use what I call a "soft reentry":

"How is it going?" or "See anything interesting?"

These questions are gentler than "Can I help you now?" They give the Customer an easy way to engage if they're ready, but they can also answer briefly and return to browsing if they're not.

If they engage, great! Transition into the Interview phase. If they still deflect, respect that and pull back again. Some Customers genuinely need to browse extensively before they're ready to interact. Your patience and respect for their process will be remembered when they are ready to talk.

The "I'm Just Looking for Someone Else" Special Case

Occasionally, Customers will indicate they're shopping for someone else: "I'm looking for a gift for my husband" or "My wife asked me to pick something up."

This requires a Welcome variation. These Customers need different help than someone shopping for themselves. They often feel out of their depth – they're in a specialty store but lack the expertise to navigate it.

Your response should immediately address this dynamic:

"I can definitely help with that! Tell me about [the recipient]. What are they into?"

This question serves multiple purposes:

- It shows you understand they need different help
- It starts gathering the information you'll need to make recommendations
- It frames you as an expert guide, which these Customers desperately need
- It makes the process collaborative rather than intimidating
- AND it moves you right in the Interview Phase!

Gift-buying Customers can be highly profitable because they often spend more (trying to get something nice) and rely heavily on your guidance (lacking personal expertise). The Welcome phase is where you establish yourself as their trusted advisor for this mission. Remember, the Customer is the hero- especially in this scenario - and you are the guide.

The Just Looking Facts

Here are the facts: **80%** of the people who come in the door will probably say "just looking." It's what they are programmed to do. It's what they know. With a professional and unique greeting, we can cut that down to **50%**. But with the Bridge, we can still get around the just looking phrase and engage them in conversation. If we cannot engage, we cannot sell. Period.

We have so many stories (hundreds and hundreds and hundreds of stories) of Customers saying, "I'm just looking." The salesperson gives up, letting the Customer go. The Customer is literally headed to the door, on their way to the parking lot, when the store manager sees them, uses a bridge, and before you know it, sells them something! Don't let that be you.

Cultural and Demographic Adaptations

The WISE Welcome described here works remarkably well across diverse Customer populations, but some adaptation may be necessary based on cultural context, demographics, or individual personality.

Age considerations: Older Customers often appreciate more formal interactions. Younger Customers typically prefer casual conversation. Adjust your level of formality accordingly. The 60-year-old Customer might appreciate "It's a pleasure to meet you, ma'am," while the 25-year-old prefers "Nice to meet you!"

Cultural variations: Different cultures have different norms around eye contact, personal space, and interaction with strangers. If you serve diverse communities, invest time learning these norms. Respectful adaptation demonstrates cultural competence and builds trust.

Personality types: Some people are naturally extroverted and love conversation. Others are introverted and find extended social interaction draining. The introverted Customer might appreciate a brief Welcome that gets to the point faster. Pay attention to cues and adjust.

Shopping with others: Customers with friends, partners, or children need different Welcome approaches. Acknowledge all people in the group but identify who's making decisions. Often, one person in a couple drives the decision while the other provides input. Engaging both without alienating either requires skill.

The principle underlying all adaptations is the same: Pay attention, stay flexible, and prioritize making the Customer comfortable over following any script rigidly.

Common Welcome Mistakes

Even after training on WISE Welcome techniques, several mistakes remain common:

Mistake 1: Greeting too early. Give Customers 30-60 seconds to orient themselves before approaching. Someone who just walked in needs a moment to adjust to the environment. Immediate greeting feels aggressive. I always say "allow the tint on their glasses to fade" before you start.

Mistake 2: Greeting too late. Wait too long, and Customers feel ignored or assume you're unavailable. The 60-second guideline exists for a reason.

Mistake 3: Greeting while occupied. If you're helping another Customer, acknowledge the newcomer with a smile and brief "Thanks for coming in. I'll be with you in just a moment!" Don't ignore them, but don't abandon your current Customer either.

Mistake 4: Insincere delivery. If you don't mean "Thanks for coming in," it shows. You can't fake genuine warmth. If you're having a bad day, take a moment to reset before greeting Customers. They don't deserve to deal with your mood.

Mistake 5: Rushing past Welcome. Some salespeople, eager to get to the "real" selling, race through Welcome perfunctorily. They say the right words but clearly want to move on. This defeats the purpose. Welcome isn't a formality; it's a foundation. Build it properly.

Mistake 6: Information dumping. When sharing Points of Pride, some salespeople launch into extensive store history or feature lists. Keep it brief – two or three distinctive points, then move on. You're orienting, not orating. It's the trailer, not the whole movie.

Mistake 7: Failing to transition. After a good Welcome, you need to move into the Interview. Some salespeople do a great Welcome but then stand there awkwardly, unsure what to say next. Practice the transition phrases so they flow naturally.

Practice and Refinement

Welcome skills require practice to feel natural. New phrases feel awkward at first. You'll stumble over words, forget to ask for names, or struggle with transitions.

This is normal. Keep practicing.

Several methods help:

Role-play with colleagues. Take turns being Customer and salesperson. Practice the complete Welcome sequence until it flows naturally. Give each other feedback on body language, tone, and phrasing.

Record yourself. Use your phone to record practice Welcome interactions. Watching yourself reveals unconscious habits – crossing arms, avoiding eye contact, speaking too quickly. You can't fix what you don't notice.

Seek feedback from Customers. After successful sales, ask Customers about their experience. "Was there anything about our interaction that made you comfortable working with me?" Their answers often highlight Welcome elements they appreciated.

Observe experts. Watch your most successful colleagues. How do they welcome Customers? What do they do that creates instant rapport? Model their techniques.

Reflect after each interaction. Spend 30 seconds after each Welcome thinking about what went well and what could improve. This reflection creates conscious learning from every repetition.

Track your "just looking" rate. How often do Customers give you the "just looking" deflection? As your Welcome improves, this rate should decrease. If it doesn't, something in your delivery needs adjustment.

Excellence in Welcome doesn't happen overnight. It develops through conscious practice, honest self-assessment, and continuous refinement. But the investment pays enormous dividends. Every subsequent phase of WISE Selling becomes easier when Welcome is executed well.

The Welcome Mindset

Technique matters, but mindset matters more. The Welcome Phase works because it's grounded in an authentic mindset: You genuinely value every Customer who walks through your door.

This isn't about faking enthusiasm or pretending every Customer is your favorite person. It's about recognizing a fundamental truth: Every Customer represents opportunity. The opportunity to help someone solve a problem. The opportunity to share expertise you've developed. The opportunity to create a positive experience in someone's day. The opportunity to build a relationship that might last years.

When you approach Welcome with this mindset, the techniques become tools for expressing genuine welcome rather than tricks for manipulating behavior. Customers sense this difference immediately.

Some days, this mindset comes naturally. You're energized, the store is busy, Customers are pleasant. Other days, it's harder. You're tired, you've dealt with difficult people, you're not feeling it.

On those hard days, the Welcome techniques become especially important. They provide a framework that helps you deliver good service even when you don't feel naturally motivated. Following the process – expressing gratitude, exchanging names, asking the connection question – creates positive interactions that often improve your mood.

But also give yourself permission to be human. If you're having a genuinely terrible day, it's better to acknowledge it to yourself, take a few deep breaths, and reset before greeting Customers. Two minutes of honest self-care prevents hours of subpar interactions.

Transition Phrase to The Solution

In order to transition from the Welcome Phase to the Interview, you need a transition phrase. In fact, you need a transition phrase to move between all of the WISE Selling phases. We have already discussed these earlier, but I wanted to hit this idea again for repetition and impact.

The transition phrase from the Welcome Phase to the Interview Phase can take on many forms, but in essence you are starting the Interview with a question like:

"Tell me about your project?" or

"Which part of your wardrobe are we working on today?" or

"Which part of your fitness routine are we working on today?" or

"Walk me through your skin care routine?" or

"Is this your first time buying a new car?"

In each of these variations, you can see that we are starting the Interview with a question. And it is not "so what are looking for?" The truth is most Customers don't know what they are looking for. They have an idea of what they are looking for, but there is still much to be decided in their mind. THIS IS WHY THEY CAME INTO A STORE VERSUS SHOPPING ONLINE!

The transition phrase must be open-ended and allow the Customer air to frame the conversation the way they want it to go. You'll also notice the consultative, guide-like approach of the phrasing of the transition. It is intentional. Based on the product you are selling, the transition phrase will take on a different shape, but craft one that sounds like you. If it's not genuine then it does not work.

Why Welcome Matters So Much

Before moving on to the Interview phase, let's reinforce why Welcome deserves this much attention.

Research on first impressions shows that people make judgments about others within the first few seconds of meeting. These judgments are surprisingly accurate and remarkably sticky – difficult to change once formed.

In retail, Customers are making rapid assessments: Is this person trustworthy? Knowledgeable? Genuinely helpful or just trying to make a sale? Do I feel comfortable with them? These assessments happen mostly unconsciously, based on tiny cues in your greeting, body language, and demeanor.

Get Welcome right, and you've earned the benefit of the doubt. Small mistakes later are forgiven. Recommendations are trusted. Objections are minimal. The entire sales process flows smoothly.

Get Welcome wrong, and you're fighting uphill the entire way. Everything you say is filtered through skepticism. Customers guard their information. Objections multiply. Even when you make the sale, it feels like work.

Welcome isn't just the first phase of WISE Selling. It's the foundation that makes everything else possible. Invest the time to master it.

In the next chapter, we'll explore the Interview phase – where you discover what Customers actually need, which is often quite different from what they think they want. Now that's exciting!

Chapter 3

Interview – The Lost Art of Listening

"Tell me about your project."

Five simple words that separate great salespeople from mediocre ones. Five words that shift the entire dynamic from pushing products to solving problems. Five words that most retail salespeople never say because they've been trained to talk, not listen.

The Interview phase – the I in WISE – is where you gather the intelligence necessary to provide genuinely helpful recommendations. It's where you discover not just what Customers say they want, but what they actually need. It's where you build trust by demonstrating that you care more about their success than your commission. And quite frankly, you cannot be the guide to their hero story without it!

It's also where most salespeople fail spectacularly.

Traditional retail training spends minimal time on questioning techniques and maximum time on product knowledge and closing tactics. This is exactly backward. Product knowledge without Customer understanding is useless – like having a fully stocked toolbox but no idea what you're building. You can't solve a problem you don't understand.

This chapter teaches you how to conduct interviews that feel like conversations, questions that feel like curiosity rather than interrogation, and listening techniques that make Customers feel genuinely heard – often for the first time in their shopping journey.

Why Customers Don't Know What They Want

Let's start with an uncomfortable truth: Most Customers who walk into your store don't actually know what they want. They think they do. They'll tell you they do. But they don't.

This isn't their fault. It's a fundamental challenge of human decision-making. We're generally poor at:

Self-diagnosis. Just as patients can't diagnose their own medical conditions (hence the need for doctors), Customers often can't accurately diagnose their own needs. They see symptoms – "My feet hurt. I need new shoes" – without understanding the underlying causes.

Understanding available options. Even extensive online research leaves gaps. Reviews provide opinions but not personalized guidance. Specification sheets list features without explaining real-world implications.

Predicting future needs. Customers focus on immediate problems without considering how their needs might evolve. The beginner woodworker buying basic tools doesn't realize they'll outgrow them in six months.

Articulating constraints. Customers know they have space limitations, budget considerations, or skill level constraints, but they struggle to weigh these factors appropriately or communicate them clearly.

Here's a real example from fitness retail: A Customer enters saying, "I need a treadmill." Seems straightforward. But an effective Interview reveals:

- They actually hate running and only think they need a treadmill because that's what they see in gyms
- Their real goal is losing weight and improving cardiovascular health
- They have knee problems that make high-impact exercise uncomfortable
- They have limited space and a busy schedule
- Their previous treadmill became an expensive clothes rack after three months

The "right" answer isn't a treadmill at all – it's probably an elliptical or recumbent bike that addresses their actual needs (reduced stress on knees, weight loss) rather than their stated wants.

This pattern repeats across every retail category. The Customer who says they need a table saw actually needs guidance on which woodworking projects match their skill level. The person shopping for face moisturizer needs education on what products they're working with and what results they're trying to achieve since skin types vary greatly. .

Without an Interview, you're stuck recommending based on stated wants, which often don't match actual needs. With a thorough Interview, you can provide solutions that genuinely serve the Customer – even when those solutions surprise them.

The Doctor Analogy

The best framework for understanding the Interview comes from healthcare. Think about visiting a doctor:

The doctor doesn't immediately prescribe. Imagine a doctor who handed you medication the moment you walked in: "Here, take these!" You'd be horrified. You'd demand to know what the medication is for, why you need it, whether it addresses your actual problem.

The doctor asks questions. What are your symptoms? When did they start? How severe are they? What makes them better or worse? Have you experienced this before? The questioning is systematic, covering multiple areas to build a complete picture.

The doctor listens carefully. They're not interrupting to tell you about medications in their sample closet. They're focused on understanding your situation. They take notes. They ask follow-up questions to clarify ambiguous responses.

The doctor considers context. Your medical history, current medications, lifestyle, age, and other factors all inform their recommendations. They're not treating symptoms in isolation; they're treating you as a complete person.

Only then does the doctor diagnose and prescribe. After gathering information, they explain what they believe is wrong and why specific treatments make sense for your situation. The prescription flows logically from the diagnosis, which flows logically from the questions.

This is exactly how the Interview should work in retail. You're the expert consultant. The Customer has a problem or goal. Your job is to understand their situation completely before recommending solutions.

Yet most retail salespeople skip straight to prescription. The Customer mentions interest in a laptop, and the salesperson immediately starts describing his favorite laptop. No questions about experience level, goals, purpose, or budget. Just laptop features rattled off rapid-fire.

Prescription without diagnosis is malpractice – **in medicine and in retail.**

The Three Focus Areas

Effective Interviews gather information in three distinct areas. Think of these as three lenses through which you view the Customer's situation. Each provides different but complementary information.

Focus Area 1: Past Experience

Past experience questions explore what the Customer has used before, what worked, what didn't, and what they learned. This historical perspective provides crucial context.

Key questions include:

- "Tell me about the [equipment/product] you're using now."
- "What do you like best about what you have?"
- "What do you like least?"
- "What's your favorite brand and why?"
- "What would you change if you could start over?"
- "Have you used anything like this at a gym or friend's house?"
- "What's your experience level with [activity]?"
- Have you had any injuries?
- How long have you been working with or using these products?

These questions reveal whether you're working with a novice who needs education or an expert who needs advanced features. They show you what the Customer values – reliability might matter most to someone burned by poor quality previously, while features matter most to someone bored with basic equipment.

Past experience questions also build rapport. People enjoy talking about their experiences. Sharing stories creates connection. When Customers describe previous frustrations, you're building trust by showing you care about avoiding those same problems. If you are selling skin care products or fashion apparel these items are very personal and people have definite opinions and experiences to share.

SIDEBAR: Don't let past experience questions become griping sessions. Some Customers will want to spend twenty minutes complaining about everything that ever went wrong. Acknowledge their frustrations – "That sounds really frustrating" – but guide conversation forward: "So that's definitely something we want to avoid this time. Let me ask about..."

Focus Area 2: Expectations

Expectation questions explore what the Customer hopes to achieve, what features matter to them, and what success looks like. This future-focused lens helps you understand their goals.

Key questions include:

- "What are you trying to accomplish with this?"
- "What would be the most important thing to consider?"
- "What have you heard or read about that interested you?"
- "If we get this exactly right, what changes for you?"
- "What are your goals for [timeframe – 6 months, 1 year]?"
- "Have you used a _____ before?"

These questions often reveal disconnects between current ideas and actual needs. A Customer might expect a basic model will meet their needs when you can see they'll outgrow it quickly. Or they might assume they need premium features that don't actually matter for their use case. It is a common fact that Customers use only 20% of the features on their smart TVs at home.

Expectation questions also help you understand decision criteria. What factors will ultimately determine whether they buy? Price? Quality? Specific features? Understanding these priorities lets you structure your solution appropriately.

In fitness, one of the most powerful expectation questions is: "What will be different about you [or your situation] in six months after you've been using this?"

This question forces Customers to think beyond the product to actual outcomes. It reveals whether they have realistic expectations or need education about what's possible. And it provides language you can use later when presenting solutions: "Remember, you said you wanted to..."

You will notice that we did not ask what features the Customer is interested in. That's intentional Customers don't know features. If they did, they wouldn't need you. They will discuss features with you and even tell you some they might like or desire in the Interview conversation. But oftentimes this is driven by the fears the Customer is dealing with that we will discuss in Chapter 8.

Never ask a Customer what features they are looking for. That is not what a guide would do. And it is not WISE Selling.

Price Expectations

Before we move on to the last focus area, let's talk about the issue of price. We all think about it, but nobody wants to talk about it. But to the Customer, one of their most important expectations often is price. So, you need to be proactive in helping them make this decision.

Your store has a large selection of products. You may intentionally cover a wide range of prices letting a Customer feel confident that they can afford your store. Plus, with the wide assortment, you also ensure that the Customer can make a solid investment by being able to strike a balance between the best product and what they want to spend.

So, with every Customer work the expectation question about price into your process. Here are some proven examples that work:

"Brad, based on what you've told me so far, we have several styles of boots that would work for you. Let me ask you this, though, which is more important to you: making sure you get the best camera or staying within a certain budget?"

Or

"Emery, as you can see we have a huge selection to choose from; but I'm curious, what's the most important thing to you? Do you want to make sure you get the best look and fit for your body or do we need to stay within a certain budget?"

Many Customers have price considerations. Some have firm budgets. Others have general ranges. Some will spend whatever it takes to get exactly the right product, while others prioritize value.

You need this information to recommend appropriately. Yet many salespeople avoid asking because:

- It feels intrusive or pushy
- They worry Customers will lie or lowball
- They're uncomfortable discussing money
- They fear being perceived as judgmental

These concerns are understandable but counterproductive. Not knowing the Customer's price expectations leads to wasted time showing inappropriate options and potentially losing sales.

You can frame the price question as helping narrow choices:

"I want to make sure I show you options that work for your situation. We have products ranging from [low price] to [high price]. To help narrow that down, what's more important to you – getting the absolute best equipment regardless of cost, or staying within a specific budget range?"

This phrasing:

- Acknowledges your wide range (you're not assuming they're cheap or wealthy)
- Frames the question as helpful, not nosy
- Offers two reasonable options, neither of which requires stating a specific number
- Gives Customers permission to prioritize either quality or budget

Most Customers will indicate their general approach. Some will volunteer specific numbers: "I was thinking around $2,000." Others will describe parameters: "I don't want the cheapest thing, but I'm not looking to spend a fortune either."

Whatever they share provides useful guidance. And if they insist money is no object, take them at their word – but also note that Customers who claim "price doesn't matter" often do have limits. They just want to see the best options first. Do you see how having this information can save you a lot of heartache down the road? Makes sense, doesn't it?

The truth is most Customers use price to mitigate risk. When they are dealing with the fear of making a mistake (Chapter 8) then they can ease that fear by spending as little as possible. This is where WISE Selling is so powerful. The more trust you build, the more confidence you exude, the more you build the relationship, the more money they are willing to invest.

Notice, that at no time did I say that a Customer will not spend more than their budget. The purpose of this question is to ascertain and assess the strategy you must use when dealing with price with your Customer. Do not feel you have to use this tool every time but do become comfortable with using it. Over time, with practice, this may become your favorite tool. I know it is one of mine.

Focus Area 3: Conditions of Use

Conditions questions explore the practical realities of how the Customer will use the product. This pragmatic lens ensures recommendations fit their actual situation.

Key questions include:

- "Where will you use this?"
- "Tell me about your work?"
- "How often will you use it?"
- "Who else will use it?"
- "What are the space constraints?"
- "Are you trying to connect this with another product?"
- "Are there any physical considerations we should know about?"

These questions catch practical showstoppers before they become problems. The perfect treadmill doesn't matter if it doesn't fit through the Customer's doorway. The ideal washer/dryer combo is useless if they don't have electrical capacity to run it.

Conditions questions also demonstrate professionalism. You're thinking ahead to implementation, not just the sale. This builds confidence that you're a consultant, not just an order-taker.

Don't skip conditions questions even when the answers seem obvious. The Customer shopping alone might be buying for a spouse with different height, weight, or strength. For example, the person shopping for home gym equipment might need recommendations considering a spouse who weighs significantly more or less. Or the person shopping is very tech-savvy, but their spouse at home is not. So, a lot of fancy features may not be the right solution. These details only emerge through careful questioning.

The Art of Open-Ended Questions

The difference between an effective and ineffective Interview lies largely in question structure. Compare these exchanges:

Ineffective (Closed Questions):

- "Do you want a treadmill?" (Yes/No)
- "Is this for weight loss?" (Yes/No)
- "Do you have space limitations?" (Yes/No)

Effective (Open-Ended Questions):

- "Tell me about your fitness goals."
- "What's your typical workout routine?"
- "Describe the space where this will go."

Closed questions can be answered with one word. They're useful for confirming specific facts, but they don't generate the rich information you need. Open-ended questions require explanation. They get Customers talking, which serves multiple purposes:

You gather more information. When people elaborate, they provide context, nuance, and details you wouldn't think to ask about. "Describe your space" might reveal not just dimensions but also that it's an unfinished basement with concrete floors and poor climate control – all factors that affect recommendations.

Customers clarify their own thinking. Articulating thoughts aloud helps people process their own needs. Many Customers discover what really matters to them while answering your questions.

You build rapport. People like talking to good listeners. The more a Customer talks and feels heard, the more they trust and like you. And the more they start to feel like it is their choice and not yours. Guide.

You demonstrate expertise. The questions you ask signal what you know. Thoughtful, probing questions show depth of expertise that builds credibility.

Craft questions that begin with words like:

- Tell me about...
- Describe...
- What...
- How...
- Why...

Avoid questions beginning with:

- Do you...
- Are you...
- Can you...
- Will you...

One exception: Occasionally use closed questions to confirm understanding or narrow options. After gathering extensive open-ended information, "So it sounds like space-saving design is your top priority with this new washer and dryer – is that right?" helps confirm you've understood correctly.

Active Listening Techniques

Asking good questions is only half of the Interview. The other half is **listening** – really listening, not just waiting for your turn to talk.

Most people are terrible listeners. My wife tells me I can be at times. We're formulating responses while others speak. We're getting distracted by our own thoughts. We're jumping to conclusions before the speaker finishes. In retail, salespeople often stop listening the moment they think they know which product to recommend.

Active listening requires conscious techniques:

Technique 1: Focus completely.

Give the Customer your full attention. Make eye contact (but don't stare). Orient your body toward them. Put away your phone. Stop mentally rehearsing your product pitch.

This sounds obvious but watch retail employees. Many are scanning the store while "listening," or clearly mentally somewhere else. Customers notice. Lack of focus communicates lack of care.

Technique 2: Use minimal encouragers.

While the Customer talks, provide small verbal and nonverbal signals that you're engaged: "Mm-hmm," "I see," "Go on," head nods. These encourage continued sharing without interrupting.

Technique 3: Paraphrase and reflect.

Periodically summarize what you've heard in your own words: "So if I understand correctly, you're looking for something that..." This serves multiple purposes:

- Confirms you understood accurately
- Shows you're paying attention
- Gives Customers a chance to correct misunderstandings
- Helps solidify information in your memory

Technique 4: Ask clarifying questions.

When something's unclear, ask for clarification immediately rather than assuming or guessing. "When you say 'compact,' what size are you thinking about specifically?"

Technique 5: Note emotions and address them.

Listen not just to words but to feelings behind them. If a Customer seems frustrated, anxious, or excited, acknowledge it: "It sounds like your previous running shoes were really frustrating" or "I can hear how excited you are about this project."

Addressing emotions builds connection and often reveals important information. The frustrated Customer might need extra reassurance. The anxious one needs patient education. The excited one is ready to buy and just needs guidance.

Technique 6: Tolerate silence.

After asking a question, be quiet and wait for the answer. Don't fill silence with more talking. Some Customers need time to think. Resist the urge to jump in with your own thoughts.

Many salespeople are so uncomfortable with conversational pauses that they start talking again within seconds, often answering their own questions. This defeats the entire purpose of asking.

Technique 7: Take notes.

For complex situations or high dollar purchases, jot down key points. This shows Customers you take them seriously and ensures you don't forget important details. It also gives you reference material for later phases.

Some salespeople worry note-taking seems impersonal or bureaucratic. Frame it positively: "I want to make sure I capture all these details so I can recommend exactly what you need. Do you mind if I jot a few notes?"

Most Customers appreciate the attention to detail.

Review

Before transitioning from Interview to Solution, always summarize what you've learned. This critical step serves multiple purposes:

Confirms accuracy. You might have misunderstood something. Summary gives Customers the chance to correct misperceptions before you base recommendations on faulty information.

Demonstrates attentiveness. When you summarize accurately, Customers recognize you genuinely heard them. This builds trust enormously.

Refreshes both memories. Interviews cover a lot of ground. Summary reminds both you and the Customer of everything discussed, ensuring nothing gets forgotten.

Creates transition. Summary naturally bridges from Interview to Solution. After reviewing what you learned, you can seamlessly use the most powerful words in selling,

"Based on you've told me..."

A good summary sounds like this:

"Let me make sure I have this right. You're working on refinishing your kitchen cabinets – nine cabinets total. You've done some small finishing projects before but nothing this scale. You're hoping to complete it over a weekend or two, working mostly alone with some help from your wife. You have garage space to work in so you can spread out. You want to go from dark stain to a lighter, more modern look. You have three young kids, so durability matters. The most important things for you are getting that lighter color, having it be durable enough for the kids, and completing the project reasonably quickly. Does that capture it?"

This summary demonstrates you listened, understood, and remember the key details. The Customer can simply confirm or add any missed elements. Then you're ready to move forward with confidence.

Common Interview Mistakes

Mistake 1: Asking leading questions.

Leading questions suggest the "right" answer: "You want the best quality, don't you?" or "Durability is important to you, right?" These don't gather genuine information; they get Customers to agree with your assumptions.

Mistake 2: Interrogating rather than conversing.

The Interview should feel like natural conversation, not a police investigation. If you're firing questions rapid-fire without natural pauses or responsiveness, you're interrogating.

Mistake 3: Jumping to solutions prematurely.

The moment you think you know which product to recommend; it's tempting to stop interviewing and start pitching. Resist this urge. Complete the Interview thoroughly. You'll often discover additional factors that change which solution is optimal.

Mistake 4: Asking irrelevant questions.

Every question should serve a purpose. Don't ask about their favorite music if you're selling televisions. Stay focused on information that affects your recommendations.

Mistake 5: Ignoring buying signals.

While thoroughness matters, don't ignore clear buying signals. If a Customer says, "That sounds perfect!" or "Where do I sign?", you don't need to ask ten more questions. Recognize when the Interview has served its purpose.

Mistake 6: Talking too much.

In an effective Interview, Customers should talk 70-80% of the time. If you're talking more than listening, you're doing it wrong.

Mistake 7: Failing to adapt.

Some Customers want extensive conversation. Others want efficiency. Some are analytical and detail-focused. Others are big-picture thinkers. Adapt your Interview style to match Customer preferences.

When Interview Goes Wrong

Sometimes, despite your best efforts, the Interview doesn't flow smoothly. The Customer is uncommunicative, evasive, or unclear. Several strategies help:

Strategy 1: Acknowledge the difficulty.

"I'm sensing you might not be sure exactly what you need yet, which is totally fine. A lot of Customers feel that way. How about I show you a few different options, and that might help clarify what works for you?"

Strategy 2: Provide structure.

Some Customers struggle with open-ended questions. Give them frameworks: "I usually find people fall into a few categories [describe categories]. Do any of these sound like you?"

Strategy 3: Start with easier questions.

If substantive questions aren't working, begin with simple, factual ones to build momentum: "How long have you been [doing activity]?" "Where are you located?" "Have you used eyeliner before?"

Strategy 4: Show first, ask second.

With some Customers, seeing products triggers helpful conversation. "Let me show you a few different options, and you can tell me which ones interest you and why."

Strategy 5: Recognize true lookers.

Occasionally, Customers genuinely are just browsing with no intent to buy today. They might be early in research or gathering ideas. That's okay. A brief Interview establishes rapport without pressuring them. Give them space, provide your card, and stay available if questions arise.

The Cultural Shift the WISE Selling Interview Requires

For salespeople trained in traditional methods, the Interview requires a fundamental cultural shift. You're redefining your role from product-pusher to problem-solver, from talker to listener, from closer to consultant. From hero to guide.

This shift can feel uncomfortable. You're giving up control. You're trusting the process. You're spending more time per Customer without immediate gratification of a quick sale.

But here's what makes it worthwhile: When the Interview is done well, the subsequent phases become dramatically easier. Solutions flow naturally from the information you gathered. Objections rarely arise because you've already addressed concerns during Interview. Closing becomes simple because the Customer already sees you as their advocate.

Traditional selling is hard throughout – difficult greeting, challenged presentation, pressure closing. WISE Selling front-loads the work into Welcome and Interview, making later phases almost effortless.

The Interview as Differentiation

In an age where Customers can research products extensively online, the Interview becomes one of your primary differentiators. Amazon can't conduct an Interview. YouTube videos can't ask about their specific situation. Review sites can't customize recommendations to their unique needs.

This human capability – understanding individual situations through conversation – is what justifies physical retail's existence. Customers who want generic product information don't need to visit stores. Customers who need genuine consultation do.

Position yourself as the consultant (guide) they cannot find online. Demonstrate that a few minutes of thoughtful Interview provides more value than hours of internet research. Help them discover needs they didn't know they had and avoid mistakes they didn't know they were making.

This is how physical retail survives and thrives: by offering something genuinely better than digital alternatives.

Practice and Improvement

Interview skills develop through deliberate practice. Several methods accelerate learning:

Record and review. Record roleplay interactions. Listening reveals patterns you don't notice in the moment – questions you ask repeatedly, topics you avoid, interrupting habits.

Role-play extensively. Practice Interview scenarios with colleagues. Take turns playing difficult Customers – the uncommunicative one, the know-it-all, the indecisive one. Develop comfort handling various personalities.

Debrief after interactions. What questions worked well? Which didn't? What information did you wish you'd gathered but didn't? Conscious reflection accelerates improvement.

Study your best performers. Watch or shadow your store's top salespeople. How do they conduct interviews? What questions do they ask? How do they handle resistance?

Read beyond retail. Books on investigative interviewing, journalism, therapy, and sales all offer valuable questioning techniques. The skills transfer across domains.

Track your improvement. Notice how interview duration, information quality, and conversion rates change as you improve. Data keeps you motivated through the learning curve.

Excellence in the Interview doesn't happen instantly. You'll ask clumsy questions. You'll interrupt at the wrong moments. You'll forget to summarize. This is all normal. Every expert was once a beginner. The only way through is practice.

Transition Phrase to The Solution

When the Interview is complete – you've explored past experience, expectations, and conditions of use; you've listened actively; you've reviewed and summarized accurately – you're ready to transition into the Solution phase.

This transition should feel natural and logical. The most powerful transition phrase is simple:

"Based on what you've told me… I have the perfect solution for you."

This phrase works because:

- It references the Interview explicitly ("based on what you've told me")
- It promises a customized answer ("the perfect solution for you")
- It positions you as the expert who synthesized their information into recommendations
- It signals that you're about to shift from asking to advising from Interviewing to guiding

Remember to use your own words. **"Based on what you've told me, I think I know exactly what you need.** or **"I think I know just what you are looking for "** or **"Based on what you've told me, I have a couple of options that you are going to love."**

Based on what you've told me is simply the most powerful phrase in selling. It works in multiple Phases of WISE Selling. It works here as the transition from the Interview to the Solution. It will work later when answering objections. And it works in the Experience Phase when you lock in the sale and say, "Based on what you've told me, you are going to love your new bike!"

What makes this so powerful is that when faced with this, it is hard to reject. It even works in marriages. My wife and I may not agree on something, but when she says "well, you said" (her version of "based on what you've told me") and I realize she's right - I'm cooked as my daughters would say.

The Customer has been talking. You've been listening. Now they're ready to hear what you learned and what you recommend. They've earned your expertise through their participation in Interview.

This is the moment where WISE Selling begins paying obvious dividends. Because you understand the Customer deeply, your recommendations will resonate. They'll recognize their own needs in your suggestions. They'll trust your guidance because you demonstrated understanding.

In the next chapter, we'll explore exactly how to present those solutions in ways that create excitement and eliminate resistance.

Chapter 4

Solution – Becoming the Expert They Need

The Interview revealed everything: your Customer's experience level, their goals, their constraints, their fears, their budget, and what success looks like to them. You've listened carefully, asked clarifying questions, summarized to confirm your understanding, and used the most powerful phrase in selling "Based on what you've told me." Now comes the moment they've been waiting for: your expert recommendation.

This is the Solution phase – the S in WISE – is where you transform the raw material of Customer information into specific, actionable recommendations that address their needs precisely.

But here's where most salespeople stumble. They know what to recommend, but they present it ineffectively. They rattle off features the Customer doesn't understand. They use technical jargon that creates confusion rather than clarity. They fail to connect product capabilities to the specific needs revealed during the Interview.

The result? Customers who should be excited about your recommendation feel overwhelmed, confused, or skeptical. The sale that should be easy becomes difficult. Objections multiply. Customers say they need to "think about it" – which usually means they're going somewhere else.

This chapter teaches you to present solutions in ways that create clarity, excitement, and confidence. You'll learn how to translate features into benefits, structure presentations for maximum impact, and handle the unique challenges of different Customer types and product categories.

Why We Call It "Solution" – Becoming the Guide, Not the Hero

There's a profound reason we call this phase "Solution" instead of "presentation" or "pitch" or "recommendation." The language matters more than you might think.

When you present a "Solution," you're fundamentally positioning yourself differently in the Customer's story. You're not the hero swooping in to save the day with your amazing product knowledge. You're not the salesperson pushing your favorite items or this month's featured merchandise.

Remember our discussion of Donald Miller and his StoryBrand book in Chapter 1? The Solution Phase is really where you start to drive home this principle -

You're the **guide** helping the Customer find **their** solution to **their** problem.

This distinction changes everything.

The Hero's Journey and Your Role in It

In every great story, the protagonist, the hero, faces a challenge and must overcome it to achieve their goal. Your Customer is on exactly this kind of journey. They walked into your store because they have a problem to solve, a goal to achieve, a need to fulfill.

They're renovating their kitchen. They're training for their first marathon. They're trying to capture better photos of their kids' sports games. They're building cabinets for their workshop. They're furnishing their first home.

They are the hero of this story.

And heroes don't need someone to rescue them. They need someone to **guide** them toward success. They need expertise, wisdom, and direction, but the victory must be theirs.

Think about every great mentor in literature and film: Gandalf guiding Frodo, Obi-Wan guiding Luke, Haymitch guiding Katniss. The mentor never takes over the hero's journey. The mentor provides knowledge, tools, and direction then trusts the hero to act.

That's your role as a WISE practitioner. You're Gandalf, not Frodo. You're Obi-Wan, not Luke.

When you call it "the Solution" and consciously frame it as **their** solution that you're helping them discover, you position yourself correctly in their story. You become the trusted guide they need, not the pushy salesperson they fear.

The Fears

As you read through this book, we will weave a consistent theme about the two fundamental fears of every Customer when they enter your store - the fear of making a mistake and the fear of looking stupid. (Deep dive on this in Chapter 8) Embedded deeply in the fear of looking stupid is a more specific fear: **the fear of being manipulated or taken advantage of by a pushy salesperson.**

Every Customer who's ever walked into a retail store has had this experience or heard horror stories about it. The salesperson who cares more about their commission than the Customer's actual needs. The one who pushes the most expensive option regardless of fit. The one who makes you feel pressured, cornered, manipulated.

That's the "hero" salesperson; the one who makes the sale about themselves, their goals, their success. "Look at what I sold! Look at how I convinced them! Look at how good I am!"

When you position yourself as the guide presenting **their** solution, you eliminate this fear completely.

Here's why: A solution, by definition, is the answer to **their** problem. Not your problem. Not your commission goals. Not your sales quota. **Their** problem that they came to you to help solve.

When you say, "Based on what you've told me, here's the solution for your situation," you're explicitly stating that this recommendation flows from **their** needs, **their** goals, **their** constraints. It's not about you at all.

This is why the phrase "Based on what you've told me" is so powerful. It reminds both you and the Customer that everything you're about to recommend comes directly from understanding their specific situation through the Interview. You're not imposing your preferences. You're reflecting back what they need.

The Solution Is Theirs; The Expertise Is Yours

Here's the beautiful balance of being the guide: The solution belongs to the Customer, but the expertise that identifies that solution belongs to you.

The Customer owns the decision. They're empowered. They're in control. They're the hero of their own story.

But they needed your expert guidance to find the right path forward. They needed your knowledge of products, your understanding of trade-offs, your experience with what works and what doesn't. They needed your Interview skills to help them articulate what they actually need. They needed your ability to connect their needs to the right products.

Without you (without the guide) they would have been lost in a sea of options, overwhelmed by specifications they don't understand, uncertain about which path to take.

With you (with the expert guide) they found **their** solution. And because it's **their** solution, they're committed to it. They own it. They believe in it.

How This Shows Up in Your Language

Listen to the difference in how these sound:

Hero language (It's about you):

- "I'm going to sell you this model because it's the best."
- "I recommend this because I love it."
- "This is what I think you should get."
- "Let me tell you what you need."
- "Trust me on this one."

Guide language (It's about them):

- "Based on what you've told me about your situation, here's the solution that fits."
- "Given your goals and constraints, this is what makes sense."
- "For your specific project, this addresses your needs."
- "Your solution includes these elements because you mentioned..."
- "This works for your situation because..."

Notice how guide language constantly references **their** situation, **their** needs, **their** goals? It's explicitly making the solution theirs, not yours.

This isn't just semantic trickery. This is fundamentally different positioning that the Customer feels at a deep level.

When you use guide language, Customers relax. Their defensive walls come down. They stop worrying about being manipulated because you're clearly not trying to impose your will on them. You're helping them find their own answer.

Why Salespeople Resist This (And Why You Shouldn't)

Many salespeople resist being "just the guide." They want to be the hero. Their ego demands it.

"Look at this amazing sale I made! Look at how I convinced that difficult Customer! Look at how I overcame their objections!"

It's all about them. Their skill. Their cleverness. Their persuasiveness.

This is natural. We all want to feel important, skilled, heroic. But here's the brutal truth: **hero salespeople get 50/50 results.**

Why? Because Customers don't trust heroes. Heroes have their own agenda. Heroes are self-focused. Heroes make the story about themselves.

Guides, on the other hand, are trusted implicitly. Why? Because guides have no agenda except helping the hero succeed. The guide's success **is** the hero's success. The guide's only goal is equipping the hero to win.

When you let go of being the hero and embrace being the guide, something magical happens: **You actually become more successful, not less.**

Because Customers trust you more. They accept your guidance more readily. They implement your recommendations more fully. They return more often. They refer more people.

Your lifetime value per Customer skyrockets not because you're manipulating or convincing better, but because you're genuinely serving better.

The guide who helps 100 customers find **their** solutions has far more success (and far more satisfaction) than the hero who forces 100 customers to accept **his** solutions.

The Solution Framework Reinforces Guide Positioning

At the risk of "skipping ahead"- notice how the entire WISE Selling framework reinforces guide positioning at every step:

Welcome: You're not pitching. You're greeting warmly and establishing that you're here to help them, not sell to them.

Interview: You're not assuming. You're asking questions to understand **their** unique situation deeply. You're listening more than talking.

Solution: You're not pushing your favorite products. You're presenting **their** solution based on **their** specific needs that you uncovered in Interview.

Experience: You're not moving on to the next commission. You're ensuring **their** success through lock-in, complete solutions, and follow-up.

Every single phase reinforces: This is about them, not you. You're the guide helping them succeed.

The word "Solution" is the linguistic manifestation of this entire philosophy. When you say "solution," you're reminding yourself and signaling to the Customer: This is **their** answer to **their** challenge, which I'm helping them discover through my expertise.

How This Should Change Your Mindset

When you truly internalize that you're presenting **their** solution, not **your** pitch, several things shift in your mindset:

You stop worrying about rejection. If they don't buy, it's not a rejection of you. Maybe the solution you identified doesn't fit their budget right now. Maybe they need time to process. Maybe they need to consult with someone. That's all fine. It's **their** decision about **their** solution.

You stop feeling pushy. You're not pushing anything. You're guiding them to what genuinely fits their needs. If you've done a thorough Interview and customized your Solution presentation appropriately, you're simply showing them the logical path forward.

You become more confident. Paradoxically, giving up the hero role makes you more confident, not less. Why? Because you're standing on solid ground - the Interview information they gave you. You're not guessing or manipulating. You're genuinely helping based on real understanding.

You care more about their success. When it's **their** solution, you're emotionally invested in whether it actually works for them. You follow up because you genuinely want to know: Did the solution work? Are they succeeding? This authentic care shows through in everything you do.

You're liberated from perfection. Heroes have to be perfect. Guides can be honest about limitations, acknowledge trade-offs, and admit when the perfect solution doesn't exist. This honesty builds trust rather than destroying it.

The Ultimate Test

Here's how you know you've fully embraced being the guide presenting **their** solution:

You can genuinely say, without any hesitation, that you would recommend the exact same solution to your best friend or family member if they had the exact same situation, goals, and constraints that this Customer described in Interview.

If you can't honestly say that you're not presenting **their** solution; you're pushing **your** agenda.

But when you genuinely believe that what you're recommending is what you'd tell your sister or your best friend if they were in this exact situation, then that's when you've become the guide.

And that's when everything changes.

The Customer feels it. They sense your authenticity. They trust your guidance. They accept your recommendations. They become loyal advocates.

Not because you're a brilliant manipulator or a gifted salesperson.

But because you helped them find **their** solution.

You became the guide they needed, not the hero you wanted to be.

And paradoxically, by letting them be the hero of their own story, **you** become the hero of your own career. A career with sustainable success, deep satisfaction, and customers who return year after year because they trust you to guide them toward their next solution.

That's the power of calling it "Solution."

That's the power of being the guide.

Now, enough lecture. Let's break the Solution down into the important selling components.

Features vs. Benefits: Understanding the Difference

Every product or service has features – objective characteristics, specifications, or capabilities. A treadmill has a motor (3.5 horsepower), a running surface (22" x 60"), incline capability (15 levels), and preset programs (12 options).

Features are facts. They're measurable, comparable, and objective. They're also completely meaningless to most Customers.

Benefits are what features do for the Customer. They answer the crucial question every Customer is silently asking: "What's in it for me?"

That 3.5 horsepower motor? The benefit is "smooth, consistent performance that won't bog down even during intense workouts." The 22" x 60" running surface? "Comfortable stride without feeling cramped, even if you're tall." The 15 incline levels? "Variety to keep workouts interesting and target different muscle groups."

Here's the fundamental principle of Solution presentation:

Features tell. Benefits sell.

Customers don't buy specifications; they buy outcomes. They don't want a table saw with a 3-horsepower motor and a cast-iron table; they want precise, safe cuts that make their woodworking projects turn out beautifully. They don't want a shirt with a moisture-wicking lining; they want the ability to run outdoors in a short that doesn't get heavy with sweat.

Yet salespeople consistently fall into the feature trap. Why? Several reasons:

Product training focuses on features. Manufacturers provide specification sheets and feature lists. Sales training teaches you what products have, not what they do for Customers. Even when the manufacturer or vendor rep comes into the store, they tell you the difference between product A and product B is based on a list of features.

Features feel objective and professional. Listing specifications seems authoritative. Benefits can feel like "mere opinion" or sales hype.

The curse of knowledge. Once you understand how features benefit Customers, the connection seems obvious. You forget that Customers don't have your expertise.

Features are easier to remember. Spec sheets provide features. Benefits require you to think through implications for different Customer situations.

Overcoming the feature trap requires conscious practice translating every feature into Customer-relevant benefits.

The "This Has, That Means" Formula

In order to avoid the traps of feature selling, we use a tool called Benefit Statements. A benefit statement has a construct that forces you to give the benefit. Most salespeople will tell you what it does and how it does it but rarely tell you why you need it. And the "why" in our scenario is based on the information you gathered during the Interview.

The simplest method for creating benefit statements uses a two-part structure:

"This has [feature]. That means [benefit for you]."

Examples:

- "This treadmill has a shock-absorption system in the deck. That means you can run longer with less stress on your knees and joints."
- "This router has electronic variable speed. That means you can adjust it perfectly for whatever material you're working with – preventing burns on hardwood or chipping on plastics."
- "This exercise bike has a self-generating power system. That means you can place it anywhere in your home without worrying about outlets or power cords."
- "This jacket has a breathable membrane liner. That means you stay comfortable during active movement without overheating, while still being protected from wind and rain."
- "These dress pants have a stretch fabric blend. That means you can move freely throughout your day – whether you're sitting in meetings or rushing between appointments – without feeling restricted."
- "This shirt has moisture-wicking technology. That means perspiration is drawn away from your skin, keeping you dry and confident even during stressful presentations or warm commutes."
- "These jeans have reinforced stress points at the knees and pockets. That means they'll last much longer through regular wear, saving you money and the hassle of frequent replacements."
- "This winter coat has synthetic insulation. That means it keeps you warm even when wet and dries quickly – perfect for unpredictable weather."
- "This washing machine has a load-sensing system. That means it automatically adjusts water levels based on your laundry size, reducing your water bills and environmental impact."
- "This refrigerator has dual cooling zones. That means your produce stays crisp longer, and your frozen foods maintain quality, reducing food waste and grocery trips."

- "This dishwasher has a third rack for utensils. That means you can fit up to 30% more items per load and free up space in the bottom racks for larger pots and pans."
- "This vacuum has HEPA filtration. That means it captures 99.97% of allergens and dust particles, creating a healthier environment for family members with allergies or asthma."
- "This oven has true convection heating. That means heat circulates evenly throughout, so you can bake multiple trays of cookies at once with consistent results on every rack."
- "This coffee maker has a thermal carafe. That means your coffee stays hot for hours without a heating plate, preserving the flavor and eliminating that burnt taste."
- "These tires have asymmetric tread patterns. That means you get exceptional handling in corners while maintaining straight-line stability, giving you confidence in all driving conditions."
- "These tires have deep circumferential grooves. That means water is channeled away quickly, reducing hydroplaning risk and keeping you safer during heavy rain."
- "This moisturizer has hyaluronic acid. That means it can hold up to 1,000 times its weight in water, keeping your skin plump and hydrated throughout the day without feeling greasy."
- "This sunscreen has broad-spectrum SPF 50. That means you're protected from both UVA and UVB rays, preventing premature aging and reducing your risk of skin damage during outdoor activities."
- "This cleanser has a pH-balanced formula. That means it cleans effectively without stripping your skin's natural protective barrier, leaving you fresh and comfortable rather than tight and dry."
- "This serum has vitamin C stabilized with ferulic acid. That means it brightens your complexion and reduces dark spots while remaining potent and effective, giving you visible results you can actually see."

Okay, that was a lot of examples, but I wanted to make my point. The typical salesperson loves to talk about how features work. But when all you do is talk about features, you are simply adding cost. And the more "cost" you are adding, the more you are triggering their fear of making a mistake. Think of it this way:

Features Add Cost Benefits Add Value

I have watched too many sales presentations where the salesperson just kept stacking up the features. To their credit, they were demonstrating an impressive amount of product knowledge. But the Customer was slowly tuning out. All they hear when you stack up features is a bunch of stuff they don't need!

The formula works because it explicitly connects feature to benefit. The Customer hears both the specification (for those who care about such details) and the practical implication (which everyone cares about).

A variation adds "Because" as a third element, explaining the mechanism:

"This has [feature]. That means [benefit]. Because [explanation]."

Examples:

- "This dovetail jig has built-in setting gauges. That means you save tons of time on setup. Because you don't have to measure and test-cut repeatedly – the gauges show you exactly where to set everything immediately."
- "This TV has a 120Hz refresh rate. That means fast-action sports and movies look incredibly smooth without blur, because the screen updates twice as fast as standard TVs, capturing every moment of movement."
- "This television has HDMI 2.1 ports. That means you can experience next-gen gaming at its full potential with 4K at 120fps, because these ports have the bandwidth to handle the massive amount of data that advanced gaming consoles produce."
- "This sofa has eight-way hand-tied springs. That means it will maintain its comfort and support for decades, because each spring is individually knotted to the frame and neighboring springs, creating a foundation that won't sag or lose shape."
- "This dining table has a solid wood top. That means it can be refinished multiple times over the years, because real wood can be sanded down and restained, allowing you to refresh its appearance or repair damage rather than replacing it."

- "This office chair has lumbar support adjustment. That means you can sit comfortably through long work sessions without back pain, because the lower back support moves up, down, and in or out to match your spine's natural curve exactly."
- "This mattress has individually wrapped coils. That means you won't feel your partner moving during the night, because each spring responds independently to pressure, isolating motion to just one area of the bed."

The three-part version works well with Customers who like understanding how things work. It's more for your experts. The two-part version is more concise for Customers who just want bottom-line benefits. It is more for the typical Customer.

Practice translating features for every product you sell. Create a mental database of benefit statements you can deploy appropriately. After all, these do not change based on the Customer. Or do they....

Customizing Benefits to the Interview

Here's where the Interview pays enormous dividends: You know exactly which benefits matter to each specific Customer. Consider this, I have a Jeep Grand Wagoneer. It is an amazing vehicle that has so many features that I never even knew it had. One early morning while I was waiting for one of my daughters to get out of practice, I started scrolling around and playing with the buttons and I discovered about 100 things that I could care less about. I'd just assume they were automatic and adjusted as needed when needed. So, if you spent time on these, then you would definitely have lost me.

But I did discover that it had night vision. I could turn it on and it would sense heat signatures at night. It actually tags an animal moving and shows it on the screen for safety. And living in the country on two-lane roads, I absolutely needed this. And this is where you move from hero to guide - you connect the Benefit Statements to the Interview. In fact, in my seminars I often confess that when I am selling I only cover features that I derived directly from the Interview in my presentation. Sure, it does a lot more, but the more I connect it to the /interview, the more it is *their* choice and not mine.

Let's go back to that detailed kitchen cabinet refinishing Interview from Chapter 3 and see how this works. The Customer mentioned:

- Working mostly alone over weekends
- Three young kids (durability matters)
- Limited woodworking experience
- Desire to avoid a drawn-out project
- Wanting a lighter, modern look

Now watch how Solution presentations (Benefit Statements) reference the Interview:

"Based on what you've told me, here's what I recommend. For stripping the old finish, this gel stripper is perfect because you mentioned working mostly alone. That means it's user-friendly for someone doing this solo – you don't need professional experience to get great results.

For your new finish, I'm suggesting this gel stain in our coastal oak color. You mentioned wanting something lighter and more modern, and this is one of our most popular choices for exactly that look. Here's the key part for your situation with three kids: this particular stain pairs with a poly finish that's extremely durable. That means it handles the daily abuse of kids without showing every fingerprint or getting damaged easily."

Notice how every recommendation explicitly references what the Customer told you. "Because you mentioned..." or "You said you wanted..." This isn't manipulative; it's demonstrating that you listened and your recommendations flow logically from *their* needs.

This customization transforms the Solution phase from a product pitch into collaborative problem-solving. The Customer recognizes their own needs in your presentation. They see that you genuinely understood them and thought carefully about their situation.

Contrast this with a generic presentation: "This is our best-selling stain. It comes in 12 colors. It has low VOC content. It dries in 4 hours. We have it in stock." None of this connects to the Customer. It's information without meaning.

The Three Types of Benefits

Not all benefits are created equal. Different Customers prioritize different value types. Understanding these categories helps you emphasize the right benefits for each Customer.

Functional Benefits: These address practical performance – what the product does and how well it does it.

Examples:

- "This elliptical has a smooth, quiet stride"
- "This saw blade makes clean cuts with minimal tear out"
- "This bookshelf has adjustable shelving"

Functional benefits matter most to Customers focused on capability and performance. Enthusiasts and professionals particularly care about functional excellence.

Emotional Benefits: These address feelings – how the Customer will feel using the product or after achieving their goals.

Examples:

- "You'll feel confident knowing this equipment won't let you down"
- "Imagine the pride when friends see your finished project"
- "You'll love reclining back in this chair and watching the game"

Emotional benefits resonate with all Customers but especially DIYers and those early in their journey. People who are anxious or uncertain need emotional reassurance as much as functional capabilities.

Economic Benefits: These address financial value – saving money, avoiding waste, protecting investment, or achieving ROI.

Examples:

- "The table's durability means you won't need to replace it in two years"
- "The washer's efficiency saves on electricity costs over time"
- "One quality tool that does the job right is cheaper than buying and replacing cheap ones"

Economic benefits matter to all Customers but particularly those on tight budgets or making significant investments. Professionals care deeply about ROI – their tools need to pay for themselves through work.

In any presentation, incorporate all three benefit types. Different elements of your solution will emphasize different benefits, creating a well-rounded picture of value.

Structuring Your Solution

How you organize your recommendations matters as much as what you recommend. Effective structure creates clarity and builds conviction. Here's a proven framework:

1. Transition from Interview

Begin with the phrases that signal you're moving into recommendations:

"Based on what you've told me, I know exactly what you need..." or "Here's what I recommend for your situation..."

This transition reminds Customers that recommendations flow from understanding their specific needs.

2. Start with the primary recommendation

Lead with your main suggestion – the core product or solution that addresses their central need:

"I'm recommending the X-series line for you..."

Be specific and confident. Don't hedge with "maybe" or "you might consider." You're the expert. Make a clear recommendation.

3. Explain why this particular option

Connect your recommendation to their situation:

"This model fits your situation perfectly because you mentioned [Interview detail]. This addresses that by [benefit]."

4. Present 2-3 key benefits

Focus on the benefits most relevant to their Interview. Don't list every feature; highlight the ones that matter to them:

"The three things that make this ideal for you are: First, [benefit based on Interview detail]... Second, [benefit based on Interview detail]... Third, [benefit based on Interview detail]..."

5. Use the "That means" structure

For each benefit, use the formula: "This has [feature]. That means [benefit relevant to their situation]."

6. Check for understanding

After each major benefit, use a **tie-down** question to confirm they understand and agree:

"Does that make sense?" "That would work for your space, right?" "That addresses your concern about _____, doesn't it?"

These check-ins prevent confusion from accumulating. If the Customer looks uncertain, you can address it immediately rather than discovering misunderstanding later.

7. Introduce supporting recommendations

After the primary solution, present complementary items:

"To complete your setup, you'll also need..."

This is where you begin the add-on process we'll discuss in depth in Chapter 10.

8. Summarize the complete solution

End with a brief recap:

"So, to solve [their goal from Interview], I'm recommending [primary solution] because [key reason], plus [supporting items] to ensure [comprehensive outcome]."

This structure works because it's logical, Customer-focused, and builds conviction progressively. Each element reinforces that you understand the Customer and have thoughtfully designed a solution for them.

Demonstrating, Not Just Describing

Whenever possible, demonstrations dramatically increase Solution effectiveness. Seeing and touching beats hearing every time.

Different product categories allow different demonstration approaches:

For equipment: Have Customers try it. Get them on the elliptical, let them operate the table saw (safely), have them feel the weight and balance of tools. When I used to sell refrigerators, I would pull out the crisper bins and jump on them to demonstrate their durability.

Physical interaction creates visceral understanding that words cannot. The Customer who actually experiences the smooth stride of an elliptical understands its quality differently than one who only hears about it.

For materials or finishes: Show samples. Let Customers touch different stain finishes, feel the difference between wood species, compare material weights.

For technical features: Use visual aids. Show diagrams, play videos, use apps or tablets to illustrate concepts.

For before/after: Show examples of completed projects. Photos of kitchen cabinet transformations, finished woodworking projects, Customer testimonials with pictures.

During demonstrations, guide but don't control. Let Customers discover benefits themselves:

"Try adjusting the incline. Notice how smoothly it moves?" "Feel that? "Here, swap between these two bits. See how the carbide one feels more substantial?"

When Customers discover benefits through their own experience, they trust those benefits more than if you simply claimed them.

Handling Multiple Options

Sometimes the Interview reveals that multiple products could work. The Customer's needs don't point to a single obvious answer.

In these cases, present 2-3 options with clear differentiation:

"Based on our conversation, I have two recommendations that could both work, but in slightly different ways..."

Then explain each option with its particular strengths:

"Option 1 is [product]. This would be the choice if [circumstance]. The advantages are [benefits].

Option 2 is [product]. This would be better if [different circumstance]. The advantages here are [different benefits].

Which of those situations sounds more like what you're looking for?"

This approach gives Customers choice without overwhelming them. You're not showing them 10 options and saying "pick one." You're narrowing to 2-3 thoughtfully selected options and helping them think through the differences.

The key is clearly articulating what makes each option distinctive and which Customer circumstances favor each. Don't just show three similar products at different price points. Show genuinely different solutions for different priorities or situations.

The Price Conversation

At some point in the Solution, price enters the conversation. Many salespeople dread this moment, fearing the Customer will balk or compare to lower prices elsewhere. We tried to setup this discussion in the Interview Phase with our expectation question.

But WISE Selling makes price conversations easier through several techniques:

Technique 1: Address price in Interview

Remember the budget question from Chapter 3? By discussing price parameters during the Interview, you've already established that recommendations will align with their financial situation.

Technique 2: Emphasize value, not price

Frame price in terms of value received:

"The investment for this complete solution is $2,400. That gives you [benefit], [benefit], and [benefit], which solves [their goal from Interview]."

Technique 3: Break down costs

Help Customers understand pricing in manageable terms:

"Over five years of regular use, that breaks down to about $400 per year, or roughly a $1 per load of laundry."

or

"The difference between the standard model at $800 and this premium version at $1,200 is $400. That $400 gets you [specific benefits]. Given that you mentioned [Interview detail], I think that $400 is worth it for your situation."

Technique 4: Compare to alternatives

Help Customers understand your price in context:

"Compared to a gym membership at $50/month, this pays for itself in about two years – and then you have your own equipment for as long as you want."

Technique 5: Acknowledge significant investments

For expensive items, recognize the decision's significance:

"This is definitely an investment. I wouldn't recommend it if I didn't think it was the right solution for what you're trying to accomplish. But given [their goal], [their constraints], and [their priorities from the Interview], this gives you exactly what you need to be successful."

Technique 6: Separate price concerns from value concerns

Oftentimes Customers say, "that's too expensive" when they really mean "I don't see enough value yet." Before addressing price, ensure you've fully explained benefits:

"Is it the dollar amount that's higher than you planned, or is it that you're not sure it delivers enough value for the price?"

If it's the value concern, revisit benefits. If it's truly budget, discuss alternatives:

"I understand that's higher than you wanted to spend. But based on what you told me, this is the best solution for your needs. However, let's talk about which features are most important to you, and we can look at options that deliver those within your budget range."

The Movie Theater Principle: Endings Matter

So, have you ever been to a movie and thoroughly enjoyed yourself until the ending? The special effects were great, the actors were great, but the ending was less than expected? How does that leave you feeling about the entire movie?

The Customer might love the product you recommended. The Interview might have been thorough. The Solution might have been perfect. But if the experience after they say "yes" is mediocre—if you don't lock in their decision, if you forget critical accessories, if you never follow up—they leave with uncertainty instead of confidence.

That uncertainty is what creates 50/50 odds instead of 98%.

Many times, we finish our presentation on the sales floor and simply stand back and say "soooo..." and wait for the Customer to make the next move. We stand there and let a great movie end badly.

Assuming the Sale: Moving Forward with Confidence

Before we dive into post-purchase Experience, let's address a critical moment that determines whether you even get to the Experience phase: **assuming the sale.**

So, when is the best time to Assume the sale and ask the Customer to buy?

Timing is everything. The best time to close the sale and ask the Customer to buy is **whenever the Customer is most likely to say yes!**

This time may be, and often times is, different for each Customer.

So, can you identify when the Customer is ready to buy? Good question.

There are two ways to know when the Customer is most likely to say yes—we watch for **verbal and nonverbal cues.**

Verbal cues are the easiest to pick up on. But you have to listen for them. Be ready for what you hear when you hear them. Keep it in mind that you have a lot of Customers who need your assistance, so in a way, you are providing a real service when you take the initiative and **Assume the Sale.**

Reading Buying Signals

Here are some examples of verbal cues we found in the store

- I really like this bike.
- How much is it?
- Does this come in other colors?

These are all buying signals. The Customer is mentally moving forward. They're imagining ownership. They're working through logistics.

Other verbal buying signals:

- "How long will this take to arrive?"
- "Do you have this in stock?"
- "Can I return it if it doesn't work?"
- "What's your warranty?"
- "My wife would love this."
- "When could I pick this up?"
- "Do you deliver?"

When you hear these signals, **assume the sale**. Don't keep presenting. Don't add more information. Move confidently toward completing the purchase.

Nonverbal Buying Signals:

- Touching or holding the product repeatedly
- Nodding while you explain benefits
- Smiling or showing positive body language
- Leaning in with interest
- Examining the product closely (checking seams, testing features)
- Checking price tag multiple times
- Looking at it from multiple angles
- Imagining where it would go or how they'd use it
- Discussing it with their shopping partner positively
- Relaxed body language (they've overcome their fears)

When you see these signals, assume the sale.

How to Assume the Sale

The assumptive close means you act as if the decision to buy has been made and you're simply moving to the next logical step.

This builds on the trust you've created through Welcome, Interview, and Solution. You've eliminated their fears through compassion and confidence. Now you move forward with the same confidence.

Weak approach (asking permission, inviting hesitation):

"So... do you want to buy this?"

"Are you ready to purchase?"

"What do you think? Should we do this?"

These questions invite hesitation and re-trigger the fear of making a mistake. You're asking them to make a scary decision.

Strong approach (assuming the sale, moving forward):

"Perfect, let me get this written up for you."

"Great, let's get you set up with this."

"Excellent choice. I'll get this rung up and we'll get you on your way."

"Let me grab this from the back in your size."

You're acting as if the decision is made. You're moving confidently to the next step. This demonstrates confidence (you know this is right for them) and shows compassion (you're making the process smooth, not pressuring them).

If they're not ready, they'll stop you: "Wait, I want to think about it" or "Can I see one more option?" That's fine. You'll handle it appropriately (we'll cover this later in this chapter).

But most of the time, when you assume the sale after clear buying signals, Customers simply move forward with you. Your confidence gives them confidence.

Assuming the Sale Across Product Categories

Bicycle Shop: [Customer test rode the bike, asked about the gear range, mentioned it feels comfortable]

"Excellent. This bike matches your riding style perfectly. Let me get this adjusted to your exact fit and rung up. Did you want to take it today or should we deliver it once the fit adjustments are complete?"

You're offering options for how to proceed, not whether to proceed.

Furniture Store: [Customer sat on the sofa twice, discussed with spouse positively, asked about delivery timeframe]

"Great choice for your family's needs. This is going to serve you well for years. Let me get your delivery information and we'll get this scheduled. What's your address?"

You're already asking for delivery information. You've assumed the sale. You're moving forward.

Jewelry Store: [Customer looking at engagement ring, asked about sizing, mentioned "she would love this"]

"This ring is exactly right for what you described about her style. Let me get your information and we'll talk about sizing and any customization. What's the best contact number for you?"

Getting their information. Moving forward. Assuming the sale.

Camera Store: [Customer has been nodding throughout your explanation, has picked up the camera three times, just asked about the warranty]

"Perfect. This camera is exactly right for photographing your kids' sports like we discussed. Let me get a box from the back and we'll get you set up. While I'm grabbing that, which memory card size makes sense for you? The 64GB or 128GB?"

Notice: You assumed the sale ("let me get a box") and moved seamlessly to ensuring they have complete solutions (memory card).

Electronics Store: [Customer asked about the return policy, checked the price twice, nodded throughout your explanation]

"This laptop handles everything you described perfectly. Let's get you checked out. I'll set up your account in our system so you get warranty coverage and can reach me if questions come up."

Moving to checkout, creating their customer profile. You've assumed the sale.

Sporting Goods Store: [Customer tried on running shoes, walked around the store in them, asked if they're good for trail running]

"These are perfect for the trail running you described. Let me get you a fresh pair from the back. Size 9.5, correct? And based on your training volume, you'll want a second pair to rotate. Let's talk about that while I'm grabbing these."

Assumed the sale, moving to get product, already thinking about their complete solution.

Garden Center: [Customer asked if the plants would survive in shade, confirmed they match the description of their yard, picked up three of them]

"Perfect. These plants will thrive in your yard conditions based on what you described. Let me get you checked out and I'll give you the planting instructions. How many of each did you want? Will three be okay or should we get you a few more for fuller coverage?"

Assuming purchase, moving to checkout, even suggesting they might need more.

Clothing Store: [Customer tried on dress, came out of dressing room smiling, asked their friend "what do you think?" and their friend said "that's beautiful on you"]

"That dress is stunning on you and perfect for the event you described. Let me grab a garment bag for this. While you're changing, I'll pull together some accessories that would complete the look like the necklace and shoes we talked about. Sound good?"

Assumed the sale, moving to complete the solution.

What If They're Not Ready?

If you assume the sale and they're not ready, they'll tell you:

"Wait, I want to think about it."

"Can I see that other option you mentioned?"

"I need to talk to my wife first."

That's perfectly fine. You haven't lost anything. You simply respond with the same compassion and confidence you've shown throughout:

"Of course, no problem. What specifically would be helpful to think through?"

Or: "Absolutely, let me show you that other option."

Or: "That makes sense. What questions should I make sure you can answer when you talk to her?"

You've simply moved from Solution to handling their concern—which is a natural part of the process.

But here's what happens most of the time: when you confidently assume the sale after clear buying signals, Customers simply move forward with you. Your confidence gives them confidence. Your assumption that this is the right decision reinforces their belief that it is the right decision.

This is compassion and confidence working together. You're making the process smooth (compassion) while demonstrating certainty (confidence). Both fears are eliminated, and the Customer moves forward.

"Based on everything we've discussed – your experience level, your project goals, your space, your budget – I'm confident this is exactly what you need to be successful. Does it feel right to you?"

This approach works because:

It's collaborative, not pushy. You're checking alignment, not forcing decision.

It invites honest feedback. If Customers have concerns, this question surfaces them for discussion rather than driving them underground.

It references the entire process. By mentioning "everything we've discussed," you're reminding them of the careful thought behind this recommendation.

It trusts their judgment. "Does it feel right to you?" respects their decision-making while confirming your expert opinion.

If the Customer says yes, great! Move forward with completing the purchase and adding on complementary items (Chapter 10).

If they express uncertainty, explore it:

"What part feels uncertain? Let's talk through that."

Often, one lingering question or concern prevents commitment. Address it and the sale proceeds smoothly.

Ultimately, you can go back to our Soften and Ask tool we learned in the Welcome Phase. But we will go into more detail on that in Chapter 11.

Common Solution Mistakes

Mistake 1: Showing too many options

More choice paradoxically makes decisions harder. Limit recommendations to 2-3 thoughtfully selected options, not 10 similar products. While ideally you only want to present the one perfect solution, the truth is very few Customers will walk away feeling like it was a remarkable experience if there are 100 TVs on the wall and you only show them one.

Mistake 2: Feature dumping

Listing every specification overwhelms Customers. Focus on 3-5 key benefits relevant to their Interview.

Mistake 3: Using jargon

Technical language alienates Customers. Use plain English. Explain terms if you must use them. And NO acronyms. This triggers the Customer's fear of looking stupid.

Mistake 4: Failing to connect to Interview

If your presentation doesn't reference the Interview, you're not demonstrating that you listened or that recommendations are customized.

Mistake 5: Neglecting demonstrations

Whenever possible, let Customers experience products directly. Descriptions can't match actual interaction.

Mistake 6: Rushing

Take time to present solutions thoroughly. Rushing suggests you care more about transactions than ensuring right fit.

Mistake 7: Being tentative

Make confident recommendations. You're the expert. Hedging with "maybe" or "you might consider" undermines your credibility.

Handling Common Concerns

Several concerns arise frequently during the Solution. Anticipate and address them proactively:

Concern: "Will I actually use it?"

The abandoned treadmill syndrome haunts many fitness equipment purchases. Address it directly:

"You mentioned wondering if you'll actually use it. That's a valid concern — nobody wants expensive equipment gathering dust. Here's what I've seen work: [specific strategies]. Also, the fact that you're asking thoughtful questions and taking time to find the right fit suggests you're approaching this seriously. That's very different from impulse purchases that become clothes racks."

Concern: "Is this too much for a beginner?"

DIYers worry about buying equipment beyond their skill level:

"Actually, getting quality equipment as a beginner is smart. Here's why: cheaper tools are harder to use because they're less precise and consistent. They make you work harder to get good results. This equipment will grow with you — it won't limit you as you get better."

Concern: "What if I'm wrong about what I need?"

Customers fear buyer's remorse:

"That's exactly why we spent so much time discussing your thoughts before we looked at any product – to make sure we understand your situation completely. Based on [specific Interview details], I'm confident this addresses your needs. Also, we have [return policy/satisfaction guarantee] if it turns out differently than expected."

Concern: "Can I get this cheaper elsewhere?"

Price shopping is inevitable:

"You might find a lower price online. Here's what you get by buying from us: [expert consultation we just provided], [setup/delivery], [service], [training], [local support]. The question is whether that value is worth [price difference]. For most Customers doing [their type of project], having that support makes a big difference in success."

When the Solution Isn't Perfect

Sometimes, even after a thorough Interview, the perfect solution doesn't exist. The Customer wants capabilities that conflict, or their budget doesn't support their needs, or their space truly won't accommodate what they want.

Don't pretend limitations don't exist. Address them honestly:

"I want to be straight with you. Given [constraint], we can't achieve [ideal outcome]. What we can do is [realistic alternative], which gets you [partial benefit]. The trade-off is [what they're sacrificing]. Is that acceptable, or would you rather wait until [constraint changes]?"

This honesty builds tremendous trust. Customers know you're not just trying to make a sale; you're genuinely helping them make the best decision possible given real constraints.

Sometimes the honest answer is "don't buy anything today":

"Based on our conversation, I don't think we have the right solution for you right now. Here's why: [specific reason]. My recommendation is [alternative approach]. When [condition changes], come back and we can revisit this."

Sending Customers away empty-handed seems counterintuitive. But it builds long-term relationships. That Customer will remember your honesty and return when the time is right. They'll also refer friends, knowing you won't push inappropriate products.

The Transition to Experience

When the Solution is complete – you've presented recommendations, demonstrated benefits, addressed concerns, and built confidence – you transition into the Experience phase (Chapter 5). Just like in our earlier Phases, you use a phrase to move forward and transition. In this instance the transition is based on the Close.

This transition often happens naturally as Customers indicate readiness:

"That sounds perfect!" "Where do I sign?" "Let's do it."

When you hear these signals, move forward confidently:

"Great! Let me get this written up for you. While I'm doing that, let me show you a few accessories that'll help you get the most out of this..."

Unfortunately, this type of Customer response is not the typical one. However, I have seen it happen dramatically more after a Sales Professional starts to use WISE Selling. So, the transition phrase that gets us from the Solution to the Experience Phase is what you have already learned…

"Since We've Agreed.."

This phrase creates a transition from Solution to Experience and into Add-Ons (more on Multiplying in Chapter 10) should feel seamless. The Customer isn't being sold anymore; they've already decided. Now you're helping them complete the purchase and ensuring they have everything they need for success. You have guided them to their Solution, not yours.

Measuring Your Solution Effectiveness

How do you know if your Solution presentations are working? Several metrics:

Conversion rate: What percentage of Customers you Interview ultimately buy? If you're interviewing thoroughly but conversion remains low, your Solution presentations need work.

Average transaction value: Are Customers buying just the core item, or are they accepting your recommendations for complete solutions? Higher transaction values suggest effective presentation of comprehensive solutions.

Return rate: High returns suggest Solution recommendations weren't actually right for Customers. Low returns confirm you're matching products to needs accurately.

Referral rate: Customers who receive genuinely helpful recommendations become your best marketers. If referrals increase, your Solutions are creating satisfied Customers.

Time to decision: How long between Solution presentation and purchase decision? Shorter times suggest clear, compelling presentations. Extended "thinking about it" suggests confusion or uncertainty.

Track these metrics for yourself and compare to colleagues. Improvement in these areas indicates developing Solution expertise.

The Expert Mindset

The WISE Selling Solution requires a specific mindset: You are an expert guide helping a client solve their problem. Not a salesperson pushing products. Not an order-taker facilitating transactions. An expert who is helping the Customer become the hero in their story.

This identity shift changes everything:

Experts make confident recommendations. They don't hedge or equivocate. They assess situations and advise clearly.

Experts educate. They help clients understand options, implications, and trade-offs. They increase client knowledge rather than exploiting ignorance.

Experts prioritize client success. They recommend what's truly best for the client, even when that's not what generates maximum immediate revenue.

Experts take pride in their work. They care about outcomes, not just transactions. They want clients to succeed and take satisfaction in enabling that success.

When you embody this expert identity, Customers perceive and treat you differently. They trust your recommendations. They accept your guidance. They value your input highly enough to pay for it (through purchasing from you rather than cheaper alternatives).

This is how specialty retail justifies its existence in an e-commerce age. You're not just selling products; you're selling expertise that Customers can't access elsewhere.

Continuous Improvement

Solution skills never stop developing. Even experts, like myself, continue learning and refining. Several practices support ongoing improvement:

Study products deeply. Go beyond specification sheets. Use products yourself. Understand them at a visceral level so you can speak authentically about them. When I used to own my own shoe stores, I made the Fit Consultants (salespeople) try on every shoe to see how it fit the shape of his or her foot. This personal experience knowledge made a huge difference in their Solutions and ultimately in our return rate.

Learn adjacent knowledge. If you sell woodworking tools, learn about woodworking techniques, wood species, finish chemistry. Deeper context makes you a better consultant.

Collect stories. Remember Customers' success stories. File away examples of how specific products solved specific problems. These become powerful illustrations during future Solution presentations.

Seek feedback. After sales, ask Customers how the product is working. Learning what succeeds and what disappoints improves future recommendations.

Watch your language. Record yourself presenting Solutions. Identify repetitive phrases, unclear explanations, or feature-focused language that needs translation into benefits.

Learn from failures. When Customers don't buy, or they return items, or they're dissatisfied, understand why. What did you misread during the Interview? How could your Solution presentation have been clearer?

Excellence in Solution is a journey, not a destination. Commit to that journey and watch your effectiveness compound over time.

In the next chapter, we explore the Experience phase – how you transform transactions into relationships that generate loyalty and referrals.

Chapter 5

Experience – Creating Moments That Matter

The Customer said yes. They're buying the television you recommended, along with accessories and installation equipment. The sale is complete.

For most retailers, this is the end of the story. Transaction finished, move on to the next Customer.

For WISE practitioners, this is where the real work begins.

The Experience phase, the E in WISE, encompasses everything that happens from "yes" through checkout, delivery, setup, initial use, and ongoing relationship. It's where you transform a one-time transaction into an ongoing relationship. Where satisfied Customers become loyal advocates. Where today's sale seeds tomorrow's referrals.

This is where 50/50 odds become 98% odds.

Remember the 50/50 Principle from Chapter 1? When you merely meet expectations, only half of Customers return. When you exceed expectations, 98% return. The Experience phase is where you exceed expectations systematically - not through grand gestures, but through dozens of small, thoughtful actions that eliminate the Customer's fears and prove you care about their success beyond the sale.

Here's something that should get your attention: Existing customers are like a gold mine for any modern business. However, many brands ignore customers right after they have made a purchase and instead focus on acquiring new ones.

Look at these numbers:

- The probability of selling to an existing customer is up to **14x higher** compared to the probability of selling to a new customer
- Around **77% of customers are willing to recommend** a brand to a friend after just one positive experience
- Increasing customer retention rates by a mere **5% can lead to an increase in profits by 25% to 95%**

The internet is full of statistics that highlight the importance of retaining existing customers rather than constantly chasing new ones.

After a customer agrees to buy, you can create a remarkable experience in-store by focusing on **personalization, valuable information, a seamless checkout, and thoughtful post-purchase gestures**. These actions transform a transaction into a relationship-building opportunity.

This chapter teaches you these critical post-purchase elements that separate 50/50 retailers from 98% practitioners.

The Buyer's Remorse Problem

Imagine this scenario: A Customer just purchased a $2,400 elliptical after a thorough Interview and Solution presentation. They seemed excited. They paid. They left smiling.

Three days later, they return it.

What happened? **Buyer's remorse**—the anxiety and second-guessing that often follows significant purchases.

Buyer's remorse is predictable and preventable. It emerges from several sources:

Post-decision dissonance: After choosing, people naturally wonder if they chose correctly. Did they miss something? Could they have done better? The fear of making a mistake returns with a vengeance.

Input from others: The Customer's spouse, friend, or colleague says "Why didn't you get X instead?" or "I saw that cheaper online." This triggers both fears—maybe they made a mistake, and maybe they should have known better.

Reality setting in: The abstract idea of purchase becomes the concrete reality of money spent and commitment made. The fear intensifies when the credit card bill arrives.

Anticipated regret: Worrying about potential problems: "What if it breaks?" "What if I don't use it?" "What if I wasted money?"

Left unaddressed, buyer's remorse leads to returns, negative reviews, and Customers who never come back to your store.

This is what creates 50/50 odds. The Customer seemed satisfied when they left, but uncertainty crept in afterward. You met expectations during the sale but didn't exceed them. 50/50.

The Experience phase prevents buyer's remorse and moves you from 50/50 to 98%. Here's how.

Locking In the Sale: Reinforcing Confidence

Locking in means actively reinforcing that the Customer made a wise decision. It's not manipulative reassurance; it's genuine confirmation based on the thorough Interview and customized Solution you provided.

Remember: Trust = Compassion + Confidence. (By the way, I will do a deeper dive on this in Chapter 8.)

You built trust during the Welcome and Interview. You demonstrated it during the Solution. Now you seal it during the Experience phase by showing both compassion (you care that they feel confident) and confidence (you're certain they made the right choice).

The lock-in conversation happens immediately after the purchase decision, often while processing payment. This is critical timing—you're catching buyer's remorse before it even starts.

Here's how it sounds:

"I have to tell you; you made a really smart decision here. Based on everything you told me about [Interview detail] and [Interview detail], this is exactly what you need. Here's why I'm confident about that..."

Then provide specific reasoning that connects their situation to your recommendation:

Fitness Equipment:
"You mentioned you've had knee problems with high-impact exercise. This elliptical's stride geometry is specifically designed to eliminate that impact. You're going to notice that difference immediately.

You also said you get bored easily with workouts. The variety of programs in this model—plus the tablet mount for streaming shows—means you'll actually stick with it, which is the key to getting results.

And remember your concern about your husband being too tall for most equipment? We specifically chose this model because it accommodates users up to 6'5" comfortably. That's exactly why I didn't recommend the compact model you first looked at."

This reinforcement accomplishes several things:

Reminds them of the careful process: They didn't impulse-buy; they made a thoughtful decision based on extensive consultation. This addresses the fear of making a mistake.

References specific needs: By citing details from their Interview, you show the recommendation was customized for them specifically, not some generic sales pitch. This shows compassion—you genuinely listened and understood.

Preempts doubts: By explicitly addressing concerns they mentioned, you prevent those concerns from festering into regret when they get home and their friend says "Why didn't you get the cheaper one?"

Demonstrates your investment: Your detailed reasoning shows you genuinely care about their success, not just hitting your sales numbers. This reinforces both compassion and confidence.

Creates social proof: Your confidence in their decision becomes external validation they can lean on when doubt creeps in. When their spouse questions the purchase, they can repeat your reasoning.

The lock-in should feel natural and genuine, not like some scripted speech you memorized. You're simply summarizing why this solution makes sense for them specifically—something that should be easy because you just spent time learning about their situation in the Interview.

Lock-In Examples Across Product Categories

Let's see how lock-in sounds in different retail environments:

Camera Store:
"You made an excellent choice. Based on what you told me—shooting your kids' sports in gym lighting, needing fast autofocus because they're constantly moving, and wanting something that grows with your skills—this Sony A7 IV is exactly right.

That autofocus system I showed you will track your son even when he's running full speed down the court. The low-light performance means those gym photos come out clear instead of grainy like what you're getting from your phone. And as your skills develop over the next few years, this camera has professional capabilities you can grow into. You're not going to outgrow this one."

Furniture Store:
"You made a really smart decision on this sofa. Remember you said you have three young kids and you need something that can handle daily family use without falling apart? This leather will actually get better-looking with age. It develops that nice patina and handles spills easily. Just wipe them up. That fabric sofa you looked at first would have been showing stains within six months with kids.

You also mentioned wanting something that doesn't look like 'kid furniture' so you're still happy with it in ten years when they're teenagers. This style is classic enough to last but modern enough to feel current. And that's why we went with this over the sectional. This fits your living room layout perfectly without overwhelming the space like that sectional would have."

Running Shoe Store:
"You made the right call with these Brooks. Based on your IT band issues you mentioned, your neutral gait pattern, and the fact you're training for your first marathon, these are exactly what you need.

Remember we talked about how stability shoes would actually cause problems for you because you don't overpronate? These give you the cushioning you need for the high mileage training without the motion control features that would mess up your natural gait and create new problems.

And with that IT band history, the softer landing you get from these will reduce the impact that aggravates that issue. I'm confident you made the smart choice here."

Electronics Store:
"This laptop is perfect for what you're doing. You mentioned video editing for your YouTube channel, running multiple programs simultaneously, and needing something that'll last you through four years of college. This has the processing power and RAM for video editing without frustrating lag, and the build quality means it'll easily last those four years without falling apart.

That cheaper model you looked at first would have frustrated you constantly with video rendering times. You'd be sitting there waiting for exports while your classmates are already uploading. This is absolutely worth the extra investment for what you're actually doing with it."

Home Improvement Store:
"Great choice on this drill. Based on your home renovation plans you shared - the deck project this summer, the cabinet building this fall, and regular ongoing home maintenance - you needed something contractor-grade, not basic homeowner-grade that'll die in six months.

This brushless motor will handle the heavy-duty work you're planning without burning out, and the battery platform means you can add other tools later that all work on the same batteries. That's that system we talked about. You really set yourself up for long-term success here instead of having to replace a cheap drill every year."

Bicycle Shop:
"You made an excellent choice. This bike matches perfectly with what you told me—mostly road riding on weekends, some longer rides building toward your first century ride, and you wanted something comfortable enough for those 50-mile days without destroying your back.

The geometry on this is specifically designed for endurance riding. It has a slightly more relaxed position than a racing bike so you're actually comfortable on those long rides instead of climbing off in pain. And the component group will handle everything you're planning without nickel-and-diming you on repairs. I'm really confident this is exactly right for your goals."

Notice the pattern? Every lock-in references specific details from the Interview and connects them directly to why this purchase was the right decision. You're eliminating the fear of making a mistake by reinforcing the logical, thoughtful basis for their choice.

This isn't manipulation. This is reminding them of the careful process they just went through so that when doubt creeps in later, they remember: "We talked through all of this. This wasn't impulsive. This makes sense."

The Psychology of Lock-In: Why It Works

Why does locking in work so powerfully?

When people make significant decisions, they enter a state of **cognitive vulnerability**. They've committed resources (money, time, social capital) based on incomplete information (they haven't actually used the product yet). This vulnerability creates anxiety which means both fears are hovering and ready to pounce.

In this anxious state, people desperately seek reassurance. They're particularly receptive to confident expertise. Your authoritative confirmation that they chose well reduces anxiety by providing expert validation they can hold onto.

This works because of **authority bias**. Humans naturally defer to experts in domains where we lack expertise. When an expert confidently says "you made the right choice," we feel relieved. Our fears diminish. We think: "Okay, if the expert says this is right, it probably is."

But here's the crucial caveat: **The expert must be credible.**

If you just met the Customer five minutes ago and conducted no Interview whatsoever, your reassurance rings completely hollow. They know you're just saying what salespeople always say. Your confidence means nothing because you haven't earned any credibility. You might meet expectations this way (50/50), but you definitely won't exceed them.

But if you spent thirty minutes understanding their specific situation, asked thoughtful questions that showed you care, provided customized recommendations based on what you learned, and explained detailed reasoning for your recommendations. You've earned genuine expert credibility through demonstrated compassion and confidence.

Now your lock-in carries real weight. Now they actually believe you. Now you're moving toward 98% instead of settling for 50/50.

WISE Selling's front-loaded work pays massive dividends here. The thorough Interview and customized Solution establish the credibility that makes locking in effective. You can't fake this. You can't shortcut it. The work you did earlier makes the lock-in possible.

Team Lock-In: Multiplying Confidence

Another powerful way to lock in the sale is through **team selling**. When the Customer is checking out and another member of your team naturally asks "What did you get today?" this creates a perfect opportunity for reinforcement.

Sporting Goods Store: [Customer checking out with running shoes]

Teammate: "What did you end up getting?"

Customer: "These Brooks Ghost."

Teammate: "Oh, excellent choice! We've heard such great things from people who run in those. You're going to love them."

This secondary confirmation from another team member multiplies the lock-in effect dramatically. It's not just one person's opinion anymore. It's team consensus. This social proof is extraordinarily powerful for eliminating the fear of making a mistake.

The Customer thinks: "Okay, it's not just the salesperson who thinks this is good. The whole team knows these are great shoes. I definitely made the right choice."

Camera Store: [Customer checking out with camera]

Teammate: "What are you getting today?"

Customer: "The Sony A7 IV."

Teammate: "Perfect camera. We get so many people coming back specifically to tell us how much they love that one. Great choice."

Furniture Store: [Customer completing purchase of sofa]

Teammate: "What did you decide on?"

Customer: "The leather sectional."

Teammate: "Smart choice, especially with young kids. That leather is going to hold up beautifully for years. We have so many families with kids who absolutely love that one."

This technique requires cultural alignment. Your whole team needs to understand and value the lock-in approach. But when your team naturally reinforces each other's recommendations, the lock-in effect multiplies dramatically.

The Customer leaves thinking: "Everyone there agreed this was the right choice. I feel really good about this."

That's exceeding expectations. That's moving from 50/50 to 98%.

Handling "I Need to Think About It"

Sometimes Customers don't commit immediately after your Solution presentation. They say they need to "think about it" or "discuss with my spouse" or "sleep on it."

These responses require careful, compassionate handling. Sometimes they're completely legitimate where the person genuinely needs time or spousal input before making a significant decision. Sometimes they're polite deflections hiding unaddressed objections.

Your job is figuring out which situation you're dealing with.

Use the same approach you learned in the Welcome phase when someone said "just looking": **Soften and Ask.**

"That makes sense. *(Soften)* But before you go, can I ask, is there something specific you'd like to think about? Maybe a question I didn't fully answer or a concern we didn't address?" *(Ask)*

This compassionate question (you're not challenging them or being pushy at all) often surfaces hidden objections:

"Well, I'm just not sure about the price..."
"I'm worried it won't actually fit in my space..."
"I don't know if I really need something this advanced..."

If objections emerge, address them right now while you still have the Customer's attention and can have a real conversation about their concerns.

If the Customer insists there's no specific concern and they genuinely just need time to process:

"I completely understand. This is a significant decision. *(Soften)* Let me make sure you have everything you need to think it through properly." *(Ask)*

Then provide helpful resources:

- Your business card with direct contact information
- Product brochures or specification sheets
- Links to reviews or additional information online
- Price quote in writing
- Information about any time-sensitive promotions or availability

Most importantly, set up a follow-up plan:

"When do you think you'll have a chance to think this through? ... Okay, how about I give you a call [day after that] to see if you have any additional questions or if there's anything else I can help clarify?"

This accomplishes several important things:

Maintains connection: You're not abandoning them the moment they don't buy immediately. This shows genuine compassion for their decision-making process.

Shows confidence: You're not desperate or pushy; you're confident enough in your recommendation to give them the time they need while remaining available as a resource.

Creates accountability: The scheduled follow-up makes it harder for them to simply forget about you or drift away to a competitor who catches them at the right moment.

Provides timeline: You know exactly when to follow up rather than randomly guessing or pestering them too early.

Important note: This technique is most appropriate for larger purchases—cars, major appliances, furniture, expensive electronics, anything over a few hundred dollars. It's honestly rare that someone buys a car when they first walk into a dealership. It's a huge life decision and many people genuinely need time to process it, talk it over with family, check their budget, whatever.

For smaller purchases though (under $200 or so) if someone says "I need to think about it," it's almost always a hidden objection that needs addressing immediately through Soften and Ask. They're not going home to ponder a $75 purchase. Something is bothering them.

Many "think about it" Customers become happy customers when handled well. They needed time, you gave it to them professionally and compassionately, and you maintained connection that brings them back when they're ready. This is exceeding expectations and moving toward 98% instead of just accepting 50/50 and moving on.

And for those of you reading this right now and "objecting" to the fact that I only spent one page on objections, fear not - Chapter 11 will make you feel better.

Multiplying the Solution: Creating Complete Success

Let's shift gears from preventing problems to actively multiplying success. The Customer has purchased your primary recommendation. Excellent! Now it's time to ensure they have everything, and I do mean everything - needed for actual success.

This is where the magic of the Experience phase really happens. This is where you separate yourself from 50/50 retailers and move decisively toward 98%.

Here's what most salespeople don't understand: **Multiplying the solution isn't about increasing your sale. It's about ensuring the Customer's success.**

When you multiply the solution properly, you're not "upselling" or being pushy. You're preventing the Customer from going home with an incomplete solution that leads to frustration, project failure, and the nagging feeling that they made a mistake.

Think about it from the Customer's perspective:

Scenario 1: Incomplete Solution (50/50 Territory)

Customer buys a router table for their woodworking projects. They're excited. They get it home, set it up, and suddenly realize they need:

- Router bits for the specific hardwoods they work with
- Safety equipment they don't have (push sticks, eye protection)
- A guide system for making accurate cuts
- Cleaning supplies for maintenance
- Proper dust collection

Now they're incredibly frustrated. They have to make another trip to the store (or multiple trips). Their project is completely delayed. They're annoyed at themselves for not thinking ahead, and honestly, they're also annoyed at you for not mentioning these essentials.

They think: "Why didn't the salesperson tell me I'd need all this other stuff? Some expert."

Will they return to your store next time? Maybe. 50/50 at best. They might just order everything online next time to avoid the hassle.

Scenario 2: Complete Solution (98% Territory)

You say: "Perfect! Now let's make sure you have absolutely everything you need to be successful with this project. You mentioned working primarily with hardwoods like oak and maple. These carbide bits are essential for that. Trying to use standard bits on hardwood causes terrible frustration. They burn out fast and give you rough edges.

You'll also want our router safety kit. This includes push sticks and eye protection specifically designed for router work. Router safety is no joke, and these tools keep your fingers where they belong.

And since you mentioned you're still learning woodworking and this is your first router table, this guide system will help you make precise cuts while you're developing your skills. A lot of beginners really struggle with freehand routing, and this eliminates that frustration completely while you're learning.

Finally, this cleaning kit keeps everything running smoothly. Dust buildup is honestly the number one cause of router problems and inaccurate cuts. Five minutes of cleanup after each session prevents hours of frustration later."

Which scenario better serves the Customer? Obviously the second one. You prevented multiple problems and ensured their project success. The Customer finishes their cabinets successfully. They're absolutely thrilled. They tell their woodworking friends. They return eagerly for their next project.

This is genuinely exceeding expectations. This is moving decisively toward 98%.

Why Multiplying the Solution Creates Remarkable Experiences

Here's what's fascinating: When done correctly, multiplying the solution actually makes Customers happier, not annoyed. Let me explain why.

The Customer didn't buy a router table because they wanted a router table sitting in their garage. They bought it because they want to build beautiful cabinets that they can be proud of. They want project success.

Anything that contributes to that success (even if it costs additional money) makes them happier in the long run because they achieve what they actually wanted: the completed project.

When you multiply the solution properly:

You demonstrate expertise: You're thinking through their entire project and identifying potential problems before they encounter them. This builds confidence in your knowledge.

You show you care: You're invested in their project success, not just ringing up a sale. This demonstrates compassion for their actual goals.

You save them time and frustration: They don't have to make multiple trips or troubleshoot problems on their own. This is incredibly valuable.

You enable their success: They actually complete their project successfully instead of giving up halfway through when they hit obstacles.

You eliminate buyer's remorse: They don't go home wondering "What else am I going to need?" because you already thought of everything.

All of this adds up to a **remarkable experience** that they remember, value, and tell others about.

The math is simple: Would you rather have a Customer spend $300 today and never return (50/50), or have a Customer spend $450 today on a complete solution, successfully complete their project, rave about you to their friends, and return for every future project (98%)?

The second customer is worth literally thousands of dollars more over their lifetime, even though you could have made the quick $300 sale and moved on.

Multiplying the solution creates remarkable experiences that move you from 50/50 to 98%.

The Four Types of Solution Multipliers

When multiplying solutions, items typically fall into four categories. Understanding these helps you think comprehensively about what the Customer needs:

1. Essential Accessories: Items absolutely required for the primary product to function as intended for their specific use.

Examples:

- Memory card for camera (can't take photos without it)
- Router bits for router (literally can't use it without bits)
- Running socks designed to prevent blisters (regular cotton socks destroy feet at distance)
- Proper hangers for clothing purchases (wire hangers damage delicate fabrics)
- Batteries or charging cables (dead product is useless product)
- Mounting hardware or installation supplies

2. Performance Enhancers: Items that significantly improve results or user experience for their specific goals.

Examples:

- Specific lens for camera that matches their shooting style (sports, portraits, landscapes)
- Jigs and guides for precision woodworking
- Heart rate monitor for fitness equipment (transforms random exercise into strategic training)
- Quality soil amendments and fertilizer for plants
- Upgraded components for their specific use case

3. Problem Prevention: Items that protect their investment or prevent the most common failure points for their use case.

Examples:

- Camera bag and lens cleaning kit (keeps expensive gear working)
- Furniture floor protectors (prevents damage to both furniture and floors)
- Equipment maintenance supplies (prevents breakdown and extends life)
- Protective cases or covers
- Anti-chafe products for athletic wear (prevents the misery of distance running/cycling)
- Plant disease prevention treatments

4. Complementary Products: Items that complete their broader goal or solution.

Examples:

- Shoes and accessories that complete the outfit for the event they described
- Nutrition strategy for the marathon training program they're starting
- Tripod to go with the camera for the landscape photography they mentioned
- Complementary furniture pieces that complete the room
- Companion plants that thrive together in their garden conditions

For each primary sale, think through 2-4 items across these categories. Not to push every possible thing, but to thoughtfully recommend what truly completes their specific solution based on what you learned in the Interview.

Multiplying Solutions Across Product Categories

Let's see how solution multiplication sounds in different retail environments:

Running Shoe Store:

Primary purchase: Running shoes for marathon training

Solution multiplication: "Perfect! Now let's make sure you're completely set up for successful training. You mentioned your long runs will be on Sundays, building up to 20 miles. Once you're past 90 minutes of running, you absolutely need a fuel strategy or you'll hit the wall hard. These energy gels are what marathoners use. Typically, one every 45 minutes after the first hour prevents that bonk where your legs just stop working.

You also said you've had IT band issues before in previous training. Using this foam roller literally just five minutes after your long runs keeps that from coming back and derailing your entire training. IT band problems are the number one reason first-time marathoners don't make it to race day.

And Body Glide for chafing prevention. I know this seems small, but at marathon distance, clothing seams become absolute torture without it. You'll thank me at mile 20.

And you'll need running-specific socks. Regular socks cause blisters after about mile 15. These have seamless toes and compression that prevents that.

These four things - shoes, fuel, injury prevention, chafing protection - address the most common reasons first-timers don't finish successfully. With all of this, you're actually set up properly."

Camera Store:

Primary purchase: Camera body for kids' sports photography

Solution multiplication: "Excellent choice! Now let's make sure you have everything to actually capture great photos at those games. You'll definitely need a memory card and this 64GB card handles about 2,000 photos, which is perfect for a tournament weekend.

This lens is significantly better for sports than the kit lens that comes with the camera. The autofocus is about three times faster for tracking your son when he's running, and it performs way better in gym lighting. The kit lens honestly struggles in gyms and you'll end up with blurry or grainy shots. This lens is the difference between capturing the moment and missing it.

You'll also want a camera bag that protects the equipment and makes it easy to carry into games without juggling everything.

And this lens cleaning kit is great. A gym environment gets surprisingly dusty, and fingerprints on your lens ruin photos. Two minutes of cleaning before the game saves you from fuzzy shots.

With all of this, you're set up to actually capture those sports moments clearly instead of getting frustrated."

Garden Center:

Primary purchase: Plants for shade garden

Solution multiplication: "Great choices! Now let's make sure these plants actually thrive instead of just surviving. This soil amendment is specifically formulated for shade plants since regular potting soil doesn't have what they need to thrive in low light conditions. This makes the difference between plants that struggle along and plants that flourish.

This fertilizer is designed specifically for shade-loving plants and gives them the nutrients they need when they're not getting as much energy from limited sunlight.

And mulch to retain moisture and suppress weeds. This is critical for shade gardens where you want the plants' limited energy going to healthy growth, not competing with weeds for resources.

With the right soil, fertilizer, and mulch, these plants will absolutely thrive in your shaded area instead of struggling."

Electronics Store:

Primary purchase: Laptop for college student

Solution multiplication: "Perfect laptop for what you're doing! Now let's make sure it stays protected and functional through four years of college. This laptop case protects it in your backpack between classes and honestly, laptops get damaged way more from the daily jostling in backpacks than from anything else. A case is basically insurance.

External hard drive for backing up your work. Losing a semester's worth of papers and projects to a hard drive failure is completely preventable with weekly backups. This is way cheaper than retaking classes.

And a wireless mouse is great. The trackpad is fine for basic use, but you mentioned graphic design work. A mouse makes that so much easier and more precise. Your hand will thank you.

With these three things, your laptop stays protected, your work stays safe, and you can actually work comfortably."

Home Improvement Store:

Primary purchase: Cordless drill for home renovation

Solution multiplication: "Great choice for those projects! Now let's make sure you have everything to actually complete them successfully. This bit set covers most home projects for you. The drill only comes with two basic bits, and you'll need different types for wood, metal, masonry, and different screw types.

An extra battery means you're not sitting there waiting for one to charge in the middle of hanging drywall or building that deck. Nothing's more frustrating than stopping work for two hours waiting on a battery.

And these impact-rated bits specifically for the deck project you mentioned—regular bits actually break when you're driving lag screws into treated lumber. These are designed for that heavy-duty work.

With all of this, you can actually complete your projects without running back to the store three times or sitting around waiting."

Notice the pattern in all of these? Each multiplication is:

- Connected directly to Interview information
- Explained as completing their specific solution
- Framed as enabling their success, not increasing the sale
- Protecting them from common frustrations or failures

This is how multiplying the solution creates remarkable experiences.

The "Did You See This?" Technique

One of the most effective and natural approaches for multiplying solutions is beautifully simple. As you walk with the Customer through the store toward checkout, point to a relevant item:

"Did you see this?"

That's it. Just draw their attention to something relevant. Then pause and let curiosity work its magic. In my book, <u>The Retail Sales Bible,</u> co-authored with retail legend Rick Segel, we called these the "4 Magic Words" because when used properly, they are magic.

Most Customers will naturally look and ask "What is that?" or "What does that do?" Now you've created a natural opportunity to describe and recommend without any pressure or pushiness. And yes, some will simply say "that's nice" and move on. But don't stop trying. Keep using the 4 Magic

Words until you get to the product that really captures the Customers attention.

Woodworking Store:
"Did you see this? This is our bench cookie system. It's genius for finishing work. It lets you elevate pieces so you can stain or seal all surfaces without having to wait for one side to dry. Based on the cabinet project you mentioned, you'd use these constantly. Makes finishing so much faster and easier."

Running Store:
"Did you see these? These are our favorite running socks. They're specifically designed to prevent blisters at long distances. The seamless toe construction and compression around the arch keep your foot stable. For marathon training, these honestly make a huge difference compared to regular athletic socks."

Camera Store:
"Did you see this lens? This is the 50mm prime and it's what most sports photographers eventually end up getting. It's significantly faster than the zoom for gym lighting and creates better background blur for isolating your subject. Given what you told me you're shooting, this would be a real gamechanger for your photos."

The phrase "Did you see this?" works brilliantly because:

- It creates curiosity without any pressure
- It feels inclusive. You're sharing something cool you noticed, not pushing a sale
- It's conversational and natural
- It allows easy escape. If they're not interested, they just say "Oh, that's neat" and you both move on
- It works repeatedly. You can use it multiple times for different items without sounding salesy

Practice making "Did you see this?" part of your natural language as you walk through your store. It transforms solution multiplication from awkward "upselling" into helpful sharing between friends.

The "To Complete Your Setup" Technique

While "Did you see this?" works beautifully during the walk through the store, you need another phrase for when you're at the checkout counter and not walking around:

"To complete your setup..."

These four powerful words frame items as necessary completions of their solution, not optional add-ons they should consider.

"To complete your setup, you'll want these refill cartridges and lubricant oil."

The phrasing naturally assumes these items are part of the solution, not additional purchases to debate. You're not asking "Would you like to add...?" You're confidently stating "To complete your setup, you need..."

Fitness Equipment:
"To complete your setup, you'll need this mat underneath to protect your flooring and reduce noise, and this heart rate monitor that integrates perfectly with the machine's training programs."

Power Tools:
"To complete your setup, you'll want this bit set that covers most home projects since the drill only comes with two basic bits and an extra battery so you're not waiting for charges in the middle of projects."

Camera:
"To complete your setup, you'll need this memory card for storage and this lens cleaning kit. It's absolutely essential for keeping your photos sharp. Dust and fingerprints are photo killers."

Running Gear:
"To complete your training setup, you'll need these running-specific socks for blister prevention and this Body Glide for chafing. Both are critical at marathon distance. Trust me on this."

This framing works powerfully because it aligns perfectly with how Customers actually think. They didn't buy a drill because they wanted a drill sitting in their garage collecting dust. They bought it to complete projects successfully. Anything necessary for successful project completion is naturally part of the solution, not some optional add-on.

Obviously, don't abuse this powerful technique. Only use "to complete your setup" for items that genuinely complete their specific solution based on what you learned in Interview. If a Customer balks or questions something, respect that immediately:

"Not a problem at all. You can always grab those later if you find you need them. But I will say, most Customers find having them from the start prevents frustration and extra trips."

Timing Your Solution Multiplication

When you present solution multiplication items matters as much as how you present them:

During the Solution phase: For absolutely critical items, introduce them as part of your primary recommendation:

"For your situation, I recommend this elliptical. To get the most from it and actually succeed with your fitness goals, you'll also need a mat underneath to protect your flooring and reduce noise, and this heart rate monitor that integrates perfectly with the machine's programs for optimized training."

While walking to checkout: Use "Did you see this?" for relevant items you pass along the way.

At the checkout counter: Final opportunity using "To complete your setup":

"To complete your setup, did we get you cleaning supplies for maintenance? These keep everything running smoothly."

The key is absolutely natural flow. Don't bombard Customers with a laundry list of add-ons. Weave recommendations naturally into conversation at appropriate moments, always connected to their specific success based on what you learned in Interview.

Lock-In Your Multiplication

Remember, every item you add to the solution is another small purchase decision that could potentially trigger buyer's remorse. Apply lock-in principles to multiplied solution items too:

"I'm really glad we got you these carbide drill bits. Regular bits would have frustrated you incredibly fast on those hardwood cabinets you're building. These will make the job so much easier and your results will look legitimately professional instead of obviously DIY."

This reinforces that solution multiplication items weren't frivolous extras; they were genuinely smart decisions that will pay off in their project success. It shows both compassion (you care deeply about their project outcome) and confidence (you know these items make a real difference).

The Final Touches

After a customer agrees to buy and you've multiplied the solution appropriately, you can create a truly remarkable experience at checkout by focusing on personalization, valuable information, and thoughtful post-purchase gestures.

Here are the specific actions that transform transactions into remarkable experiences:

Express Genuine Appreciation

Offer a sincere and personalized "thank you" using the Customer's name. Simple politeness is absolutely key to a positive experience.

"Thank you so much, Sarah. I really enjoyed helping you with this project today."

This sounds obvious, but you'd be shocked how many salespeople just robotically process checkout without any personal acknowledgment.

Share Product Knowledge and Tips

Provide valuable advice, care instructions, or unexpected uses for the product they purchased. This helps them get full value from their purchase and demonstrates your genuine expertise.

"One thing I always tell people about this router table: take five minutes after each use to blow out the dust before it builds up. Dust buildup is honestly the number one thing that causes accuracy problems down the line."

Or:

"With these running shoes, alternate them with another pair if you can. Letting the foam fully decompress between runs extends their life significantly. With this you'll get about 500 miles instead of 350."

These little tips show you're thinking about their long-term success, not just today's transaction.

Ensure a Smooth Checkout

Be genuinely efficient with the payment process. If a line is forming behind them, acknowledge waiting Customers with eye contact and a quick friendly greeting to manage their expectations. But don't rush the Customer you're currently serving.

"Thank you for your patience. I'll be with you in just a few minutes."

Then continue giving your current Customer full attention. Rushing through checkout to get to the next person destroys the remarkable experience you just spent thirty minutes building.

Before the Customer Leaves the Store

Right before the Customer walks out, you have a final opportunity to exceed expectations:

Offer Help Carrying Items

For large or multiple purchases, offer to help carry items to their car without being asked. Don't wait for them to struggle.

"Here, let me help you carry this out to your car."

This small gesture of service is incredibly memorable, especially for larger or awkward items. It's the kind of thing people mention in reviews: "They even helped me carry everything to my car!"

The Two-Card Technique

Give Customers two of your business cards:

"Here are two of my cards. One is for you to keep it with your paperwork or in your wallet. If you have any questions about the project or need anything else, call me directly. I'm here to help.

The second card is for a friend. When someone compliments your new cabinets or asks where you got your tools, you can give them my card. I'll take just as good care of them as I did you."

This accomplishes several things simultaneously:

- Provides easy contact method for follow-up questions
- Creates psychological commitment (they have your card; they're more likely to use it)
- Plants the referral seed naturally
- Flatters them (assumes their project will turn out well enough for compliments)

Express Interest in Their Success

"When you finish those cabinets, I'd love to see a photo! We feature customer projects on our social media sometimes if you're willing, but even if not, I'd personally love to see how they turn out."

Or:

"Let me know how the 5k goes! I want to hear how the training worked out."

This genuine interest in their outcome, not just their purchase, is what creates truly remarkable experiences that people remember and talk about.

The Referral Invitation

As they're literally walking toward the door, issue a clear referral invitation:

"Tell your friends about us! When they have projects, send them my way."

That final phrase -"Tell your friends about us!" - is crucial. It explicitly gives permission and encouragement to refer. Many satisfied Customers would refer but genuinely don't think of it unless prompted. You're giving them permission to talk about you.

Post-Purchase Follow-Up: Extending the Remarkable Experience

The Customer left the store. For traditional 50/50 retailers, the relationship is essentially over at this point. They hope the Customer returns someday but do nothing to make it happen.

For WISE practitioners moving toward 98%, systematic follow-up is absolutely essential. This is where you prove the relationship matters beyond the transaction.

Follow-Up 1: Thank You (Within 24 Hours)

Send a thank-you note, email, or text message:

"Sarah,

Thanks again for coming in yesterday. I'm excited for you to start that cabinet project. With everything we talked about, you're completely set up for success.

If you think of anything else you need or have any questions as you get started, don't hesitate to reach out. I'm here to help. Looking forward to seeing photos of the finished cabinets!

—Michael"

This accomplishes several things:

- Reinforces their purchase decision (lock-in continues beyond the store)
- Maintains the relationship connection
- Reminds them you're a resource for questions
- Shows genuine interest in their project success

This is genuinely exceeding expectations. Most stores never contact Customers after the sale unless there's a problem. You did and it was within 24 hours. Just to say thanks and reiterate your support. That's remarkable. That's 98% territory.

Follow-Up 2: Check-In (1-2 Weeks Later)

Call, text, or email to see how things are actually going:

"Hi Sarah, Michael from [Store Name]. I wanted to check in and see how the router table is working out for your cabinet project. Do you have any questions about using it or anything else you need?"

This accomplishes crucial things:

- Catches any problems early (before they become returns, negative reviews, or silent defections)
- Demonstrates ongoing interest in their success
- Provides opportunity to answer questions that came up
- Reinforces that you're a resource, not just a salesperson

This is exceeding expectations. The Customer thinks: "Wow, they actually care if this is working out for me. They're not just counting their commission and forgetting about me."

This kind of follow-up transforms 50/50 experiences into 98% experiences.

Follow-Up 3: Periodic Touch-Base (Quarterly)

Every few months, reach out to regular Customers:

"Hi Sarah, just touching base. How did that cabinet project turn out? Any new projects coming up? We just got in some new finishing products you might be interested in based on the work you're doing..."

This keeps you top-of-mind for future needs. When they're ready for their next project, you're the obvious choice because you've maintained the relationship.

Measuring Experience Success: From 50/50 to 98%

How do you know if your Experience phase execution is actually working? Track these specific metrics:

Leading Indicators (immediate feedback on your actions):

- Lock-in completion rate (are you locking in every purchase consistently?)
- Solution multiplication rate (what percentage of transactions include solution multipliers?)
- Contact information capture rate (should be 100%)
- Follow-up completion rate (are you actually following up like you said you would?

Lagging Indicators (results over time - the 50/50 to 98% measures):

- **Repeat purchase rate**: What percentage of Customers actually return for future purchases? (This is the ultimate metric—moving from 50% to 90%+)
- **Referral rate**: How many new Customers come from existing Customer referrals?
- **Return rate**: Lower returns suggest Customers remain satisfied post-purchase
- **Customer lifetime value**: What's the total revenue per Customer over their entire relationship with your store?
- **Net Promoter Score**: Surveys asking "How likely are you to recommend us to a friend?" (Moving from 50% to 98%)

Improvement in these metrics, especially repeat purchase rate and referral rate, indicates successful Experience execution. The goal is clear: **move every metric from 50/50 territory toward 98% territory.**

The Multiplier Effect: Why 98% Changes Everything

Here's why the Experience phase matters so profoundly: It's multiplicative, not additive. Let me show you the actual math.

50/50 Scenario:

Customer spends $1,000 today. You met their expectations adequately. Based on the research we discussed earlier, there's about a 50% chance they return for future purchases.

Expected lifetime value: $1,000 × 1.5 (accounting for 50% return probability) = $1,500 total

You're constantly replacing the 50% who don't return. You're on an exhausting treadmill of customer acquisition. You're working twice as hard as you need to.

98% Scenario:

Customer spends $1,000 today. You exceeded their expectations through proper lock-in, complete solution multiplication, and thoughtful follow-up. Based on the research, there's approximately a 98% chance they return.

They return six months later for $500 more. They refer a friend who spends $800. They return again a year later for another $600. They continue returning for years because you've earned their loyalty.

Expected lifetime value: $1,000 + $500 + $800 (referral) + $600 + continuing future purchases = $3,000+ over just three years, and it keeps going.

That's literally 2-3x more revenue from the same initial Customer through systematically exceeding expectations in the Experience phase.

And that Customer might continue for literally decades, generating many multiples of the initial purchase value. I have customers who've bought from me for fifteen years. That's tens of thousands of dollars in lifetime value from a relationship that started with a few hundred-dollar purchase.

Traditional retail optimizes obsessively for transaction size today. WISE Selling optimizes intelligently for relationship value over time and moving from 50/50 odds to 98% odds.

The former might extract slightly more money today through pressure tactics and aggressive upselling. The latter builds genuinely sustainable business for years through systematically exceeded expectations.

The math is absolutely clear:

- Acquiring brand new Customers costs 7-8x more than retaining existing ones
- Referrals from satisfied Customers cost literally nothing
- Customer lifetime value dramatically dwarfs individual transaction value
- 98% return rates compound exponentially over time

The Experience phase is where these long-term relationships are created. It's where 50/50 odds become 98% odds. It's where transactions transform into relationships. It's where Customers become enthusiastic advocates. It's where your business builds genuinely sustainable competitive advantage that online retailers simply cannot match.

The Experience Framework

Here's your complete framework for the Experience phase:

1. Lock in the decision immediately after purchase by referencing specific Interview findings and confidently reinforcing why this was absolutely the right choice for their specific situation

2. Multiply the solution by ensuring they have complete solutions for success using "Did you see this?" during the walk and "To complete your setup" at checkout

3. Lock in the multipliers by reinforcing how each contributes specifically to their project or goal success

4. Create a remarkable checkout experience through genuine appreciation, helpful tips, smooth process, and personal attention

5. Finish strong before they leave by offering to carry items, giving two business cards, expressing interest in their success, and inviting referrals

6. Follow up systematically by sending a thank you within 24 hours, check-in within 1-2 weeks, quarterly touch-base for regular Customers

This framework transforms the Experience phase from a forgettable afterthought into your most powerful tool for exceeding expectations and moving decisively from 50/50 to 98%.

Master these elements - locking in decisions, multiplying solutions properly, and following up consistently - and you'll finish every single interaction strong. You'll create experiences where Customers leave feeling confident, equipped for genuine success, and absolutely certain they made the right choice working with you.

That's how you exceed expectations.

That's how you create genuinely Remarkable Experiences.

That's how you move from 50/50 to 98%.

Chapter 6

The Four Sales Before the Sale

Walk into any sporting goods megastore and you'll see the problem immediately. Rows of athletic shoes stretch toward the horizon. Treadmills and ellipticals crowd the fitness section. Golf clubs lean against walls in precise formations. Everything organized by category, price point, and brand.

And standing in the middle of it all, a Customer looks completely lost.

That Customer – let's call him Everett – came in looking for running shoes. He's training for his first 5K. He's read reviews online, watched YouTube videos comparing models, and checked prices on three different websites. He knows what he wants. Sort of.

Except Everett doesn't actually know what he needs. He doesn't know his foot strike pattern, his arch type, his pronation tendency, or whether the shoes he researched online are appropriate for his biomechanics. He doesn't know that the "best shoe of 2026" according to that magazine might be terrible for his specific running style.

More importantly, Marcus is making four unconscious judgments before he even considers which shoes to buy:

1. Should I trust this salesperson?
2. Is this store worth my time?
3. Am I having a good experience here?
4. Only then: Which product should I buy?

Traditional retail assumes Customers walk in ready to buy products. WISE Selling recognizes that before Customers buy any merchandise, they must first buy you, your store, the experience you provide, and only then – if those first three sales succeed – will they consider buying products.

This chapter explores these four prerequisite sales and how to make each one successfully. Miss any of the first three, and the fourth becomes exponentially harder or impossible. These sales are not *before* you start selling; they are during the entire process.

Sale #1: Selling Yourself

Everett has been in the store for thirty seconds when a salesperson approaches. In those thirty seconds, Everett's brain has already begun assessing: Friend or foe? Helper or predator? Trustworthy or suspicious?

These assessments happen mostly unconsciously; driven by evolutionary threat-detection systems we discussed in Chapter 2. But they determine everything that follows.

The first sale you must make is yourself. The Customer must decide: "I like this person. I trust this person. I want to work with this person."

This isn't about being naturally charismatic or extroverted. Some of the best WISE practitioners are introverts. It's about demonstrating specific qualities that trigger trust and rapport.

Quality 1: Genuine Interest

People detect authenticity instantly. Fake enthusiasm registers as threatening rather than welcoming. Genuine interest in helping – actually caring about the Customer's success – creates connection.

Everett can tell the difference between:

"Welcome to the Athletic Zone! I'm here if you need anything!" (performed, disengaged)

versus

"Hey, thanks for coming in. I'm James. What are you working on today?" (genuine, present)

The second feels like the start of a conversation with someone who might actually be helpful. The first feels like retail theater where both parties are obligated to perform.

Practice genuine interest by remembering: Every Customer represents someone trying to solve a problem or achieve a goal. Your job is helping them succeed. That's inherently interesting if you let it be.

Quality 2: Competence Signals

Customers need to believe you know what you're talking about. Competence signals include:

- Speaking confidently about products
- Asking insightful questions that show expertise
- Referencing specific technical details appropriately
- Admitting what you don't know rather than bluffing
- Sharing relevant experience ("I run regularly too, so I understand...")

For Everett looking for running shoes, competence means understanding gait analysis, shoe construction, injury prevention, and training principles – not just brand names and prices.

Quality 3: Non-Neediness

Desperation repels. If Customers sense you need the sale too badly, they become suspicious. What are you trying to hide? Why are you so pushy?

Demonstrate non-neediness through:

- Taking time to understand rather than rushing to pitch
- Being willing to let Customers leave if timing isn't right
- Recommending what's best for them even if it's not most profitable for you
- Showing patience with their process

This sounds counterintuitive – act less eager to sell? – but it works because it signals confidence in your value and respect for their autonomy.

Quality 4: Respect

Customers need to feel respected, not judged or patronized. Respect manifests in:

- Listening without interrupting
- Taking their concerns seriously
- Not dismissing their online research even if some of it's misguided
- Treating beginners and experts with equal dignity
- Acknowledging budget constraints without judgment

When Everett mentions he's training for his first 5K, the disrespectful response is: "Oh, you're just getting started. You probably don't need anything fancy."

The respectful response: "That's great! Training for your first race is exciting. Tell me about your training so far and what you're experiencing."

The Likeability Formula

Psychologists have studied what makes people likeable. Three factors consistently emerge:

1. Similarity – We like people who seem like us
2. Reciprocity – We like people who like us
3. Familiarity – We like people we've interacted with positively

You can deliberately activate all three:

Similarity: Listen for common ground during the Interview and acknowledge it naturally. "Oh, you run trails? I love trail running too – the hills are brutal, but the scenery makes up for it."

Reciprocity: Show genuine positive regard for the Customer. People sense when you like them and tend to reciprocate. "I appreciate you doing research before coming in – it makes my job easier when Customers know what questions to ask."

Familiarity: Multiple positive interactions build rapport. This is why the Welcome phase matters so much – it creates that crucial first positive interaction that makes subsequent ones more comfortable.

Sale #2: Selling Your Store

Everett likes James, the sales consultant. Good start. But he's still uncertain about the store itself. Should he buy here or keep shopping elsewhere?

The second sale is your store. Customers must believe your store is worth their time and money despite other options. I have been teaching this for years, but with the advent of same day online purchase and delivery, the store sale has become even more important.

This sale is partly made before the Customer arrives – through reputation, marketing, location. But it's heavily influenced by first impressions and how you position the store's value.

First Impressions Matter Enormously

Everett's brain processes the store environment in milliseconds:

- Cleanliness and organization signal professionalism and care
- Lighting affects mood (bright and warm feels welcoming; dim or harsh feels unwelcoming)
- Sound levels impact comfort (too loud is stressful, too quiet feels sterile)
- Smell matters more than we realize (fresh is good; musty or chemical is bad)
- Crowding affects perception (some activity signals success; chaos suggests poor management)

You might not control all these factors, but awareness helps. If you notice the store feels chaotic, acknowledge it: "Sorry about the crowd today – we're busier than usual. Let me make sure you get good attention despite the rush."

Points of Pride

During the Welcome phase, share 2-3 distinctive facts about your store that justify shopping there rather than elsewhere. These "Points of Pride" might include:

Specialization: "We focus exclusively on running and triathlon – not general sporting goods. That means our staff are all serious runners who actually use what we sell."

Service: "We do complimentary gait analysis for every running shoe purchase. It takes about ten minutes but ensures you get shoes that actually match your biomechanics."

Expertise: "Our team has 150 combined years of competitive running experience. Whatever questions you have, someone here has dealt with it personally."

Selection: "We stock 40 different running shoe models in full size runs – more than any other store in the region. If we don't have your size, I'll be shocked."

Community: "We host weekly group runs from the store every Saturday morning. All paces welcome – it's a great way to stay motivated and meet other runners."

Values: "We're locally owned, and we sponsor 15 local running clubs and races. Supporting us means supporting the local running community."

Choose Points of Pride that are genuinely distinctive and verifiable. Don't claim "best selection" if your competitor has more. Don't tout "expert staff" if your team turns over every six months.

For Everett, hearing "We focus exclusively on running and triathlon" immediately differentiates this specialty running store from the megastore he visited earlier where the same person selling running shoes also sells golf clubs.

Handling the "But I Can Get It Cheaper Online" Reality

Everett knows he can probably find these shoes for $10 less online. He's thinking about it. You need to address this elephant in the room proactively.

The worst response: "But we price match!" This signals that price is the only factor that matters. It also trains Customers to always demand price matching.

A better response: "You might be able to find a lower price online, but here's what you get by purchasing from us: [specific value]."

Then articulate concrete value that online can't provide:

"We're doing a gait analysis to ensure these shoes actually match your biomechanics. Amazon can't do that. We're making sure they fit perfectly – not just the right number on the box, but actually comfortable for your foot shape. And when you have questions three weeks from now about hot spots or whether you're lacing them optimally, you can come back and we'll help. You're not buying shoes – you're getting a running consultant who's invested in your training success."

This positions price as one factor among many rather than the only factor. Some Customers still choose online based on price alone. That's fine. They weren't your ideal Customers anyway. Your ideal Customers value expertise and service enough to pay a modest premium.

The Store as Community Hub

One powerful way to differentiate your store: position it as a community hub, not just a retail location.

For running stores, this might mean:

- Weekly group runs
- Training clinics and workshops
- Race registration and packet pickup
- Bulletin boards for race information
- Social events for runners
- Relationships with local running clubs

For other retailers:

- Skills clinics (golf swing analysis, tennis lessons)
- Try-before-you-buy programs
- Demo days with manufacturer reps
- Local celebrity appearances and meet-and-greets
- Charity events and fundraisers

These community aspects create reasons to visit beyond just purchasing. They build loyalty because the store becomes part of Customers' athletic identity, not just a place that sells stuff.

Sale #3: Selling the Experience

Everett likes James. He's impressed with the store's specialization and services. But how does he feel right now, at this moment? Is this experience enjoyable, or is it stressful and time-consuming?

The third sale is the experience. Customers must feel that their time in your store is valuable, pleasant, and productive.

The Experience Economy

Retail research increasingly emphasizes that Customers aren't just buying products; they're buying experiences. The reason is simple: products are abundant and accessible. Anyone can buy running shoes online. But experiences are scarce and valuable.

Consider two scenarios:

Scenario A: Everett enters a big-box sporting goods store. He finds the running section. He sees 200 shoe options. No one helps him. He picks up several boxes based on brand names he recognizes. He tries them on. They feel... fine? He's not sure. He checks prices on his phone. He leaves to think about it.

Scenario B: Everett enters a specialty running store. James greets him warmly, learns about his 5K training, conducts a brief gait analysis, recommends three specific models based on his findings, explains exactly why each suits Everett's foot strike and training goals, ensures perfect fit, and shares tips for breaking in new shoes. Everett leaves confident he made a smart decision.

Which experience does Everett value more? Which would you value more? Which creates loyalty and referrals?

The experience you create determines whether Customers view you as a commodity (comparison shop based on price) or a resource (worth paying premium for expertise).

Components of Exceptional Experience

What makes an experience feel exceptional? Several elements:

Attention: Customers feel truly listened to and understood. This is why the Interview phase matters so much.

Expertise: Customers learn something valuable. They leave knowing more than when they arrived. For Everett, understanding his overpronation and how it affects shoe selection is knowledge he'll value forever.

Efficiency: Customers' time is respected. You're thorough without being slow. Processes are streamlined. There's no unnecessary waiting or bureaucracy.

Comfort: The physical environment is pleasant. Seating is available for trying on shoes. The temperature is comfortable. Music isn't too loud.

Discovery: Customers encounter something new and interesting. Maybe it's a product they didn't know existed. Maybe it's information that changes their perspective. Discovery makes experiences memorable.

Confidence: Customers leave feeling confident about their decision. No anxiety, no second-guessing, just satisfaction that they made a smart choice.

Connection: Customers feel human connection. Not a transaction with a robot, but a conversation with someone who cared.

Every interaction provides opportunities to deliver these elements. Stay alert for where you can add value beyond the basic transaction.

The Micro-Experiences Matter

Experience isn't just the overall arc; it's composed of dozens of micro-moments. Each creates a small positive or negative impression that accumulates into the overall feeling.

Positive micro-experiences:

- Greeting within 60 seconds of entry
- Offering water on a hot day
- Suggesting sitting down while trying shoes
- Sharing a relevant tip without being asked
- Laughing together about something
- Acknowledging their patience if there's a wait
- Walking them to their car with purchases

Negative micro-experiences:

- Ignoring them while you finish a personal phone call
- Sighing or seeming annoyed by questions
- Being unable to answer basic product questions
- Disappearing to the back room for extended periods
- Making them repeat information you should have remembered
- Rushing through explanation because you're busy
- Hovering uncomfortably or following too closely
- Checking your cell phone while with them

Be conscious of these micro-moments. Each one matters more than you think.

The Last Two Minutes Principle (Revisited)

As mentioned in Chapter 5, Customers disproportionately remember the last two minutes of an interaction. Make them count:

For Everett, the last two minutes might include:

- Final fit check to ensure the shoes feel perfect
- Tips on break-in process specific to this model
- Information about the Saturday morning group run
- Invitation to return with questions
- Genuine enthusiasm for his 5K training
- Warm thanks for choosing your store

These final moments leave a lasting impression that colors how Marcus remembers the entire experience.

Sale #4: Selling the Merchandise

Only after successfully selling yourself, your store, and the experience can you effectively sell merchandise.

This might seem backward. Traditional retail starts with product. But think about your own purchasing behavior: Do you buy from people you dislike? Stores you don't trust? Experiences that feel frustrating?

Of course not. You buy products from people, stores, and experiences you feel good about. Your Customers are identical.

Why Product Is Fourth, Not First

When Customers trust you (Sale #1), believe your store adds value (Sale #2), and enjoy the experience (Sale #3), product recommendations become easy. They're receptive to your guidance. They believe your recommendations. They don't second-guess extensively.

Without those first three sales, product recommendations face enormous resistance. Customers skeptically evaluate every claim. They comparison-shop aggressively. They look for reasons not to buy. Your job becomes difficult or impossible.

This is why WISE Selling front-loads effort into Welcome, Interview, Solution, Experience. You're setting up conditions where the product sale happens naturally.

Let's see how all four sales play out:

Sale #1 (Selling Yourself): James greets Everett warmly, learns he's training for a 5K, asks genuine questions about his training and goals, and demonstrates knowledge about running biomechanics and injury prevention. Everett thinks: "This person actually knows what they're talking about and seems to care about my success."

Sale #2 (Selling the Store): James mentions the store specializes exclusively in running, conducts complimentary gait analysis, and hosts weekly group runs. Everett thinks: "This store offers value I can't get online or at generic sporting goods stores."

Sale #3 (Selling the Experience): James conducts a brief gait analysis, explains Everett's mild overpronation and what that means for shoe selection, recommends three specific models with clear reasoning, ensures perfect fit, and shares tips for his training. Everett thinks: "This was actually helpful and educational. I learned things I didn't know and feel confident about my decision."

Sale #4 (Selling the Product): At this point, the product sale is simple. James has built trust, demonstrated the store's value, and created a positive experience. When he says, "Based on your gait and training goals, I recommend these shoes," Everett trusts the recommendation. The product sale happens naturally, without pressure or resistance.

If James had skipped to Sale #4 immediately – "Here are our running shoes. These are on sale." – Everett would have felt like a transaction, not a valued Customer. He might buy, but he probably wouldn't return or refer others.

The Sequence Matters

The four sales must happen in order. You can't jump ahead.

Attempting to sell products before selling yourself creates resistance. Customers think: "Why should I trust your recommendation? I don't even know you."

Attempting to sell products before selling your store creates price-focused competition. Customers think: "If this store offers no distinctive value, I'll just find the cheapest price."

Attempting to sell products before creating a good experience generates buyer's remorse. Customers think: "This felt rushed and impersonal. Did I make the right choice?"

The sequence is: Yourself → Store → Experience → Product

Get those first three right, and the fourth becomes easy.

Adapting the Four Sales to Different Contexts

While the sequence remains constant, emphasis varies by context:

High-End Specialty Retail: Heavy emphasis on Sale #1 (yourself). Customers at premium stores expect consultative relationships with knowledgeable staff. Your expertise and personal attention justify premium pricing.

Community-Focused Stores: Heavy emphasis on Sale #2 (your store). Customers value the store as a community hub, not just a retail location. The relationships and activities around the store matter as much as what you sell.

Experiential Retail: Heavy emphasis on Sale #3 (experience). Think stores with extensive try-before-you-buy, demo programs, or in-store experiences. The experience itself is a primary product.

Volume Retail: More balanced across all four. No single element dominates, but all must be present for success.

For running specialty stores, all four sales are critical. Customers can buy running shoes anywhere. They choose specialty stores for expertise (Sale #1), community (Sale #2), services like gait analysis (Sale #3), and then products (Sale #4).

When Customers Skip Sales

Sometimes Customers arrive having already made some sales:

Loyal Customers: They already bought you, your store, and trust the experience. They skip straight to products: "Hey James, I need new shoes – what do you recommend?"

With loyal Customers, you can move quickly through early phases while still maintaining the relationship: "Good to see you! How are those shoes from last time working? ... Great. What's your mileage looking like now? ... Okay, based on that, I'm thinking we should try..."

Referred Customers: Someone they trust recommended you. They arrive with Sale #1 partially made. They're predisposed to trust you because of the referral.

Acknowledge the referral: "Sarah sent you? She's great – I helped her find trail shoes last month. Did she tell you about our gait analysis service?"

Brand-loyal Customers: They arrive wanting a specific product. They've pre-decided on the merchandise.

This seems like they've jumped to Sale #4, but actually they've just decided on product category. They still need Sales #1-3 for the specific purchase and to become loyal to your store: "You want the Brooks Ghost? Good choice – that's a versatile shoe. Let me make sure we get the right fit for you specifically..."

Even when Customers seem ready to skip ahead, briefly touch each sale. It builds relationship foundation for future visits.

Common Mistakes in the Four Sales

Mistake #1: Jumping to Product

This is by far the most common error. Salespeople assume Customers are ready to buy products and skip straight to showing merchandise. It works occasionally with highly motivated buyers but fails with most Customers.

Mistake #2: Neglecting Sale #1

Some salespeople focus on store benefits (Sale #2) or product features (Sale #4) while failing to build personal rapport (Sale #1). Customers might be impressed with the store but don't connect with the salesperson specifically.

Mistake #3: Over-Emphasizing Sale #2

Bragging extensively about your store gets boring fast. Two or three Points of Pride, then move on. Customers don't need the complete corporate history.

Mistake #4: Taking Sale #3 for Granted

Assuming the experience will naturally be positive without actively working to make it so. Experience requires conscious effort and attention to detail.

Mistake #5: Treating Sales as Checkboxes

Going through the motions – greeting mechanically, reciting store benefits without enthusiasm, conducting Interview perfunctorily – without genuine engagement. Customers sense when you're just following a script.

Here's the beautiful thing about the four sales: They compound.

Doing each one well makes the next easier. Successful Sale #1 makes Sale #2 more believable. Successful Sales #1 and #2 make Sale #3 more enjoyable. Successful Sales #1-3 make Sale #4 almost effortless.

Conversely, failing at any sale makes subsequent sales harder. If Customers don't trust you (Sale #1 failed), they'll be skeptical of your store's value (Sale #2 struggles), they'll view the experience negatively (Sale #3 suffers), and they'll resist product recommendations (Sale #4 becomes difficult).

This compounding is why WISE Selling works. You're not just executing a sales process; you're building momentum that makes each phase naturally lead to the next.

Measuring Success Across the Four Sales

Track indicators for each sale:

Sale #1 Success Indicators:

- Customers engage in conversation rather than deflecting
- They share personal information (goals, concerns, experiences)
- They ask for your opinion and advice
- They return and ask for you specifically
- They mention you by name when referring friends

Sale #2 Success Indicators:

- Customers comment positively on store differentiators
- They participate in store events and programs
- They choose your store despite knowing they could find lower prices elsewhere
- They understand and articulate your store's unique value

Sale #3 Success Indicators:

- Customers spend appropriate time (not rushed, not dragging)
- They seem engaged and interested throughout
- They thank you specifically for the experience
- They return even for small purchases
- They bring friends or family to experience your store

Sale #4 Success Indicators:

- Conversion rate (what % of engaged Customers buy)
- Average transaction value
- Return rate (low returns suggest right products sold)
- Satisfaction scores
- Repeat purchase rate

If one sale consistently shows poor indicators, focus improvement efforts there.

The Four Sales in Employee Training

When training new team members, explicitly teach the four sales framework. Many new employees assume their job is selling products (Sale #4) and neglect the foundational sales that make product sales possible.

Training should emphasize:

"Your first job is making Customers trust and like you. Your second job is helping them understand why our store adds value. Your third job is creating an experience they enjoy and find valuable. Only then (after those three jobs) does selling products become your focus. Do the first three well, and the fourth happens naturally."

This framing helps employees understand that time spent on Welcome, Interview, and building rapport isn't "wasted time before getting to the sale." It's the essential foundation that makes sales possible.

Beyond Transactional Relationships

The four sales framework ultimately transforms retail from transactional to relational.

Transactional retail: "I sell products. You buy products. Transaction complete."

Relational retail: "I help you achieve athletic goals. You trust my expertise. We build an ongoing relationship where I'm your resource for equipment, advice, and support."

The difference is profound. Transactional retail competes primarily on price and convenience — areas where physical retail struggles against e-commerce. Relational retail competes on expertise, service, and community — areas where physical retail has sustainable advantages.

Everett can buy running shoes online. He can't get personalized gait analysis, expert recommendations based on his specific biomechanics, and ongoing support for his training journey from Amazon.

When you successfully execute all four sales, you're not competing with online retail. You're offering something fundamentally different and more valuable to Customers who care about success over price.

In the next chapter, we'll explore the four distinct types of Customers you'll encounter and how to adapt WISE Selling for each type to maximize effectiveness.

Chapter 7

Know Your Customer – The Four Personality Types

Sarah walks into a home improvement store. She needs a drill. She's renovating her first house and has researched extensively. She's read reviews, compared specifications, created spreadsheets analyzing features across fifteen models. She knows exactly what torque rating she needs, why brushless motors matter, and which battery platform offers the best long-term value. She has questions (lots of them) and she needs detailed, accurate answers.

Tom walks into the same store. He also needs a drill. He's a contractor running three crews, and one of his drills died this morning. He doesn't have time for a lengthy conversation. He knows what he needs: reliable, durable, gets the job done. He wants to walk in, grab it, and get back to the job site. Time is money.

Jennifer walks into that same store. She needs a drill too. She's hanging pictures in her apartment, and her neighbor said she should get a drill instead of hammering nails. She's not interested in specifications or technical details. She just needs something that works for her immediate project, doesn't cost too much, and won't sit unused taking up space afterward.

Marcus walks into that same store. He needs a drill as well—but not just any drill. He wants the latest model with the newest technology. He saw it featured on a tech review site. It has smart connectivity, LED work lights, and looks incredible. He's documenting his home renovation on Instagram and wants tools that look as impressive as they perform.

Same store. Same product category. Four completely different people.

Traditional retail training treats all four identically: "May I help you find a drill?" This one-size-fits-all approach fails because Sarah, Tom, Jennifer, and Marcus have fundamentally different ways of making decisions, building trust, and evaluating purchases.

WISE Selling recognizes four distinct personality types. This chapter teaches you to identify which type you're working with within the first two minutes and adapt your entire approach - Welcome, Interview, Solution, Experience - to match how they naturally think and decide.

The Four Personality Types

Across virtually every retail category and every culture, Customer personalities fall into four patterns. These aren't about what they're buying; they're about how they think, decide, and build trust.

Type 1: The Analytical
They're research-driven, detail-oriented, and specification-focused. They want data, comparisons, and thorough understanding before deciding. They think carefully and slowly.

Type 2: The Driver
They're results-focused, efficiency-oriented, and impatient with unnecessary details. They want quick answers, clear recommendations, and to make decisions fast. Time is their most valuable resource.

Type 3: The Practical
They're needs-focused, value-conscious, and pragmatic. They want products that solve their immediate problem without paying for features they won't use. Function over flash.

Type 4: The Trendsetter
They're innovation-focused, aesthetically-driven, and socially aware. They want the latest, the newest, the most impressive. They care how products look and what they say about them.

These aren't about expertise level—you can have an Analytical novice and a Driver expert. These are about fundamental personality patterns that shape how people process information and make decisions.

Understanding these patterns is critical because **each type builds trust differently**. What makes an Analytical feel confident (detailed specifications and thorough comparisons) makes a Driver feel frustrated and impatient. What makes a Practical feel served (focusing on their immediate need) makes a Trendsetter feel underwhelmed.

Let's break down each type in detail.

The Analytical Customer

Characteristics

Analyticals are Sarah - the researcher with spreadsheets. They:

- Research extensively before shopping (and continue during shopping)
- Ask detailed, specific questions
- Want to understand how things work
- Compare multiple options systematically
- Take their time making decisions
- Value accuracy and thoroughness
- Get uncomfortable with pressure or rushing
- Need to feel confident they've made the informed choice
- Often second-guess decisions if information was incomplete

How Analyticals Build Trust:

Analyticals build trust through **confidence in your competence**. They need to believe you know what you're talking about and will give them accurate, complete information.

They lose trust when you:

- Provide vague or incomplete answers
- Try to rush their decision process
- Show impatience with their questions
- Can't explain technical details
- Seem to be glossing over important information

They gain trust when you:

- Answer questions thoroughly and accurately
- Provide detailed comparisons when asked
- Take their research seriously
- Give them time and space to process
- Acknowledge complexity rather than oversimplifying

Identifying Analyticals

You'll recognize them within 2 minutes by:

Language patterns:

- Technical terminology and specific questions
- "I've been researching..." or "I read that..."
- Comparisons: "How does this compare to...?"
- Detailed feature questions: "What's the torque rating?" "What's the battery chemistry?"

Behavior:

- May arrive with printed research, notes, or spreadsheets
- Pull out phone to cross-reference information
- Ask follow-up questions to your answers
- Seem methodical and unhurried
- May revisit previous topics to clarify

Body language:

- Focused, attentive listening
- Taking mental or physical notes
- Studying products carefully
- Not easily swayed by emotional appeals

WISE Selling Adaptations for Analyticals

Welcome Phase:

Keep it professional and straightforward:

"Thanks for coming in. What brings you in today?"

Don't be overly enthusiastic or chatty as Analyticals find this distracting. Get to the point.

Interview Phase:

Let them explain their research. Ask questions that show you respect their preparation:

"What have you learned so far in your research?"
"What factors are most important in your decision?"
"What questions came up during your research that you'd like me to address?"
"Are there specific models you're comparing?"

Listen carefully. Take notes if they're providing detailed information—this shows you value their input.

Solution Phase:

Provide thorough, accurate information. Use benefit statements that include the mechanism:

"This has a brushless motor. That means it runs cooler and lasts about twice as long because there are no carbon brushes wearing out. Because heat buildup is the primary failure point in motors under sustained use, this design significantly extends tool life—typically 800-1000 hours versus 400-500 for brushed motors."

Compare options when asked. Be honest about trade-offs:

"The Milwaukee has slightly more torque, about 1,800 inch-pounds versus 1,600. The DeWalt has better ergonomics for extended use due to the grip angle. For the cabinetry work you mentioned, where precision and control matter more than raw power, I'd lean toward the DeWalt. But if you're also doing structural work where maximum torque is important, the Milwaukee might be better despite the less comfortable grip."

Provide backup: "Here's the specification sheet. You can take this home to review."

Don't rush: Give them time to process. Silence is okay. They're thinking.

Experience Phase:

Lock-in should reference the thoroughness of their research:

"Based on all the research you've done and the questions we've worked through today, I'm confident you've made an informed decision. The specifications on this model match your requirements exactly. The torque rating, battery platform compatibility, and three-year warranty all align with what you identified as priorities."

Follow-up should invite further questions:

"If any other questions come up as you use this or as you continue researching, feel free to call me directly. I want to make sure you have all the information you need."

Common Mistakes with Analyticals

Mistake 1: Getting impatient with their questions. This destroys trust instantly. They interpret impatience as either incompetence (you don't know the answers) or dishonesty (you're trying to hide something).

Mistake 2: Providing vague answers. "This one's pretty good" is useless to an Analytical. They need specific information.

Mistake 3: Trying to rush the decision. "This is a great deal but only today!" backfires. Analyticals don't respond to pressure tactics. They see them as manipulation.

Mistake 4: Acting like their research is excessive. Never say "You're overthinking this." To them, you're being dismissive of their legitimate due diligence.

The Driver Customer

Characteristics

Drivers are Tom - the contractor who needs a drill now. They:

- Value efficiency and speed above all
- Want bottom-line recommendations, not lengthy explanations
- Make decisions quickly once they have key information
- Get frustrated by unnecessary details or process
- Prefer direct, confident guidance
- Have low tolerance for indecision or ambiguity
- May seem impatient or abrupt (it's not personal; it's their pace)

How Drivers Build Trust:

Drivers build trust through **confidence in your efficiency and decisiveness**. They need to believe you won't waste their time and that you can cut through complexity to give them clear direction.

They lose trust when you:

- Take too long to get to the point
- Seem uncertain or wishy-washy
- Provide excessive detail they didn't ask for
- Make the process complicated
- Can't give them a direct answer

They gain trust when you:

- Respect their time by being efficient
- Provide clear, confident recommendations
- Give them the key information without fluff
- Make the process smooth and fast
- Show decisiveness yourself

Identifying Drivers

You'll recognize them within 2 minutes by:

Language patterns:

- Brief, direct statements
- "I need..." rather than "I'm looking for..."
- "What do you recommend?" (wanting your expert opinion quickly)
- "How fast can I get this?"
- May cut you off if you're providing detail they don't need

Behavior:

- Walk with purpose
- Check watch or phone frequently
- Stand rather than browse leisurely
- May multitask (taking calls, checking messages)
- Want to make decisions and move on

Body language:

- Direct eye contact
- Impatient gestures if you're taking too long
- Energy and urgency in their movements
- May literally start walking toward checkout

WISE Selling Adaptations for Drivers

Welcome Phase:

Get straight to business:

"What do you need today?"

No lengthy small talk. No detailed store tour. Respect their time immediately.

Interview Phase:

Ask efficient, focused questions:

"What are you using this for?"
"How often will you use it?"
"What's your timeline?"

Three to five focused questions maximum. Get the critical information and move to Solution.

If they seem rushed: "I have a few quick questions to make sure I recommend the right thing, then we'll get you out of here fast."

This acknowledges their time pressure while explaining why you need brief information.

Solution Phase:

Lead with your recommendation and brief reasoning:

"For what you're doing—job site use, daily operation, durability priority—I recommend the Milwaukee M18 Fuel. It's contractor-grade, survives job site abuse, has the power you need, and the battery platform means your existing M18 batteries work with it. That's the one I'd get."

Brief and direct. Don't bury your recommendation in options unless they ask for alternatives.

Use benefit statements, but keep them concise:

"This has a brushless motor. That means it lasts twice as long under heavy use which is critical for job site work where tool failure costs you money."

If they want more detail, they'll ask. Otherwise, assume less is more.

Provide options only if needed: "There's a model that's $40 less with slightly less power that is adequate for your use but won't last as long. Or this model with more power for $60 more. Based on your volume of work, I'd go with the middle option."

Three options maximum. More creates decision paralysis for Drivers.

Experience Phase:

Lock-in should be brief and confident:

"You made the right call. This handles the work you described perfectly, and it'll last. You're set."

Don't overexplain. They've decided. Move to checkout efficiently.

Checkout should be fast. Have their items ready, process payment quickly, get them on their way.

Follow-up should respect their time:

"Quick check-in: How's the drill working out? Any issues I can address?"

Brief text or email. Don't call unless there's a problem that requires it.

Common Mistakes with Drivers

Mistake 1: Providing extensive detail they didn't request. This frustrates them and makes them feel like you're wasting their time.

Mistake 2: Showing uncertainty. "Well, you could try this one... or maybe this one..." drives Drivers crazy. Be decisive.

Mistake 3: Slow checkout process. After they've made a quick decision, don't slow them down with lengthy checkout, excessive small talk, or complex processes.

Mistake 4: Taking their abruptness personally. Drivers aren't being rude - they're being efficient. Don't let their pace throw you off.

The Practical Customer

Characteristics

Practicals are Jennifer. She just needs to hang pictures. They:

- Focus on their immediate, specific need
- Want value and functionality, not premium features
- Don't care about specifications they won't use
- Appreciate straightforward, no-nonsense guidance
- May have limited budget or don't want to overspend
- Prefer simple over complex
- Want products that do the job without extras
- Are skeptical of upselling or unnecessary features

How Practicals Build Trust:

Practicals build trust through **confidence that you're serving their actual needs** without trying to oversell them. They need to believe you're helping them solve their problem efficiently and economically.

They lose trust when you:

- Try to sell them features they don't need
- Push expensive options when simpler ones work
- Use technical jargon or complexity unnecessarily
- Make them feel like they need more than they do
- Seem to prioritize your sale over their need

They gain trust when you:

- Focus on their specific stated need
- Recommend appropriately (not always the most expensive)
- Explain simply and clearly
- Respect their budget constraints
- Show you're solving their problem, not maximizing your sale

Identifying Practicals

You'll recognize them within 2 minutes by:

Language patterns:

- Focused on specific task: "I need to hang pictures"
- Value-conscious: "I don't need anything fancy"
- Budget mentions: "I'm on a budget" or "What's reasonable for this?"
- Simplicity preference: "I just need something basic"

Behavior:

- Not browsing extensively
- Looking at price tags
- May ask about cheaper options

- Want reassurance they're not overspending

Body language:

- Practical, no-nonsense demeanor
- May seem skeptical of sales recommendations initially
- Relaxes when they feel you're being straight with them

WISE Selling Adaptations for Practicals

Welcome Phase:

Be straightforward and helpful:

"Thanks for coming in. What project are you working on?"

Interview Phase:

Focus on their specific need without overcomplicating:

"Tell me what you're trying to do."
"Have you done this kind of work before?"
"What's your budget range?"

Respect budget from the start. Asking about budget isn't pushy with Practicals. It shows you respect their constraints.

Solution Phase:

Recommend what they actually need, not the premium option:

"For hanging pictures in an apartment, you don't need a professional-grade drill. This cordless model will handle everything you're describing - drywall, maybe a few light projects around the apartment. It's $60, and it'll last you years for occasional home use."

Use practical benefit statements:

"This has a lithium battery. That means it holds its charge for months sitting in the closet, so when you need it next time, it's ready. Older batteries would be dead."

Address value directly:

"You could spend $180 on the professional model, but you'd be paying for power and durability features you won't use for picture-hanging. This gives you what you need without paying for what you don't."

Multiplication should focus on essentials only:

"You'll need these drill bits. The basic set is $8 and handles most home projects. That's really all you need for what you're doing."

Don't push accessories they don't need. Practicals will appreciate this restraint and trust you more.

Experience Phase:

Lock-in should emphasize you gave them the right solution for their need:

"This drill handles the picture-hanging perfectly, and it's appropriately priced for occasional home use. You got exactly what you need without overspending on features you wouldn't use. Smart choice."

Follow-up should be helpful without being salesy:

"Just checking in to see if the picture-hanging go smoothly? Any questions about using the drill?"

Common Mistakes with Practicals

Mistake 1: Trying to upsell them to premium options they don't need. This destroys trust instantly. They feel like you're taking advantage of them.

Mistake 2: Using technical jargon unnecessarily. Keep it simple and practical.

Mistake 3: Pushing multiplication items that aren't essential. Recommend only what they truly need.

Mistake 4: Making them feel cheap or uninformed for choosing value options. Never be condescending about budget consciousness

The Trendsetter Customer

Characteristics

Trendsetters are Marcus. He wants the latest with the best design. They:

- Care about innovation and what's new
- Value aesthetics and design as much as function
- Are influenced by what's popular, featured, trending
- Want products that make a statement
- Follow influencers, reviews, and lifestyle media
- Appreciate brands with strong identity
- May share purchases on social media
- Want to be early adopters
- Care how products look and what they say about them

How Trendsetters Build Trust:

Trendsetters build trust through **confidence that you understand current trends** and can guide them to products that are innovative, well-designed, and socially validated. They need to believe you're knowledgeable about what's new and what's good.

They lose trust when you:

- Seem out of touch with trends or innovations
- Push outdated models or designs
- Dismiss aesthetics as unimportant
- Don't know what's popular or what influencers recommend
- Treat their design preferences as superficial

They gain trust when you:

- Demonstrate awareness of current trends
- Take design and aesthetics seriously
- Reference what's popular or getting attention
- Show enthusiasm for innovation and new releases
- Validate that style matters

Identifying Trendsetters

You'll recognize them within 2 minutes by:

Language patterns:

- "I saw this on [Instagram/YouTube/TikTok]..."
- "What's the newest model?"
- "What colors does this come in?"
- "Is this the same one [influencer] uses?"
- "What are most people getting right now?"
- References to design, aesthetics, style

Behavior:

- Examining products for design details
- Taking photos of products
- Checking social media for product information
- Asking about limited editions or exclusive versions
- Browsing with attention to packaging and presentation

Visual cues:

- Fashion-conscious personal style
- Latest tech/accessories
- Brand awareness in their own choices
- Overall aesthetic attention in appearance

Body language:

- Confident and engaged
- Visually oriented (touching, examining, photographing)
- Excited about new or distinctive products

WISE Selling Adaptations for Trendsetters

Welcome Phase:

Acknowledge their style awareness:

"Thanks for coming in! I noticed you're looking at the new Milwaukee line. You have a great eye, that just launched last month and it's getting incredible attention."

Reference trends or newness early to show you're tuned in.

Interview Phase:

Ask questions that respect design and trends as legitimate priorities:

"What drew you to this particular model?"
"Are you looking for something that matches a specific aesthetic?"
"Have you seen this featured anywhere—reviews, social media?"
"How do you envision this looking in your space?"
"What appeals to you about this versus other options?"

These questions validate that design matters. You're not dismissing their priorities; you're taking them seriously.

Solution Phase:

Lead with what's new and distinctive:

"This is actually our newest model that just launched last month. It's getting a lot of attention because of the innovative design. Milwaukee completely redesigned the tool body with this matte black and red accent colorway. It's showing up all over tool Instagram right now."

Combine aesthetics with function:

"The performance is exceptional. This is the same motor technology as their professional line, so you're getting serious capability. But what sets it apart is the design. That matte black finish with the copper accents is trending hard in home design right now. It looks as good sitting on your workbench as it performs."

Use social proof:

"This model was featured in Popular Mechanics and recommended by [relevant influencer]. It's definitely having a moment. We've sold a ton of these in the last month."

Discuss brand story when relevant:

"DeWalt redesigned their entire line with sustainability in mind like recycled materials, carbon-neutral manufacturing. They're one of the first major tool brands to make that commitment, which resonates with a lot of people."

Highlight exclusivity when available:

"This colorway is actually exclusive to specialty retailers, so you won't find it at big box stores. Only a few hundred units were produced, so you're getting something distinctive."

Connect to their lifestyle:

"Based on what you mentioned about documenting your renovation on Instagram, this tool photographs incredibly well. A lot of our Customers who share their projects love how this looks in progress shots. The design is striking enough to feature rather than hide."

Multiplication should emphasize the complete aesthetic:

"To complete the look, you'll want the matching impact driver and work light. The whole kit creates that cohesive aesthetic and functionally, being on the same battery platform makes sense."

Experience Phase:

Lock-in should validate their choice as trendy and well-informed:

"You made an excellent choice. This is one of the most popular models right now for good reason. Milwaukee nailed the combination of performance and design. When you're using this on your renovation, it's going to look and perform exactly how you want."

Encourage social sharing:

"When you complete that project, tag us on Instagram! We love seeing how our Customers use these tools. We often feature Customer projects on our feed."

Keep them in the loop:

"I'm going to add you to our list for new product announcements. You'll get early access when new releases arrive. And you seem like someone who appreciates being first to know about innovations."

Follow-up can reference their project documentation:

"How's the renovation coming along? I'd love to see some progress shots if you're sharing them!"

Common Mistakes with Trendsetters

Mistake 1: Dismissing aesthetics as superficial. "You shouldn't care what color it is—performance is what matters." This alienates them completely. Design IS important to them.

Mistake 2: Being unaware of trends. If you don't know what's popular, new, or getting attention, you can't build trust with Trendsetters.

Mistake 3: Pushing older models. Even at a discount, Trendsetters don't want last year's model. They specifically want what's current.

Mistake 4: Ignoring social validation. Failing to mention what's popular or what influencers recommend misses key trust-builders.

Mistake 5: Being judgmental. Some salespeople look down on Customers who care about brands and design. This attitude kills trust and sales.

Mistake 6: Leading only with technical specs. While Trendsetters want quality, drowning them in specifications bores them. Lead with innovation, design, and brand story.

Personality Type Examples Across Categories

Let's see how these four types show up across different retail environments:

Running Shoe Store

Analytical: "I've been researching pronation control and cushioning systems. Can you explain the difference between your stability shoes' medial posting versus guide rails? I've read conflicting reviews about which approach provides better biomechanical support for overpronators."

Driver: "I need running shoes. I overpronate, run 30 miles a week, mostly road. What do you recommend?"

Practical: "I'm starting to run a few times a week for exercise. I don't need anything fancy just something comfortable that won't hurt my knees and doesn't cost a fortune."

Trendsetter: "I saw these Hoka One Ones on a running influencer's Instagram. That maximalist cushioning look is everywhere right now. Do you have them in the new colorway that just dropped?"

Camera Store

Analytical: "I'm comparing the Sony A7 IV versus the Canon R6 Mark II. Can you walk me through the autofocus algorithm differences? I've read Sony's eye-tracking performs better in low light, but Canon's subject recognition seems more reliable for erratic movement. What's your experience?"

Driver: "I need a camera for photographing my kids' sports. Fast autofocus, good in gym lighting. What's the best option under $2,000?"

Practical: "I want to take better photos of my family than my phone gives me, but I don't need professional quality. What's a good camera that's not too complicated and reasonably priced?"

Trendsetter: "I'm looking at the Fujifilm X-T5 in silver. That retro aesthetic is perfect for my style. I saw it featured on PetaPixel. Is this the one a lot of photography influencers are using right now?"

Furniture Store

Analytical: "I'm researching construction methods. Can you explain your joinery techniques? I've read mortise-and-tenon is more durable than dowel joints for frame furniture. What joining method does this sofa use, and how does that affect longevity?"

Driver: "I need a sofa for my living room. Durable, comfortable, seats four. I have kids, so it needs to handle daily use. What do you recommend?"

Practical: "I need a couch that's comfortable and will last a few years. I don't need anything fancy just something functional that doesn't break the bank."

Trendsetter: "I'm looking for something in that modern minimalist aesthetic with clean lines, maybe in that warm cognac leather color that's trending. I saw something similar in Architectural Digest. Do you have anything like that?"

See the pattern? Same products, completely different approaches needed for each personality type.

Adapting Mid-Interaction

You might initially misidentify a Customer's type. That's fine just adapt when you recognize the mismatch.

If you're giving an Analytical brief answer and they keep asking detailed questions:

"I can see you're really interested in the technical details. Let me go deeper into how this works..."

If you're giving a Driver lengthy explanations and they seem impatient:

"Let me cut to the bottom line for you..."

If you're trying to sell a Practical premium feature and they seem skeptical:

"You know what, let me back up. For what you're actually doing, here's what you really need..."

If you're giving a Trendsetter only technical specs and they seem bored:

"Let me shift gears and talk about what makes this distinctive from a design and innovation standpoint..."

Flexibility and awareness are key.

Overlap and Evolution

These types aren't rigid boxes. Some Customers show characteristics of multiple types:

Analytical + Practical: Researches extensively but ultimately chooses based on value and need, not premium features.

Driver + Trendsetter: Wants the latest and best but wants to decide quickly without lengthy deliberation.

Analytical + Trendsetter: Deeply researches new innovations and wants both cutting-edge and thoroughly understood.

Additionally, Customers evolve over time. A Practical buying their first product in a category might become an Analytical as they develop interest and knowledge.

Building Trust: The Universal Key

Regardless of personality type, building trust requires both compassion and confidence from Chapter 8. But HOW you demonstrate each varies by type:

For Analyticals:

- Compassion = Respecting their research and giving them time
- Confidence = Demonstrating deep technical knowledge

For Drivers:

- Compassion = Respecting their time and efficiency needs
- Confidence = Being decisive and direct

For Practicals:

- Compassion = Respecting their budget and not overselling
- Confidence = Showing you understand their real needs

For Trendsetters:

- Compassion = Respecting that design and innovation matter
- Confidence = Demonstrating you're current with trends

Same trust equation. Different application for each type.

The Universal Application

These four personality types appear across every retail category, every culture, every demographic. The principles for identifying and serving each remain constant even as specific products change.

Master this framework and you'll dramatically improve your effectiveness with the full spectrum of Customers who walk through your door.

Chapter 8

The Psychology of Trust – Fear, Compassion, and Confidence

Every Customer who walks through your door carries two invisible companions: fear and hope.

The fear whispers: "What if I make the wrong choice? What if I waste money? What if this salesperson takes advantage of me? What if I look foolish?"

The hope whispers: "Maybe this time will be different. Maybe this person can actually help. Maybe I'll find exactly what I need. Maybe this will work out well."

Your job as a WISE practitioner is simple to state but challenging to execute: Quiet the fear. Amplify the hope. Build trust.

Trust is the foundation of all successful retail relationships. Without it, Customers guard their information, resist recommendations, comparison-shop obsessively, and frequently walk away to "think about it." With it, they share openly, accept guidance, and make confident purchase decisions.

But what is trust, exactly? How do you build it? Can it be created systematically, or is it simply chemistry between people?

This chapter explores the psychology of trust in retail contexts and introduces a powerful framework: **Trust = Compassion + Confidence**.

Master these two elements, and you'll transform your effectiveness with every Customer type.

The Invisible Wall: Understanding the Defensive Barrier Customers Build

More specifically, every Customer walks in with two fundamental fears that shape every interaction, every question they ask, and every decision they make:

The fear of making a mistake.
The fear of looking stupid.

Think of these fears as an invisible wall the Customer builds the moment they walk through your door. It's a defensive barrier designed to protect them. And here's what you need to understand: this wall is completely rational from their perspective. They've been burned before. They've made bad purchases. They've felt talked down to by salespeople who made them feel ignorant.

So, they arrive with their guard up, walls high, ready to defend themselves against two catastrophic outcomes: wasting their money on the wrong thing or being exposed as clueless.

These twin fears drive more retail behavior than any other factors. They explain why Customers research obsessively online before coming to your store. They explain why someone will spend thirty minutes deciding on a $50 purchase. They explain the defensive body language, the skeptical questions, and the hesitation to commit.

The fear of making a mistake whispers: "What if I waste my money? What if this doesn't work? What if I choose the wrong one and regret it? What if there's a better option I'm missing?"

The fear of looking stupid whispers: "What if I ask a dumb question? What if this salesperson thinks I'm clueless? What if I don't understand what they're explaining—will they take advantage of me? What if everyone else knows something I don't?"

Understanding How These Fears Work

Before we explore how to build trust and break down these walls, let's understand these fears more deeply, because they affect different Customers in different ways.

The Fear of Making a Mistake

This fear is fundamentally about consequences. Customers worry about:

- **Financial waste**: "I'm spending hard-earned money. What if I choose wrong and can't return it?"
- **Project failure**: "I need this for something important. What if it doesn't work for my specific situation?"
- **Regret**: "What if I discover a better option tomorrow? What if I overpay?"
- **Time waste**: "What if I have to come back and go through this whole process again?"

This fear gets worse with:

- Higher price points
- Complex decisions with many options
- Products the Customer is unfamiliar with
- Past experiences of making poor purchases
- Pressure to get it right (gifts, important projects, limited budgets)

The Fear of Looking Stupid

This fear is fundamentally about social judgment and self-esteem. Customers worry about:

- **Revealing ignorance**: "Everyone else probably knows this. I'll look clueless if I ask."
- **Asking the wrong questions**: "What if my questions reveal I don't understand the basics?"
- **Being judged**: "This salesperson probably thinks I'm an idiot."
- **Being taken advantage of**: "What if they realize I don't know anything and try to sell me things I don't need?"
- **Making obvious mistakes**: "What if I miss something obvious that everyone else would catch?"

This fear gets worse with:

- Technical or specialized products
- Salespeople who seem impatient or condescending
- Other Customers who appear more knowledgeable
- Gender stereotypes (especially in traditionally gendered categories like tools or technology)
- Past experiences of feeling embarrassed in retail settings

What These Fears Look Like in Action

Understanding how these fears show up in Customer behavior helps you recognize and address them:

The fear of making a mistake often appears as:

- Repeated questions about the same features
- Requests to see products multiple times
- Extensive price comparison discussions
- Hesitation even after seemingly reaching a decision
- "Let me think about it" or "I need to do more research"
- Seeking reassurance: "Are you sure this is the right one?"

The fear of looking stupid often appears as:

- Apologizing for questions: "This might be a dumb question, but..."
- Claiming knowledge they don't have: "Oh yes, I know about that" (when they clearly don't)
- Avoiding questions entirely, preferring to figure it out themselves
- Defensive or aggressive posture to hide insecurity
- Bringing a friend or partner as a "safety" person
- Deflecting to price or features rather than admitting confusion

Some Customers show one fear more than the other. Many show both simultaneously, creating a complex emotional state that traditional sales approaches fail to address.

Your job? Systematically dismantle both sides of this defensive wall.

The Trust Equation: How to Tear Down the Wall

Here's the breakthrough insight from research in psychology, neuroscience, and behavioral economics: trust isn't mysterious. It's built from two distinct components that directly attack both Customer fears:

Trust = Compassion + Confidence

Compassion eliminates the fear of looking stupid. When Customers believe you genuinely care about their success and won't judge them, the wall comes down. They feel safe asking questions, admitting uncertainty, and revealing their true level of knowledge.

Confidence eliminates the fear of making a mistake. When Customers believe you're competent enough to guide them correctly, they trust that following your recommendations will lead to good outcomes, not regret. The wall protecting them from bad decisions comes down.

Here's the critical part: both elements are necessary. Neither alone is sufficient.

Think about what happens when one is missing:

High Compassion + Low Confidence: The Customer feels emotionally safe with you. They're not afraid of looking stupid. The wall protecting their ego comes down. But they're still afraid of making a mistake because they don't trust your competence. The wall protecting their wallet stays up.

Result: "That salesperson was so sweet, but they couldn't answer my questions, so I ordered online." The fear of making a mistake remains, so no sale happens.

Low Compassion + High Confidence: The Customer believes you know your stuff, which reduces their fear of making a mistake if they follow your advice. The wall protecting their wallet starts to come down. But they're afraid to reveal their true level of knowledge or ask "stupid" questions. The wall protecting their ego stays up.

Result: "That guy knew his stuff, but I felt like he was just trying to upsell me." The fear of looking stupid remains, leading to guardedness and distrust of your motives. They buy the minimum or leave.

Low Compassion + Low Confidence: Both walls stay fully intact. No trust whatsoever. The Customer leaves immediately or endures the interaction only if they have no alternatives.

High Compassion + High Confidence: Both walls come down completely. The Customer feels safe admitting what they don't know (compassion) and confident that following your guidance won't lead to mistakes (confidence). This is where sales happen easily and relationships are built.

Real-World Examples: Breaking Down the Wall in Different Retail Environments

Let's look at how this plays out practically across various retail formats.

Example 1: Electronics Store

The Situation: A 50-year-old woman walks into your electronics store looking for a laptop. She's holding her phone with notes, clearly has been researching, but looks overwhelmed and uncomfortable.

The Wall She's Built:

- *Fear of making a mistake*: "I've wasted money on technology before. I don't understand specs. What if I spend $800 on the wrong thing again?"
- *Fear of looking stupid*: "My kids are tech-savvy. This salesperson probably deals with people who know way more than me. I'm going to sound like an idiot."

Watch her body language. Arms slightly crossed. Making brief eye contact but looking away quickly. She's braced for judgment.

Traditional Approach (Fails): "Hi! What are you looking for today? What's your budget? Are you familiar with the difference between Intel and AMD processors?"

This approach immediately triggers both fears. "What's your budget?" feels intrusive before trust exists. "Are you familiar with..." directly tests her knowledge, confirming her fear that she's supposed to know things she doesn't.

Both walls get higher. She'll either leave or buy the cheapest option to escape.

WISE Approach - Building Compassion (Eliminates fear of looking stupid):

"Hi! Thanks for coming in. I'm Jason. Laptop shopping can be incredibly confusing - the manufacturers don't make it easy to understand what actually matters. A lot of people come in feeling overwhelmed by all the specs and options. No judgment here whatsoever. Let me ask you a few questions about what you'll actually be using it for, and I'll translate all the tech-speak into plain English. Sound good?"

What this does:

- Acknowledges that confusion is normal (not her fault)
- Explicitly removes judgment: "No judgment here"
- Positions him as translator, not examiner
- Makes it safe to not know things
- The wall protecting her ego starts to come down

WISE Approach - Building Confidence (Eliminates fear of making a mistake):

After she explains she mainly uses it for email, documents, Netflix, and storing photos...

"Okay, perfect. Based on what you've told me - mostly email, documents, streaming, and photo storage - here's what actually matters and what doesn't. Processor power? You don't need much. Any modern i5 or Ryzen 5 handles everything you described easily. Where I want to focus is storage. You mentioned you take a lot of photos. Here's what I see happen constantly: people buy a laptop with 256GB storage because it's cheaper, seems like plenty. Six months later, their photos have filled it up, everything slows down, and they're scrambling to buy an external hard drive for another $100. Then they're frustrated because they have to remember to plug it in.

I'm recommending you get at least 512GB, ideally 1TB. It costs about $150 more upfront, but you'll never worry about space. Based on helping hundreds of people with similar needs, that's where people get the most real-world value. The mistake I'm trying to help you avoid is under-buying storage and regretting it six months from now."

What this does:

- Shows deep understanding of her actual use case
- Explains what matters (storage) and what doesn't (processor power)
- Steers her away from a common mistake with specific reasoning
- Uses real experience: "Here's what I see happen constantly"
- Directly addresses her fear: "The mistake I'm trying to help you avoid"
- The wall protecting her wallet starts to come down

The Result: Both walls are down. She asks follow-up questions without apologizing. She trusts both that you care about her success (compassion) and that you know how to prevent her from making a mistake (confidence). She buys the right laptop, thanks you by name, and tells her friends about the helpful person at the store.

Example 2: Running Shoe Store

The Situation: A 35-year-old guy walks in. He's been training for his first marathon, has clearly spent hours researching online, and looks overwhelmed by conflicting information.

The Wall He's Built:

- *Fear of making a mistake*: "If I get the wrong shoes, I could get injured and blow four months of training. This is too important to screw up."
- *Fear of looking stupid*: "Everyone in running stores seems super-serious about running. I'm just a regular guy trying not to die during 26 miles. They probably think I'm a poser."

Traditional Approach (Fails): "So you're training for a marathon? Nice! What's your weekly mileage? What's your PR? Do you pronate?"

This immediately makes him feel tested. He doesn't know what his "PR" is, he's not sure about pronation, and now he feels like an amateur.

WISE Approach - Building Compassion:

"Marathon training! That's awesome! First one? The shoe question is a big one, and honestly, there's so much contradictory information online that it creates more confusion than clarity. Here's the thing: every runner is different. What works for someone else might not work for you. No stupid questions here. I'd rather spend 30 minutes making sure we get this right than have you walk out unsure. Cool?"

What this does:

- Validates that shoe selection is legitimately important
- Acknowledges the confusion from online research
- Explicitly removes "stupid questions" fear
- Creates collaborative, not hierarchical, relationship
- His ego-protection wall starts coming down

WISE Approach - Building Confidence:

After watching him walk/jog and asking questions about his training...

"Okay, so you've got neutral pronation, you're a midfoot striker, and you're building up to 40 miles per week. Based on those three factors, I'm recommending the Brooks Ghost over the Adrenaline, and here's specifically why.

The Adrenaline is designed for runners who overpronate. Their foot rolls inward too much. It has stability features to correct that. You don't need that correction. If you wear a stability shoe when you don't need it, it actually fights against your natural mechanics and can create problems that don't exist now.

The Ghost is designed for neutral runners like you. It's got enough cushioning for marathon distance, which you absolutely need at 26 miles, but not so much that you lose ground feel, which matters for your midfoot strike pattern.

I've fit about 200 marathon runners per year. When I see someone with your gait pattern and your mileage, this is consistently what works. The mistake I'm helping you avoid is wearing the wrong type of shoe for your mechanics. That's where overuse injuries come from."

What this does:

- Demonstrates sophisticated understanding beyond generic advice
- Explains the specific reasoning for this specific person
- Explains what would go wrong with the alternative
- References extensive relevant experience
- Directly addresses his injury fear with expert guidance
- His wallet-protection wall comes down

Example 3: Home Improvement Store

The Situation: A young woman, first-time homeowner, walks into the tool section looking for a power drill. She looks intimidated since she's in the "guy section" and clearly feels out of place.

The Wall She's Built:

- *Fear of making a mistake*: "I don't know anything about tools. What if I buy something that doesn't work for what I need? What if I pay too much for features I don't need?"
- *Fear of looking stupid*: "This is such a guy domain. The employee probably assumes I'm clueless about tools. Which I am. But I don't want to confirm the stereotype."

Traditional Approach (Fails): "Looking for a drill? What are you going to use it for? Do you know what voltage you need? Brushed or brushless motor?"

This immediately confirms her fears. She doesn't know what these terms mean, and now she's been exposed as ignorant - exactly what she feared.

WISE Approach - Building Compassion:

"Hey! Tool shopping, huh? It's confusing. The manufacturers make it way more complicated than it needs to be. Before I worked here, I didn't know anything about this stuff either, so I get it. Let me ask you a few questions about what projects you're working on, and we'll figure out exactly what you need. No technical knowledge required on your end—that's what I'm here for."

What this does:

- Normalizes not knowing about tools
- Shares his own previous ignorance (creates empathy)
- Removes the "I should know this" pressure
- Makes it explicitly safe to not know technical terms
- Completely gender-neutral approach focused on her needs

WISE Approach - Building Confidence:

After she explains she needs it for furniture assembly, hanging pictures, maybe some shelves...

"Perfect. Based on what you're doing - furniture assembly, picture hanging, occasional shelf work - here's my recommendation and why.

You're looking at this 12-volt model and that 20-volt model. The 20-volt has more power, which sounds better, right? But here's the thing: for your projects, you don't need that extra power. And that extra power comes with two downsides.

First, it's 2.5 pounds heavier. That might not sound like much, but when you're holding it over your head hanging pictures, or you're assembling furniture for an hour, that weight really matters. You'll get fatigued way faster.

Second, it's $85 more expensive. You're paying for power you'll literally never use for these projects.

I've helped dozens of first-time homeowners, and this 12-volt handles everything you've described easily, it's lighter so you won't get tired, and it's cheaper. Here's what I'd do with that $85 you save: get a good bit set. That's actually where you'll see the difference in how well things work. A good bit set with the 12-volt drill beats a cheap bit set with the 20-volt drill for what you're doing.

The mistake I'm saving you from is spending extra money on power you don't need, when what actually matters for your projects is having the right bits."

What this does:

- Breaks down the decision in clear, practical terms
- Explains trade-offs honestly (weight matters for overhead work)
- Steers away from overspending on unnecessary features
- Shows genuine interest in the right solution, not the biggest sale
- Redirects money to what actually matters for her projects
- Demonstrates real expertise through practical application knowledge

Example 4: Camping/ Hiking Store

The Situation: College student planning his first multi-day backpacking trip. Limited budget. Has spent weeks researching online and is now more confused than when he started.

The Wall He's Built:

- *Fear of making a mistake*: "I'm going into the wilderness. If my gear fails, it's not just disappointing; it could be dangerous. And I can't afford to buy everything twice."
- *Fear of looking stupid*: "These outdoor store employees have probably been backpacking for decades. I'm a college kid who's never spent more than one night outside. They're going to think I'm a total beginner."

Which, of course, he is. But he doesn't want to be treated like one.

WISE Approach - Building Compassion:

"First backpacking trip? Awesome! Yeah, researching gear online is a rabbit hole—you end up with 50 browser tabs and more questions than when you started. Everyone goes through that. I remember my first trip; I was so worried about having the wrong stuff.

Here's what we're going to do: you tell me about your specific trip like where you're going, how long, what time of year and your budget. Then we'll talk about what's actually essential versus what's nice-to-have. No judgment about budget. I'd rather help you spend your money on the right things than waste it on gear you don't need. Sound good?"

What this does:

- Validates that research confusion is normal
- Shares his own beginner experience
- Respects budget limitations without judgment
- Creates collaborative planning approach
- Makes it safe to be a beginner

WISE Approach - Building Confidence:

After learning it's a July trip in the Sierras, 40 miles over 4 days, $400 budget...

"Okay, July in the Sierras, 40 miles. Here's how I'd prioritize your budget, and I'll tell you exactly why.

Your biggest investment needs to be your sleeping system with a bag and pad because staying warm at night in the high country makes or breaks your trip. I'm recommending this 30-degree synthetic bag at $180 instead of that $120 bag. Here's why: First, the temperature rating is more reliable. That 35-degree bag over there sounds close enough, but I've seen too many people underestimate how cold it gets at 10,000 feet at night, even in July. You'll be miserable and possibly unsafe if you're cold. Second, synthetic insulation still works if it gets wet. Sierra summer afternoons bring thunderstorms, and if your bag gets damp, you need it to still work. Down is better weight-to-warmth ratio, but at this price point, synthetic is safer for your first trip.

Now, for your tent. Honestly? For July in the Sierras, you don't need an expensive tent. This $90 tarp-and-bivy setup will be totally fine. Save that money for better boots. That's where beginners often make expensive mistakes.

Here's the mistake I see all the time: people spend $250 on a fancy four-season tent for a summer trip where a simple shelter is fine, then they cheap out on boots and suffer for 40 miles. Your feet matter way more than your tent for this trip. That's $200 I want you to put toward quality footwear instead."

What this does:

- Prioritizes based on safety and trip-specific conditions
- Explains the reasoning: temperature ratings, wet-weather performance
- References real-world experience: "I've seen too many people..."
- Steers away from common beginner mistake (over-spending on tent, under-spending on boots)
- Shows he's thinking about the student's total experience, not maximizing this sale
- Demonstrates practical wilderness knowledge

Example 5: Jewelry Store - Engagement Ring

The Situation: Young man walks in to buy an engagement ring. He's clearly nervous, has done some online research, and is terrified of disappointing his girlfriend with the wrong choice.

The Wall He's Built:

- *Fear of making a mistake*: "This is the biggest purchase I've ever made. If I choose wrong, I'll ruin the proposal and disappoint her. This has to be perfect."
- *Fear of looking stupid*: "I know nothing about diamonds, cuts, clarity, color—any of it. This jeweler is going to know immediately that I'm clueless."

WISE Approach - Building Compassion:

"Engagement ring shopping is exciting, and I know it can feel like a lot of pressure. Here's the thing: diamond terminology is deliberately confusing. It's designed to make you feel like you need a geology degree. You don't. Most guys walk in here with the same level of diamond knowledge, which is basically zero, and that's completely fine.

What I care about is understanding what she likes - her style, what you've noticed about her jewelry - and making sure you feel confident about your choice. No dumb questions here. I'd rather you ask me everything you're wondering about than walk out uncertain. Deal?"

What this does:

- Acknowledges the emotional pressure
- Normalizes diamond ignorance
- Explicitly removes judgment
- Focuses on her preferences, not technical specs
- Creates safe space for questions

WISE Approach - Building Confidence:

After learning about her style preferences, her existing jewelry, budget...

"Based on what you've told me, she likes classic, timeless looks, not trendy designs, and you've noticed her jewelry tends to be understated and elegant. Here's what I recommend and why.

I'm suggesting this round brilliant cut in the 0.9-carat range instead of pushing you toward 1.0 carat. Let me explain the reasoning because this is where I can save you real money without sacrificing what she'll actually notice.

The round brilliant cut maximizes sparkle and light return - it's the most classic cut for a reason, and it fits the timeless aesthetic she prefers. Now, here's the insider knowledge: the visual difference between a 0.9-carat and a 1.0-carat diamond is imperceptible unless you're a jeweler with a loupe. Nobody can tell the difference by looking at her hand. But you'll save about $1,200 by staying under that psychological 1.0-carat threshold.

Here's what I want you to do with that $1,200: upgrade the color from H to F grade. That's something she will notice in daily wear. It's visibly whiter and brighter, especially against her skin tone which you mentioned is cooler. It makes the whole ring look higher quality.

I've done this with hundreds of guys. The ones who get the best response? They maximize overall appearance and sparkle, not technical specs. Nobody asks about carat weight. They notice if the ring is beautiful and sparkly.

The mistake I'm saving you from is the one tons of people make: sacrificing color and clarity to hit that magic 1.0-carat number, when what actually shows is the overall beauty, not a spec on a certificate nobody ever sees."

What this does:

- Connects recommendations to her specific preferences
- Explains industry pricing psychology (threshold premiums)
- Provides budget optimization that shows he's on the customer's side
- Steers away from common mistake with clear reasoning
- References extensive experience: "I've done this with hundreds of guys"
- Focuses on the outcome that matters: her reaction

Trust Equation + WISE Process

Now that you've seen real examples, let's break down how Compassion and Confidence work systematically through each phase of WISE Selling to tear down both walls:

Welcome Phase

Compassion Signals (reducing fear of looking stupid):

- Genuine warmth - not fake cheerfulness, but real human welcome
- "Thanks for coming in" Appreciation makes them feel valued, not judged
- Respectful name exchange when natural
- Open body language
- Comfortable, unhurried atmosphere. No pressure

Confidence Signals (reducing fear of making mistakes):

- Professional appearance and demeanor
- Organized, clean store environment
- Knowledgeable reference to your specialties (Points of Pride)
- Competent, efficient manner

Interview Phase

Compassion Signals:

- Questions about their specific situation, not generic scripts
- Never assuming they know things they might not know
- Active listening without interruption
- Genuine interest in their goals
- Acknowledging constraints without judgment
- Creating explicit safety: "Have you used products like this before?"
- Normalizing confusion: "A lot of people find this confusing at first..."
- Summarizing what you heard to confirm understanding

Confidence Signals:

- Asking insightful questions that show you understand what determines success
- Recognizing patterns from other Customers with similar needs
- Asking questions in logical sequence
- Knowing what information you need to guide them correctly
- Understanding when to dig deeper into specific areas

Solution Phase

Compassion Signals:

- Explaining clearly without talking down
- "Let me explain how this works..." rather than assuming knowledge
- Patience without visible frustration
- Checking understanding: "Does that make sense, or should I explain it differently?"
- Welcoming questions: "What questions do you have?" (not "Do you have questions?")

Confidence Signals:

- Clear, confident recommendations with explicit reasoning
- "Based on what you've told me, here's what I recommend and why..."
- Honest trade-off discussion
- Specific examples and comparisons
- Deep product knowledge
- Anticipating questions before they're asked
- Steering them away from choices that would lead to regret
- Explaining expectations: "Here's what will happen when you first use this..."
- Being honest even when it means a smaller sale

Experience Phase

Compassion Signals:

- Teaching how to use products without assuming knowledge
- "A lot of people wonder about this at first..."
- Making post-purchase questions welcome
- Following up to ensure satisfaction

Confidence Signals:

- Providing specific tips that ensure success
- "Here's exactly how to set this up for best results..."
- Connecting them to ongoing resources
- Confident reassurance: "You made a great choice for your situation"
- Professional handling of all logistics
- Clear instructions and expectations
- Availability for questions: "If anything doesn't work the way you expect, come back and see me"

The Behaviors That Keep the Walls Up (or Make Them Higher)

Certain behaviors immediately amplify one or both fears. Avoid these religiously:

Behaviors that make the fear of looking stupid worse:

- Showing any condescension or impatience with basic questions
- Interrupting or dismissing their concerns
- Using jargon without explanation
- Making them feel like they should know things they don't
- Comparing them unfavorably to other Customers
- Visible judgment of their knowledge level
- Saying "Everyone knows that" or similar phrases
- Testing their knowledge: "You know what [technical term] means, right?"

Behaviors that make the fear of making a mistake worse:

- Being dishonest or exaggerating product performance
- Pushing them toward higher-priced options without clear reasoning for their specific needs
- Not being able to answer reasonable questions
- Not explaining trade-offs or limitations
- Creating fake urgency or pressure
- Being vague or tentative in recommendations
- Telling different Customers different things
- Not following up after purchase
- Dismissing concerns: "Don't worry about that"

A single condescending response can trigger such intense fear of looking stupid that it persists through the entire interaction and they never come back. A single obvious lie can trigger such strong fear of making a mistake that they'll research for hours elsewhere before trusting any purchase decision.

The Compound Effect: Why This Matters Long-Term

Here's what makes this approach so powerful: trust compounds over time.

Each positive interaction makes the next one easier. When that Customer from the laptop example comes back six months later, she walks in with both walls already partially down. She remembers that you didn't make her feel stupid and that your recommendation worked perfectly. The second interaction takes half as long and results in an easier, higher-value sale.

That's why WISE Selling emphasizes long-term relationships over short-term transactions. The initial investment in building trust involves taking extra time, being thorough, sometimes recommending lower-priced options. It pays returns for years through repeat business and referrals.

It's also why one negative interaction damages so much. It doesn't just lose one sale. It re-triggers both fears so strongly that the Customer may never return. And they'll tell others, spreading those fears to potential Customers who haven't even met you yet.

Most salespeople are naturally better at one than the other:

Some people are naturally compassionate - warm, empathetic, great listeners. But they lack product knowledge or confidence in their recommendations. Customers like them but don't trust their guidance. Result: low conversion rates.

Others are naturally confident - knowledgeable, articulate, decisive. But they come across as arrogant or pushy. Customers respect their expertise but don't trust their motives. Result: resistance and defensiveness.

Master both. Build your product knowledge until you can confidently guide any Customer. Cultivate genuine compassion until you naturally make every Customer feel safe asking questions. When both elements are present, the walls come down, trust is built, and selling becomes natural and enjoyable for everyone involved.

In the next chapter, we'll explore benefit statements. These are the specific language patterns that translate features into value Customers understand and care about, further building confidence and reducing the fear of making a mistake.

Chapter 9

Benefit Statements – Speaking the Language of Value

Here's what happens in retail stores every single day:

A Customer stands in front of two products. Both look similar. One costs $150. The other costs $275.

The salesperson says: "This one has a brushless motor, and this one has a brushed motor."

The Customer nods politely, having no idea what that means or whether it's worth an extra $125.

They leave to "think about it." Translation: they're going to Google "brushless vs brushed motor" because you didn't explain why it matters.

Now watch what happens when you speak the language of value instead of the language of specifications:

"Both of these are great tools. The difference is this: This one has a traditional brushed motor. It will do everything you need for the occasional projects you mentioned. This one has a brushless motor, which means it runs cooler and lasts about twice as long because there are no carbon brushes wearing out. For someone doing projects every weekend like you described, that means fewer replacements over the years. The question becomes: do you want to save money now, or invest in something that'll last longer for your regular use?"

Now the Customer understands. Now they can make an informed decision. Now that $125 difference makes sense.

This is what we're covering in this chapter: how to translate features into benefits and how to speak the language your Customers actually understand and care about.

The Problem: We Speak Product, They Speak Outcome

Here's the fundamental disconnect in most retail interactions:

What salespeople say: "This mattress has individually wrapped coils and a cooling gel layer."

What Customers hear: "Blah blah technical stuff blah blah."

What Customers actually want to know: "Will I sleep better? Will my back stop hurting? Will I stop waking up hot and sweaty?"

Most salespeople get stuck describing what products *have* and what products *do*. They never get to what actually matters: what products *do for the Customer*.

And here's why this matters so much: remember those two fears from the last chapter?

The fear of making a mistake gets worse when you only talk about features. The Customer thinks: "I have no idea if these specifications matter. I could be wasting my money on things that don't matter or missing things that do. How do I know?"

The fear of looking stupid gets worse too. The Customer thinks: "I should probably know what these terms mean. Everyone else probably understands this. I don't want to ask and reveal how clueless I am."

So, they nod along, pretending to understand, then leave to research online—where they'll probably get more confused and might never come back.

Your job is to eliminate both fears by translating technical stuff into plain English outcomes that matter to their life.

The Three Levels: Feature, Advantage, Benefit

Let's break down the three levels of product information, because most salespeople stop at level one or two when they need to get to level three:

Level 1 - Feature: What it has or what it is
This is a specification, characteristic, or attribute. It's objective and measurable.

Level 2 - Advantage: How it works or what it does
This describes the mechanism or capability.

Level 3 - Benefit: Why it matters to THIS Customer
This answers "What's in it for ME?"

Here's the same product described at all three levels:

Example 1: Electronics Store - Laptop

Feature (what most salespeople say):
"This laptop has an SSD."

Advantage (what better salespeople say):
"This laptop has an SSD, which is faster than a traditional hard drive."

Benefit (what WISE practitioners say):
"This laptop has an SSD instead of a traditional hard drive. That means when you open it in the morning, it's ready to use in about 10 seconds instead of sitting there for two minutes waiting to boot up. And when you click on a program, it opens instantly—no more staring at that loading circle. For

someone working from home like you mentioned, that saves you probably 20 minutes of frustration every day just in waiting time."

See the difference? The benefit connects to their specific life and explains why they should care.

Example 2: Paint Store

Feature:
"This paint has a ceramic additive."

Advantage:
"The ceramic additive makes it more washable."

Benefit:
"This paint has a ceramic additive that makes it extremely washable. You mentioned you have three kids under eight, right? That means when they inevitably get marker or crayon on the walls—and they will—you can wipe it clean without the paint coming off or leaving a dull spot. Most parents who've used regular paint know that frustration of scrubbing a mark and creating a bigger mess. This eliminates that problem."

Example 3: Running Shoe Store

Feature:
"This shoe has a carbon fiber plate."

Advantage:
"The carbon fiber plate provides propulsion."

Benefit:
"This shoe has a carbon fiber plate in the midsole. What that means for your marathon training: it acts like a spring with every step, giving you a little extra push-off. For the 26-mile distance you're targeting, that energy return adds up. You'll feel less fatigued in those final miles when you need it most. It's like having slightly fresher legs at mile 20."

Example 4: Furniture Store

Feature:
"This sofa has eight-way hand-tied springs."

Advantage:
"Eight-way hand-tied springs provide better support than typical construction."

Benefit:
"This sofa has eight-way hand-tied springs, which is old-world construction. What that means practically: you mentioned your current sofa has that saggy spot where everyone sits? This won't do that. The springs are individually knotted in eight directions, so they support each other and maintain shape. Ten years from now, this will sit like it does today with no sagging and no loss of support. Given you said you watch TV here every night, that daily-use durability matters."

The Problem: Why Salespeople Stop Too Early

Here's what I see constantly: salespeople learn product knowledge and get excited about features. They memorize specifications. They understand how things work. And then they stop there.

Why? A few reasons:

Reason 1: They assume Customers understand what they understand
You've sold this product 100 times. You know what "dual evaporator" means. You forget that Customers have no idea.

Reason 2: They think features sound impressive
"This has a quad-core processor with 16GB RAM" sounds sophisticated and knowledgeable. But it's meaningless to most Customers.

Reason 3: They weren't taught to translate
Most retail training focuses on product knowledge - memorizing specs. Almost no training teaches *translation* of those specs into Customer value.

Reason 4: It requires more work
Rattling off features is easy. Connecting to each Customer's specific situation requires listening during the Interview and customizing your presentation. That's harder.

But here's the reality: when you stop at features or advantages, you're making the Customer do the work of figuring out why they should care. And they won't. They'll just leave confused.

Worse, you're amplifying their fears. They're afraid of making a mistake, and you're giving them specifications without explaining what difference those specifications make. You're confirming their fear: "I don't know enough to make a good decision."

They're afraid of looking stupid, and you're using technical terms they don't understand. You're confirming their fear: "I'm supposed to know what these things mean, and I don't."

The Simple Formula: "This Has, That Means"

The easiest way to force yourself to get to benefits is this simple formula:

"This has [feature]. That means [benefit for YOU]."

The words "that means" force you to complete the translation. You can't say "that means" and then give another feature. You have to explain the outcome.

Let's practice this across multiple retail categories:

Garden Center

Wrong (feature only):
"These are zone 5 hardy perennials."

Right (feature plus benefit):
"These are zone 5 hardy perennials. That means they'll survive our winters and come back every spring. You plant them once and enjoy them for ten years or more instead of replanting annuals every season."

Mattress Store

Wrong:
"This mattress has individually wrapped coils."

Right:
"This mattress has individually wrapped coils instead of traditional connected springs. That means when your partner gets up in the middle of the night, you mentioned he's a restless sleeper, you won't feel it on your side of the bed. You'll sleep through the night undisturbed instead of waking up every time he moves."

Bike Shop

Wrong:
"This bike has hydraulic disc brakes."

Right:
"This bike has hydraulic disc brakes instead of rim brakes. That means consistent stopping power even in wet conditions. For the commuting you described, especially in Seattle weather, that means you can brake confidently when a car pulls out, regardless of whether it's raining. Safety improvement where it really matters."

Appliance Store

Wrong:
"This refrigerator has dual evaporators."

Right:
"This refrigerator has dual evaporators that provides separate cooling systems for the fridge and freezer. That means your food stays fresher longer without absorbing odors from other items. No more ice cream that tastes like onions. The air doesn't circulate between compartments, so everything maintains its own flavor."

Pet Store

Wrong:
"This dog food is grain-free."

Right:
"This dog food is grain-free, using sweet potato as the carb source instead. You mentioned your dog has been having stomach issues after eating, right? That means it's easier for him to digest, which often reduces that uncomfortable gas and gurgling you've been noticing. A lot of dogs are sensitive to grains without owners realizing it."

Tool Department

Wrong:
"This drill has a brushless motor."

Right:
"This drill has a brushless motor instead of a traditional brushed motor. That means it runs cooler, lasts about twice as long because there are no carbon brushes wearing out, and holds its charge better. For the regular DIY projects, you mentioned doing every weekend, that means fewer replacements over the years. This is probably the last drill you'll need to buy for ten years."

See the pattern? Every single time, "that means" forces the translation from specification to outcome.

Making It Personal: Connect to What They Told You

Generic benefits are weak. Personalized benefits, connected specifically to what the Customer told you during the Interview, are powerful.

Compare these two approaches:

Example: Furniture Store

Generic approach:
"This sofa has high-density foam cushions. That means it maintains its shape and comfort for years."

That's okay. But watch what happens when you personalize it:

Personalized approach:
"This sofa has high-density foam cushions. Remember you mentioned your current sofa has sagging cushions that hurt your back after watching TV? That means this one will maintain that firm support you need and won't develop those uncomfortable sag spots. Your back will actually feel better after sitting here for a couple hours instead of worse."

The personalized version does three things:

1. References something specific they said
2. Solves a specific problem they have
3. Uses their own language ("hurt your back," "after watching TV")

The Customer recognizes their own needs in your recommendation. That builds trust and eliminates resistance.

Let's see more examples of personalization:

Example: Camera Store

Generic:
"This camera shoots 20 frames per second. That means you can capture fast action."

Personalized:
"This camera shoots 20 frames per second continuous. You mentioned photographing your daughter's soccer games, right? That means when she's taking that shot on goal, you're capturing the entire sequence - her approach, the kick, the ball in the net. You're virtually guaranteed to get that perfect moment instead of hoping you pressed the shutter at exactly the right instant. For sports photography, that's the difference between one good shot per game and ten great ones."

Example: Kitchen Store

Generic:
"This Dutch oven is 7 quarts. That means it holds a lot."

Personalized:
"This Dutch oven is 7 quarts. You said you're cooking for six people regularly now that the kids are older, right? That means you can make one large batch of chili or stew instead of cooking in stages like you've been doing. That Sunday meal prep you mentioned? You'll cut your time in half by using one pot instead of using multiple pans."

Example: Auto Parts Store

Generic:
"These wiper blades have a beam design. That means better contact with the windshield."

Personalized:

"These wiper blades have a beam design instead of the traditional frame style. You mentioned you drive a lot for work, including at night, right? That means more consistent clearing across the entire windshield with no streaks in the center that block your view. Especially for night driving on the highway, that clear visibility makes a huge difference for safety."

Every time you say "Remember you mentioned..." or "You said..." you're showing the Customer you listened, you understood, and you're solving their specific problem—not giving a generic pitch.

The Three-Part Formula: Adding "Because"

Some Customers - particularly technical types - want to understand *how* something works. For them, add a third element:

"This has [feature]. That means [benefit]. Because [explanation of how it works]."

Example: Outdoor Store

"These hiking boots have Gore-Tex lining. That means your feet stay dry in wet conditions while not overheating when you're working hard on the trail. Because Gore-Tex is waterproof from the outside but breathable from the inside. It blocks water droplets but lets sweat vapor escape so crossing streams or hiking in rain, your feet stay dry, but unlike rubber boots, they don't turn into swamps from your own perspiration."

Example: Music Store

"This guitar has a solid spruce top instead of laminate. That means the sound will actually improve over time as you play it. It gets richer and more resonant. Because solid wood continues to vibrate and open up with use, while laminate is basically plywood that stays static. Five years from now, this guitar will sound noticeably better than it does today."

Example: Electronics Store

"This router has Wi-Fi 6 instead of the older Wi-Fi 5 standard. That means when your whole family is streaming on different devices - you mentioned everyone's on their tablets at night - nobody experiences buffering or lag. Because Wi-Fi 6 can handle multiple devices simultaneously more efficiently, rather than serving them sequentially like older routers, so everyone gets full bandwidth at the same time."

The three-part formula satisfies the "but why?" question while keeping focus on the outcome rather than drowning in technical details.

The Categories of Benefits: Match to What Customers Care About

Different Customers care about different types of benefits. Here's what you need to understand about benefit categories:

1. Functional Benefits (What it does)

"This tent has a full-coverage rainfly. That means you'll stay completely dry even in sideways rain since the vestibule keeps water from coming in when you open the door, so you're not choosing between fresh air and staying dry."

2. Economic Benefits (Money saved or protected)

"This energy-efficient washer uses 40% less water than standard models. You mentioned doing 8-10 loads a week with your family size, right? That means you're saving about $120 annually on utility bills. It costs $150 more upfront, but it pays for itself in 15 months. After that you're just saving money."

3. Time Benefits (Time saved or gained)

"This rice cooker has a delay start timer. That means you load it in the morning before work, set it to finish at 6:00 PM, and dinner's ready when you walk in the door. No more scrambling to cook when you're already exhausted from the commute you mentioned. Saves you 30 minutes of evening stress."

4. Emotional Benefits (How you'll feel)

"This bedding has that hotel-quality feel you said you loved at the resort. That means every night when you slide into bed, you'll have that 'I'm on vacation' feeling. Your bedroom becomes your personal retreat instead of just where you sleep."

5. Safety/Health Benefits (Risk reduction)

"These shoes have the stability system built into the sole. That means they support your ankles on uneven trail terrain, reducing injury risk. For the hiking you're planning, especially carrying a full pack, that ankle support means you can handle rocky trails confidently without worrying about a twisted ankle ending your trip."

6. Social Benefits (How others see you or how it affects relationships)

"This wine consistently wins awards and is critically acclaimed. That means when you serve it at your dinner party next month, your guests will be impressed. You'll be the person who knows their wine without spending $100 a bottle."

7. Aesthetic Benefits (How it looks, design appeal)

"This countertop comes in this matte black finish. That means it creates that modern, sophisticated look you showed me in the magazine photo - clean lines, contemporary aesthetic. Your kitchen will look like something out of a design magazine instead of builder-grade basic."

Here's the key: Different Customer types prioritize different benefits.

Enthusiasts care most about functional and aesthetic benefits. They want it to perform well and look great.

Professionals prioritize functional, economic, and time benefits. Show them ROI and efficiency.

Novices value emotional, safety, and functional benefits. Make them feel confident and safe.

Trendsetters emphasize aesthetic, social, and emotional benefits. Help them look good and feel current.

Adapt your benefit emphasis based on what you learned about this specific Customer during the Interview.

Adding Tie-Downs: Confirming They Get It

After you present a benefit, confirm the Customer understood and agrees:

"That solves the problem you mentioned, right?"
"That matters for your situation, doesn't it?"
"Can you see how that would help?"
"That's important given what you told me, isn't it?"

These tie-down questions serve multiple purposes:

1. **Confirmation**: Makes sure they understood the benefit
2. **Agreement**: Gets small commitments that build toward the larger buying decision
3. **Course correction**: If they hesitate, you discover the benefit doesn't resonate and can explore why
4. **Engagement**: Keeps them actively participating rather than passively listening

Example: Luggage Store

"This suitcase has four spinner wheels instead of two rollers. That means you can navigate it through crowded airports with one finger instead of dragging it behind you. That means you'll arrive at your gate less exhausted. For someone traveling for work weekly like you mentioned, that reduced physical strain really adds up, doesn't it?"

Example: Toy Store

"These building blocks are compatible with the major brands. That means your daughter can combine them with the collection she already has - you're expanding possibilities rather than starting over with something incompatible. That's important given how much she's already invested in her current set, right?"

Example: Auto Shop

"These tires have a 70,000-mile warranty. That means based on your annual mileage you mentioned, about 15,000 miles, they'll last you almost five years. No more replacing tires every two years like you've been doing. That makes a difference for your budget planning, doesn't it?"

Watch their response. If they nod enthusiastically, you've hit something that matters. If they hesitate or look uncertain, dig deeper: "What concerns you about that?" or "Is that not as important to you?"

The Deadly Mistake: Feature Dumps

The opposite of good benefit statements is what I call the "feature dump" - rattling off a list of specifications without explanation, translation, or prioritization.

Here's what this looks like in real life:

Bad Example: TV Sales

Feature Dump:
"This TV has 4K resolution, 120Hz refresh rate, HDR10+ and Dolby Vision support, HDMI 2.1 ports, variable refresh rate, auto low latency mode, quantum dot technology, local dimming with 384 zones, and built-in Google TV."

Customer's internal response:
"Uh...okay. I guess that's good. I have no idea what half of those things mean or whether I need them. I should probably go home and Google all this. This person clearly knows more than me, which makes me feel stupid for not understanding. I don't want to ask and reveal my ignorance."

Both fears activated. Sale probably lost.

Now watch the benefit-focused approach:

Benefit Statement Approach:

"Let me focus on the three things about this TV that really matter for what you told me - watching a lot of sports and some gaming with your kids.

First, the 120Hz refresh rate. That means fast sports action stays crystal clear without blur. When you're watching football, you'll see every detail of quick plays—no motion blur on fast receivers. You'll notice the difference immediately compared to your current TV.

Second, the gaming features. That means when your son uses his PlayStation, the TV automatically switches to low-latency mode. It has no lag between when he presses the controller and when action happens on screen. He'll notice the improved responsiveness.

Third, the local dimming feature. That means dark movie scenes actually look dark while keeping bright areas bright. You'll see detail in shadows instead of everything being washed-out gray. That makes a huge difference for evening movie watching.

Those three things address exactly what you said matters most. There are other technical specs that are great, but these are the ones that will impact your daily viewing. Make sense?"

This approach:

- Limits to 3-4 key benefits instead of overwhelming with ten features
- Connects explicitly to what they said they'd use it for
- Uses plain language, not technical jargon
- Explains why each benefit matters to their specific life
- Invites questions instead of assuming understanding

Handling Different Customer Types

Technical Customers (Often Enthusiasts)

Some Customers actually want technical details. Don't skip benefits, but include more depth:

Example: Camera Store

"This lens has ED glass elements. What that means technically: reduced chromatic aberration across the frame. Practically for the landscape photography you mentioned: sharper images with better color accuracy, especially at the edges. When you're shooting at f/16 for depth of field, you want corner sharpness. You'll see the difference in high-contrast situations - think sunset shots where you have bright sky meeting dark mountains. No purple fringing around high-contrast edges."

You're still explaining benefits, but you're also satisfying their desire to understand the mechanism.

Non-Technical Customers (Often Novices)

For Customers who don't want technical depth, simplify further:

Example: Same Camera Lens

"This lens has special glass that keeps colors accurate and images sharp, especially around the edges of your photos. That means when you're shooting landscapes like those mountain scenes you mentioned loving. The corners look just as crisp as the center. No softness or weird color fringing. Professional-quality results."

Same product, same benefit, different level of technical detail based on the Customer.

Using Comparison to Clarify Benefits

When Customers are choosing between two options, use benefit statements to clarify differences:

Example: Jewelry Store

"Both of these watches are excellent. The difference comes down to your priorities.

This Seiko has a quartz movement. That means it's incredibly accurate and virtually maintenance-free. Set it and forget it for years. Battery changes every few years, that's it.

This Omega has a mechanical movement. That means traditional craftsmanship with visible working parts. You can see the mechanics through the case back. It needs servicing every few years, but watch enthusiasts love the artistry and the fact that it's powered by your movement rather than a battery.

The question becomes: do you want set-it-and-forget-it reliability, or are you drawn to the traditional craftsmanship even though it requires more care?

Both will tell time perfectly; it's really about which experience you value more."

Example: Outdoor Store

"These are both excellent boots for your needs. Let me break down the practical difference.

This Salomon is lighter and more flexible. That means it feels more like a trail runner, minimal break-in needed, and your feet stay less fatigued on long days. Think comfortable immediately.

This Asolo is heavier and stiffer. That means more ankle support on technical terrain and longer durability. These will last you twice as many miles, but they'll take a few hikes to break in completely.

Given you mentioned doing mostly day hikes on maintained trails and not technical mountaineering, I'd lean toward the Salomon. The immediate comfort advantage outweighs the durability benefit for your specific use. But if you were planning to progress to more challenging terrain, the Asolo investment makes more sense."

The comparison technique helps Customers understand not just what each product offers, but which benefits align with their specific needs.

The Story Technique: Benefits Wrapped in Real Experience

Sometimes the most powerful benefit statements come wrapped in stories about other Customers:

Example: Furniture Store

"Let me tell you about this dining table. Last year, a woman bought this same walnut table. She has four kids under ten so you can imagine the chaos. Birthday parties, art projects, homework, daily meals.

She came back six months ago, and I thought she was going to complain. Instead, she wanted matching chairs because the table had held up so beautifully. She said something I'll never forget: 'It's gotten more beautiful with use. Every scratch and ding tells a story about my family.'

That's what solid wood does that laminate or veneer can't because it ages gracefully. You're not buying furniture that needs to stay pristine to look good. Ten years from now, after thousands of family dinners, this table will have character and stories, and it'll still be rock-solid. That's the benefit of investing in quality construction; it becomes part of your family history.

Stories work because:

- They provide social proof (other people are happy with this)
- They make abstract benefits concrete (you can imagine the family using it)
- They create emotional connection (it's about family memories, not specifications)
- They're memorable (you'll remember the story more than specs)

Common Mistakes to Avoid

Mistake 1: Using Jargon Without Translation

Wrong: "This has a HEPA filter."

Right: "This has a HEPA filter, which means it traps allergens that other vacuums just recirculate back into your air. You mentioned allergies are bad this season - you'll notice less sneezing and easier breathing, especially when you're vacuuming."

Mistake 2: Too Many Benefits = Information Overload

Wrong: Listing seven benefits for each of five features.

Right: Focus on 2-4 key benefits that matter most to THIS Customer based on the Interview.

Mistake 3: Generic Benefits That Apply to Anyone

Wrong: "This is really durable."

Right: "This has reinforced stitching at stress points. You mentioned cramming this backpack full for weekend camping trips. That means the seams won't split like cheaper bags when you're stuffing in your sleeping bag and trying to zip it closed. That failure point on budget packs won't happen here."

Mistake 4: Explaining Without Demonstrating

When possible, let them *experience* the benefit instead of just hearing about it.

Example: Mattress Store

Don't just say: "This has motion isolation."

Do this: "Lie down here for a second. I'm going to sit on the other side and bounce. Notice how you don't feel that movement? That's what I mean by motion isolation - when your partner moves at night, you won't feel it."

Example: Outdoor Store

Don't just say: "This jacket is waterproof and breathable."

Do this: "Put your hand inside this jacket. I'm going to pour water over it. See? Completely dry. Now feel the inside. There is no clamminess, no trapped moisture. That's what Gore-Tex does. It blocks water from outside while letting sweat escape from inside."

Experience beats explanation every time.

Mistake 5: Talking About Features the Customer Doesn't Care About

Just because a feature is impressive doesn't mean this Customer values it.

Example: A Customer buying their first entry-level guitar doesn't care about hand-wound pickups or Brazilian rosewood. They care about: "This stays in tune well, which means you'll spend more time playing and less time twisting tuning pegs. That matters when you're learning because frustration over tuning kills motivation."

Let the Interview guide which benefits matter.

The Hierarchy: Which Benefits to Lead With

Some benefits are more compelling than others. When prioritizing, emphasize:

1. Benefits that solve painful problems

Pain avoidance is more motivating than gain seeking.

"This prevents the back pain you've been experiencing" beats "This is comfortable."

2. Benefits connected to goals they mentioned

"This helps you train for that marathon you mentioned" resonates more than generic fitness benefits.

3. Unique benefits

What can they only get from this product? Commodity benefits don't differentiate.

4. Surprising benefits

Benefits they didn't expect create delight. "I didn't realize it could do that!" is powerful.

5. Emotional benefits

How will owning and using this make them feel? Pride, confidence, security, peace of mind.

Practice Makes Perfect

Here's the reality: benefit statements feel awkward at first. You'll stumble. You'll forget. You'll catch yourself feature-dumping.

That's normal.

Excellence comes from deliberate practice:

Practice Method 1: For every product you sell, write three benefit statements using "This has, that means" formula. Force yourself to complete the entire statement. Say them out loud until they feel natural.

Practice Method 2: Record yourself (audio on your phone). Listen back. Count how many times you mention features without translating to benefits. Work to reduce that number.

Practice Method 3: After Customer interactions, reflect: Which benefit statements got head nods? Which ones got blank stares? Why?

Practice Method 4: Listen to experienced colleagues. When they give great benefit statements, steal them. When they feature-dump, mentally practice how you'd translate those features to benefits.

Practice Method 5: Ask Customers after purchases: "What ultimately convinced you?" Their answers reveal which benefits mattered most and that is what to emphasize with future Customers.

The Payoff: Why This Matters

When you master benefit statements, several things happen:

1. You eliminate the fear of making a mistake

By explaining why features matter, you help Customers understand what they're getting. They can make confident decisions instead of guessing.

2. You eliminate the fear of looking stupid

By translating jargon into plain English, you make it safe to not know technical terms. They don't feel ignorant; they feel informed.

3. You differentiate yourself

Most retail salespeople feature-dump. When you speak the language of value, you stand out as genuinely helpful instead of just reciting specifications.

4. You increase transaction value

When Customers understand value, they're willing to invest more for benefits that matter to them.

5. You build trust faster

Explaining benefits shows you understand their needs and care about helping them get the right solution and not just moving products.

Start practicing today. Pick one product. Write three benefit statements. Practice saying them until they sound natural. Then do another product. Then another.

In six months, speaking the language of value will be automatic. Customers will thank you for explaining things clearly. Your sales will increase. And you'll never go back to feature-dumping again.

In the next chapter, we'll explore the multiplication effect—how to expand transactions from single items into comprehensive solutions that serve Customers better while increasing transaction value naturally.

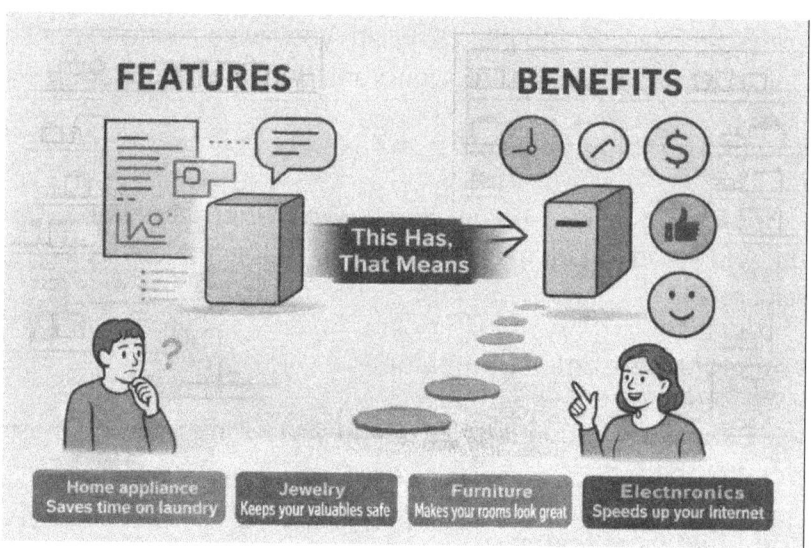

Chapter 10

The Multiplication Effect – Crafting Complete Solutions

A woman walks into a sporting goods store. She needs running shoes. She's training for her first marathon, and her current shoes have 400 miles on them and are well past their useful life.

The average salesperson conducts a brief interview, recommends appropriate shoes, rings up the $140 sale, and sends her on her way feeling good about helping her.

Three weeks later, she's back. Frustrated. She hit the wall at mile 18 during her long run because she had no fuel strategy. She has painful chafing from her sports bra. Her IT band is flaring up again. She's discouraged and wondering if she can actually finish this marathon.

The salesperson helped her with shoes but sent her out incomplete. She's now dealing with preventable problems that are threatening her goal.

Now watch what the WISE practitioner does differently:

After helping her select perfect shoes, the conversation continues:

"Okay, you're set with shoes. Now let's make sure you have everything you need to actually finish this marathon successfully. You mentioned your long runs are on Sundays, how are you handling nutrition once you're past 90 minutes?"

[Customer looks uncertain]

"Here's what happens to almost every first-time marathoner who doesn't have a fuel strategy: around mile 18, you hit the wall hard. Your body runs out of glycogen and basically shuts down. These energy gels prevent that. They're easy to carry and digest on the run. For your training distance, you'd use one every 45 minutes after the first hour."

[Pulls product]

"Second thing, and trust me on this, Body Glide for chafing prevention. At mile 18, those seams on your running clothes become torture without it. This is one of those things you don't think about until it's too late and you're in serious pain."

"Third, you mentioned summer training. These electrolyte tablets prevent cramping better than just water. Drop one in your water bottle for anything over an hour."

"Last thing. You said you've had IT band issues before. This foam roller. Five minutes after long runs prevents that from flaring up. I've seen IT band problems end dozens of training cycles. This prevents it."

The Customer leaves with running shoes, energy gels, Body Glide, electrolyte tablets, and a foam roller. Total purchase: $247 instead of $140.

But here's what really matters: She's actually equipped to finish her marathon. She'll avoid the preventable problems that derail most first-timers. She'll have a better training experience. And she'll remember this store as the place that set her up for success, not just sold her shoes.

This is the multiplication effect. It's not about inflating sales for your benefit. It's about making sure Customers have complete solutions so they can actually achieve their goals.

This chapter teaches you to identify multiplication opportunities, present them in ways that build trust rather than trigger fear, and integrate them seamlessly so Customers see them as essential components of success, not optional add-ons you're pushing.

Why Multiplication Matters: The Incomplete Solution Problem

Here's what happens when you don't multiply effectively:

Scenario 1: Customer buys a power drill but no bits. Gets home, can't use it, frustrated. Returns it or leaves it in the garage unused. Never comes back to your store.

Scenario 2: Customer buys expensive camera but no memory card. Takes it on vacation, camera says "no card," can't take photos. Vacation partially ruined. Annoyed at camera, annoyed at store.

Scenario 3: Customer buys nice furniture but no floor protectors. Scratches their hardwood floors moving it. Associates the furniture purchase with the floor damage. Negative memory of the entire transaction.

Scenario 4: Customer buys ingredients for a recipe but not all of them. Gets halfway through cooking, realizes they're missing something critical. Dinner plans ruined.

In every case, you made a sale but failed the Customer. They didn't achieve their goal. And they blame the product, the store, or themselves - often all three.

Now think about this through the lens of the two fears from Chapter 8:

Fear of making a mistake: When you send Customers out with incomplete solutions, you're *letting* them make a mistake. You knew they'd need those items and didn't tell them. Their fear was justified.

Fear of looking stupid: When they realize later they needed things you didn't mention, they feel stupid for not knowing. "I should have known I needed bits for a drill. What an idiot." You made them feel exactly what they feared.

Both fears are confirmed. Trust is damaged. They probably don't come back.

Multiplication Done Right: Building Trust Through Completeness

Now flip it. When you multiply effectively:

You eliminate the fear of making a mistake by ensuring they have everything needed for success. They can't forget something critical because you thought of it for them.

You eliminate the fear of looking stupid by proactively addressing things they didn't know to ask about. "Oh, I didn't realize I needed that—thanks for thinking of it." You made them feel taken care of, not ignorant.

You build massive trust because you demonstrated you're thinking about their success, not just your sale. You proved you have their back.

This is how multiplication becomes a trust-building tool instead of an upselling tactic. The difference is entirely about framing, timing, and genuine intention.

The Two Types of Multiplication (And Why Only One Builds Trust)

Bad multiplication (triggers fear, damages trust):

- Presented as optional extras after the main sale
- Feels like the salesperson is trying to squeeze more money out
- No clear connection to Customer success
- Customer thinks: "Are they recommending this because I need it or because they get commission?"

Example of bad multiplication: [After ringing up shoes] "Do you want socks with that? They're on sale."

The Customer thinks: "I have socks at home. This person is just trying to add to my bill. What else are they trying to sell me that I don't need?"

Good multiplication (eliminates fear, builds trust):

- Presented as essential components of the complete solution
- Clear connection to preventing problems or achieving goals
- Based on information from the Interview
- Customer thinks: "They're making sure I have everything I need to succeed. They're looking out for me."

Example of good multiplication: "Okay, shoes are perfect for you. Now let's make sure you're set up to train without the common problems that trip up first-timers. You mentioned you're running in summer heat, so you'll need a hydration strategy. And you said you've had IT band issues before, so we need to prevent that from coming back. Here's what actually works..."

The Customer thinks: "This person knows what they're doing. They're protecting me from problems I didn't even know to worry about. I trust their guidance."

See the difference? Same products recommended. Completely different impact on trust and fear.

The Four Categories of Multiplication

Not all multiplication items are equal. Understanding the categories helps you prioritize and present effectively:

Category 1: Essential Accessories

What they are: Items necessary for the primary product to function properly or safely.

Examples:

- Memory cards and batteries for cameras
- Safety glasses and proper bits for power tools
- Helmet and lights for bicycles
- Proper utensils for new cookware
- Floor protectors for furniture

Why they build trust: These are obvious needs once mentioned. When you proactively include them, Customers think: "Thank goodness they thought of that or I would have gotten home and been stuck."

How to present them: "You'll need a memory card since the camera doesn't come with one. This 64GB card holds about 2,000 photos, which should get you through your vacation. Without it, the camera literally won't take pictures."

Direct, matter of fact, obviously necessary. No fear of being oversold because the need is clear.

Category 2: Performance Enhancers

What they are: Items that improve results, extend product life, or significantly increase satisfaction.

Examples:

- Moisture-wicking socks that prevent blisters (running)
- Surge protector for expensive electronics
- Quality soil and fertilizer for new plants
- Premium brushes for painting (better finish)
- Professional-grade bits for power tools (better results, longer life)

Why they build trust: These items address the fear of making a mistake by improving the likelihood of success. "I'm investing in this project/goal—these items help ensure I don't waste that investment."

How to present them: "These moisture-wicking socks prevent blisters on long runs. You mentioned training through summer. Regular cotton socks create friction when they get sweaty. These stay dry, seamless construction. The difference is massive for marathon distance. Most serious runners consider these non-negotiable."

Connect to their specific situation, explain the mechanism, reference what experienced people do.

Category 3: Problem Prevention

What they are: Items that prevent common problems, protect investment, or provide peace of mind.

Examples:

- Insurance appraisal for jewelry
- Waterproofing treatment for outdoor gear
- Extended warranty for expensive appliances
- Screen protectors for devices
- Rust prevention for tools

Why they build trust: These directly address both fears. Fear of making a mistake: "This protects my investment." Fear of looking stupid: "I didn't know that could happen - glad you told me."

How to present them: "Last thing. Waterproofing treatment for these boots. They're water-resistant out of the box, but after a few muddy hikes, that breaks down. Treat them every few months and they'll stay waterproof for years. Skip this, and by next season they'll be leaking. Ten minutes of work prevents $200 replacement."

Honest about what happens without it. Clear cause-and-effect. Framed as protection, not upselling.

Category 4: Complementary Products

What they are: Items that complete the Customer's broader goal or significantly enhance the overall experience.

Examples:

- Running accessories for marathon training (gels, hydration, foam roller)
- Workout clothes that coordinate with fitness equipment
- Recipe book specific to new appliance
- Photography accessories that expand shooting capabilities
- Ergonomic keyboard to complete home office setup

Why they build trust: These show you understood their complete goal, not just the immediate purchase. "This person gets what I'm trying to accomplish and is helping me succeed at the whole thing."

How to present them: "You mentioned wanting to cook healthier meals for your family. This Instant Pot you're getting is perfect for that. This cookbook is specifically designed for it—every recipe has macro breakdowns and cooking times optimized for the pressure cooker. Takes the guesswork out of learning a new cooking method and keeps you focused on your health goal."

Connect to the broader goal they mentioned. Show how it serves that goal specifically.

How to Present Multiplication Without Triggering Fear

Remember: Customers walk in with those two fears already active. Your job is to quiet those fears, not make them worse. Here's how multiplication fits:

Bad Approach (Amplifies Fear):

[After selecting shoes, walking to register]

Salesperson: "Do you want to add socks? What about insoles? We have this foam roller on sale. Oh, and you should probably get Body Glide. Want to look at running shorts while you're here?"

Customer's internal response:

- *Fear of making a mistake*: "Is all this necessary or are they just trying to run up my bill? How do I know what I actually need? I'm going to waste money on things that don't matter."
- *Fear of looking stupid*: "I should probably know if I need these things. I don't want to ask and reveal I'm clueless. I'll just say no to everything to be safe."
- *Trust*: Damaged. "This person cares more about their commission than my success."

Good Approach (Eliminates Fear):

[After selecting shoes]

Salesperson: "Perfect. These shoes are exactly right for your training. Now let's make sure you're set up to actually finish this marathon without the problems that sideline most first-timers.

You mentioned this is your first marathon and you're doing long runs on Sundays. Once you're past 90 minutes, your body needs fuel or you'll hit the wall hard around mile 18. These energy gels are what marathoners use - one every 45 minutes after the first hour. This prevents that experience of completely running out of gas.

Second thing. You said you've had IT band issues before. That will come back with marathon mileage unless you prevent it. Use this foam roller for five minutes after long runs and it keeps that from flaring up. I've seen IT band problems end dozens of training attempts. This simple tool prevents it.

Last thing is Body Glide for chafing. This seems minor until mile 15 when clothing seams become torture. Trust me, $8 now prevents serious pain later."

These three things - fuel, injury prevention, chafing protection - address the most common reasons first-time marathoners either don't finish or have miserable experiences. With your shoes plus these items, you're set up properly."

Customer's internal response:

- *Fear of making a mistake*: Eliminated. "This person is protecting me from mistakes I didn't even know existed. They're preventing me from wasting my $140 shoe investment by failing the marathon."
- *Fear of looking stupid*: Eliminated. "They explained things I didn't know in a way that made me feel informed, not ignorant. They're not assuming I should know this stuff."
- *Trust*: Built. "This person genuinely cares about my success. They're thinking about my complete goal, not just making a sale. I trust their recommendations."

The difference is entirely in framing, specificity, and connection to Interview information.

The Language of Multiplication: Words That Build Trust vs. Trigger Fear

How you phrase multiplication recommendations matters enormously. Compare these:

Words That Trigger Fear (Sound Like Upselling):

"Do you want to add...?"

→ *Implies optional, maybe unnecessary, possibly money-grab*

"Can I interest you in...?"

→ *Sounds like selling, not helping*

"These are on sale today..."

→ *Motivation is moving product, not serving Customer*

"Most people buy..."

→ *Peer pressure, not personalized reasoning*

"You should really get..."

→ *Vague and pushy without clear reasoning*

Words That Build Trust (Sound Like Completing):

"To make sure you succeed with this, you'll also need..."

→ *Assumes these are part of success, not extras*

"The last piece of your solution is..."

→ *Positions as completing something, not adding to it*

"This prevents the most common problem people have..."

→ *Protection from mistakes, serving them*

"Remember you mentioned [problem]? This solves that..."

→ *Shows you listened, personalizes the recommendation*

"Everyone I work with who succeeds with this uses..."

→ *Social proof from successful people, aspirational*

"Let me make sure you're protected from..."

→ *Guardian role, looking out for them*

The second set of phrases assumes the items serve the Customer. The first set questions whether they're necessary. Start from service, not sales.

The "Complete Solution" Frame: Integration, Not Addition

The most powerful multiplication technique is presenting everything as one integrated solution from the start.

Bad: Addition Approach

[After showing shoes] "Okay, these shoes are $140. Did you want anything else?"

Good: Integration Approach

[After understanding their marathon goal] "Based on what you've told me about training for your first marathon, here's the complete solution I recommend:

Foundation: These Brooks Ghost shoes match your neutral gait and provide the cushioning you need for the high mileage you're building to.

Fuel strategy: These energy gels and electrolyte tablets keep you fueled and hydrated during those Sunday long runs. This prevents hitting the wall at mile 18.

Injury prevention: This foam roller addresses the IT band issues you mentioned having before. Five minutes after long runs prevents problems.

Comfort for distance: Body Glide prevents the chafing issues that become serious problems at marathon distance.

This complete package sets you up for successful training. You won't be dealing with the preventable problems that derail most first-time marathoners."

Notice the framing:

- "Complete solution" not "shoes plus extras"
- Each item has a clear role with benefit statement
- Connected to specific things they mentioned
- Positioned as problem prevention, not upselling

The Customer sees a system designed for their success, not a list of add-ons designed to increase your sale.

Prioritizing: What to Recommend When You Can't Recommend Everything

You can't recommend everything. Too many items overwhelms and triggers the fears ("I can't afford all this," "I don't know which things actually matter"), and damages trust.

Here's how to prioritize:

Priority 1: Essential for Safety or Basic Function

Always recommend. Non-negotiable.

"You'll need safety glasses for this power tool. This isn't optional, after all, eye protection is required for safe use."

Priority 2: Prevents Problems Customer Specifically Mentioned

They told you their concerns. Address them.

"You said you're worried about scratching your floors. These felt pads go under the furniture feet and prevents scratching completely. $12 protects your floors."

Priority 3: Significantly Improves Success Likelihood

Items that dramatically increase chances of achieving their stated goal.

"For marathon success at the distance you're targeting, a fuel strategy isn't optional. These gels are the difference between finishing strong and hitting the wall at mile 18."

Priority 4: Protects Significant Investment

For expensive primary purchases, protection becomes more important.

"This camera is a $2,000 investment. This bag protects it properly. Think of it as insurance - $80 protects $2,000."

Priority 5: High Impact Relative to Cost

An inexpensive item that prevents expensive problems or dramatically improves results.

"This $8 tube of Body Glide prevents painful chafing that can end your marathon. Relative to your total training investment, this is a no-brainer."

The sweet spot: 2-4 multiplication items per transaction for most retail scenarios. More than that starts to feel overwhelming. Less might leave critical gaps.

Practical Examples Across Retail Formats

Let's see complete multiplication scenarios across different retail environments:

Example 1: Camera Store

Customer: First-time DSLR buyer, moving up from phone photography, going on an African safari in two months.

Primary sale: Camera body and kit lens

Multiplication conversation:

"Great choice on this camera. Now let's make sure you're set up for safari success without the problems that ruin once-in-a-lifetime trips.

First, memory cards. The camera doesn't include one and you literally can't take photos without it. For a two-week safari, I recommend two 128GB cards. Here's why two: if one fails or gets lost, you don't lose all your photos. Split your storage as backup insurance.

Second, extra battery. The kit includes one, but on safari you won't have charging opportunities during game drives. A second battery means you never miss a shot because your camera died. $50 prevents the frustration of a dead camera when lions appear.

Third, this bag. The camera needs protection from dust and as you know, safari vehicles are incredibly dusty. This bag seals against dust and protects from bumps in the Land Cruiser. Your $1,800 camera investment needs proper protection.

Last thing. A cleaning kit. Dust will get on your sensor and lens no matter how careful you are. This kit lets you clean it properly without damage. Trying to clean with a t-shirt ruins expensive optics.

These four things - memory cards, extra battery, protective bag, cleaning kit - are standard for anyone doing serious photography in harsh conditions. Without them, you're risking equipment damage or missing unrepeatable moments."

Why this works:

- Connected to specific trip (safari)
- Clear reasoning for each item
- Framed as problem prevention
- References equipment value
- Sets them up for actual success

Example 2: Home Improvement Store - First Tile Project

Customer: Homeowner doing first DIY bathroom tile project, watched YouTube videos, feeling both excited and nervous.

Primary sale: Tile for 90 square feet

Multiplication conversation:

"Love this tile choice for your bathroom. Now let's make sure you have everything to do this right the first time. You mentioned this is your first tile project, so I want you to have professional results without amateur mistakes.

Adhesive: You'll need this specific thinset. It's formulated for bathroom moisture. Using standard adhesive in a bathroom leads to failure when moisture gets behind tiles. This prevents that.

Tools: This notched trowel creates the right adhesive coverage. Wrong coverage causes tiles to pop off later. These spacers ensure consistent grout lines and that's what separates pro-looking jobs from amateur ones.

Grout: This epoxy grout is waterproof and stain-resistant. Costs $30 more than standard grout, but standard grout discolors in bathrooms within a year. This stays pristine.

Cutting: For 90 square feet, you need this tile saw. You can't do quality work with a hand cutter; you need clean cuts around toilets and fixtures. You can rent one for $75 or buy this one for $140. If you're doing the whole bathroom, buying makes sense.

Protection: These knee pads. Trust me, two days on a hard tile floor without these and you'll be in agony. $15 saves serious pain.

This complete setup means you'll get results you're proud of. I've seen hundreds of first-time tile jobs. The difference between success and failure is usually having the right materials and tools, not skill level. This sets you up properly."

Why this works:

- Acknowledges their novice status without condescension
- Each item prevents a specific failure mode
- Uses benefit statements: "This prevents that"
- Positions as success enabler, not upselling
- References experience with other first-timers

Example 3: Pet Store - New Puppy

Customer: First-time dog owner, just got 8-week-old lab puppy from breeder, overwhelmed and wanting to do everything right.

Primary sale: Premium puppy food

Multiplication conversation:

"Congratulations on your new puppy! Labs are wonderful. Let's make sure the first few weeks go smoothly instead of being the nightmare some first-time owners experience.

Crate: This is critical for house training - not optional. Dogs naturally don't soil their den, so crating works with their instincts. This size accommodates the adult size your lab will reach. Without proper crating, house training takes months instead of weeks.

Cleaning supplies: This enzyme cleaner breaks down urine at the molecular level. Regular cleaners just mask odor, which doesn't prevent repeat accidents. The dog can still smell it and thinks 'this is my bathroom spot.' This actually eliminates it.

Chew toys: These are puppy-safe with no small parts to swallow. Puppies need to chew, it's not optional. Either you provide appropriate chew outlets or they choose your furniture and shoes. These redirect that natural behavior.

Training guide: This book covers the critical first 90 days including house training, bite inhibition, and socialization. Following this prevents the common problems that make people rehome puppies. The first three months determine everything.

You mentioned wanting to do this right. These items - crate, proper cleaner, appropriate toys, guidance - set you up for success. They prevent the frustration that makes people regret getting a puppy."

Why this works:

- Addresses their stated desire to "do everything right"
- Each item prevents a specific common problem
- Explains the "why" clearly
- References what happens without these items
- Positions as success framework, not product pushing

Example 4: Running Shoe Store - Marathon Training

Customer: 35-year-old training for first marathon, currently at 25 miles per week, building to 50, has historically gotten minor injuries.

Primary sale: Stability running shoes

Multiplication conversation:

"These shoes are perfect for your training needs. Now let's address injury prevention. You mentioned you've had issues before, and marathon training at 50 miles per week will expose any weaknesses. Here's what actually works.

Foam roller: You said you've had IT band trouble. This will flare up at higher mileage unless you prevent it. Five minutes of rolling after runs keeps the IT band from tightening. Every runner I work with who stays healthy through marathon training does this religiously.

Nutrition strategy: Once your long runs exceed 90 minutes, your body needs fuel. These energy gels are what marathoners use. They do one every 45 minutes after the first hour. Without this, you'll hit the wall hard around mile 18. I've seen it end training cycles.

Body Glide: This prevents chafing. Seems minor now, but at marathon distance, clothing seams without this become serious medical issues. Every marathoner uses this. It's $8 insurance against painful problems.

Quality socks: These have moisture-wicking and seamless construction. You mentioned getting blisters before and that's usually moisture and friction. These address both causes. At your training volume, proper socks matter.

These four items cost $85 total. They address the most common reasons people fail marathon training - IT band injuries, hitting the wall, chafing, and blisters. Small investment to protect your entire four-month training commitment."

Why this works:

- Directly addresses their injury history
- Each item prevents specific training failure
- Uses social proof: "Every marathoner..."
- Frames as small investment protecting large time investment
- References their specific training volume

When Customers Resist: "I Just Want the Shoes"

Sometimes Customers push back on multiplication:

"I just want the shoes. I don't need all this other stuff."

Bad response (backs down, fails the Customer): "Okay, no problem! Just the shoes then."

You've now sent them out incomplete. They'll struggle. They might blame you, the shoes, or themselves. Trust potentially damaged.

Good response (respectful but advocates):

"I understand. It does feel like a lot at once. Let me prioritize for you. Of everything I mentioned, the two most critical for your marathon success are fuel strategy and injury prevention.

Without fuel on your long runs, you'll hit the wall around mile 18. I've worked with tons of marathoners over 15 years and I've never seen anyone succeed without addressing nutrition at this distance. These gels solve that.

The foam roller prevents IT band problems you specifically said you've had before. Five minutes of rolling after long runs keeps that from coming back and ending your training.

The other items are helpful, but these two directly prevent the most common reasons first-time marathoners don't finish. Can I at least include these two?"

Why this works:

- Respects their resistance
- Prioritizes to reduce overwhelm
- References their specific situation (IT band, marathon distance)
- Cites experience ("hundreds of marathoners over 15 years")
- Gives them choice while still advocating

Alternative response (when they're truly resistant):

"I respect that. Here's what I'll do. I'm giving you this list of items I'd recommend. Many runners come back for these after their first long run when they realize they need them. At least you'll know what to look for. If you have problems - hitting the wall, chafing issues, IT band pain - these are the solutions that work."

Hand them a written list. Many Customers return for these items after experiencing exactly the problems you predicted. They'll remember you tried to help them avoid the pain.

The Budget Objection: When Cost Is the Real Issue

Sometimes "I don't need all that" really means "I can't afford all that."

Listen for signals:

- Hesitation when they see total
- Checking phone (probably calculator app)
- "That's more than I planned to spend"
- Looking at partner with concerned expression

Don't ignore this. Acknowledge it directly:

"Help me understand. Is it that you don't think these items are necessary, or is the total investment more than you'd budgeted?"

If it's budget:

"I completely understand. If you need to prioritize due to budget, here's what I'd do: Start with the shoes and the Body Glide. The Body Glide is only $8 and prevents a problem that can end training. Add the gels and foam roller over the next month as budget allows. You won't need the gels until your long runs exceed 90 minutes which is probably three weeks from now. This spreads the investment while still protecting you."

Why this works:

- Acknowledges budget reality without judgment
- Prioritizes most critical items
- Creates a timeline that aligns with their training progression
- They leave with something complete enough to start successfully

Multiplication Across Customer Types

Different Customer types need different multiplication approaches:

Enthusiasts

- Present multiplication as optimization
- Use technical reasoning
- Reference best practices in the community
- They often actively seek complete solutions

"You mentioned wanting to set up a home darkroom for film photography. Beyond the enlarger, here's what serious film photographers consider essential: a grain focuser for critical sharpness, these graduated cylinders for precise chemistry mixing, and this timer for accurate exposures. These separate okay results from excellent results. Every darkroom I've seen that produces exhibition-quality work has these items."

Professionals

- Emphasize ROI, time savings, problem prevention
- Frame as business necessities
- Focus on durability and reliability
- Connect to business outcomes

"For job site use, you need contractor-grade bits, not consumer bits. Consumer bits break constantly under professional use, costing you time and money. These cost $40 more but last ten times longer. You'll save money within three months of daily job site work, plus you're not losing time running to the store for replacements."

Novices

- Emphasize problem prevention and success enablement
- Provide clear education about why each item matters
- Reduce overwhelm by limiting to true essentials
- Build confidence through protection

"I know this seems like a lot for your first camping trip. Let me simplify: tent, sleeping bag, pad, and headlamp. Those four items mean you'll be comfortable and safe. Everything else is nice but not essential for your first trip. Start here, then add items as you discover what matters to you personally."

Trendsetters

- Present items that enhance aesthetic or complete the look
- Reference what style-conscious people use
- Emphasize items that photograph well
- Connect to aspiration and identity

"Everyone I see on Instagram who's serious about home coffee has these three things: the grinder you're getting, a gooseneck kettle, and a good-looking scale. Together they create that 'coffee ritual' aesthetic worth documenting. Plus, they genuinely improve your coffee quality. It's both functional and beautiful."

The Ethical Foundation: When to Recommend, When to Stop

Multiplication builds trust when it genuinely serves the Customer. It destroys trust when it serves only you.

The test: Would you recommend this item to your mother/best friend/someone you care about in this exact situation? If not, don't recommend it to Customers.

Recommend when:

- The item prevents a problem they'll likely encounter
- It significantly improves their chance of success
- It protects their investment
- It addresses a concern they specifically mentioned
- Most successful people in the category use it

Don't recommend when:

- You're recommending hitting a sales target, not serve them
- A cheaper version would work fine but you want the margin
- It's solving a problem they won't actually have
- You're creating unnecessary fear to push the product
- You wouldn't use it yourself in their situation

Your long-term business grows from Customers who trust you, return repeatedly, and refer others. That trust is built on serving their success, not maximizing today's transaction value.

Making Multiplication Systematic

Make multiplication habits, not random afterthoughts:

System 1: Mental checklist for each category

Running shoes → fuel strategy, foam roller, Body Glide, socks

Camera → memory cards, extra battery, bag, cleaning kit

Power tools → safety gear, appropriate bits, extension cord, storage case

System 2: Store organization
Place multiplication items near primary products. Running accessories near running shoes. Camera accessories in camera section. Makes recommendations natural.

System 3: Complete solution displays
Create displays showing complete setups: "Everything for Marathon Training" or "Complete Home Office Setup" or "First Apartment Kitchen Essentials." These educate and normalize complete solutions.

System 4: Keep feedback logs
When Customers return and thank you for recommending something, note it. When they return items or complain about something you recommended, note that too. Adjust based on patterns.

The Ultimate Proof: What Happens After

Good multiplication proves itself:

Positive signals:

- Customers return and specifically mention how helpful certain items were
- Low return rates on multiplication items
- Customers ask for you by name
- Referrals that mention "they made sure I had everything I needed"

Negative signals:

- High return rates on specific multiplication items
- Customers complain about feeling oversold
- Multiplication items don't get used
- Negative reviews mentioning pushiness

Adjust based on reality. If Customers consistently thank you for recommending Body Glide, keep recommending it. If Customers consistently return foam rollers unused, either you're recommending to the wrong people or you're not explaining use clearly enough.

Let Customer success be your guide.

The Bigger Picture: Multiplication as Trust-Building

Here's what I want you to remember: multiplication done right is one of the most powerful trust-building tools you have.

When you send Customers out with incomplete solutions, you've eliminated neither fear. They'll make mistakes (confirming their fear), feel stupid when they realize what they needed (confirming their fear), and not trust you next time.

When you send Customers out with complete solutions, you've eliminated both fears. They succeed (no mistakes), they feel taken care of (not stupid), and they trust you deeply.

That trust becomes referrals. Becomes repeat business. Becomes asking for you by name. Becomes your reputation.

This isn't about selling more stuff. It's about completing what you started when you greeted them at the door: helping them achieve their goal successfully.

In the next chapter, we'll explore how to handle objections—those moments when Customers hesitate, resist, or push back, and how to address their concerns while maintaining and building trust.

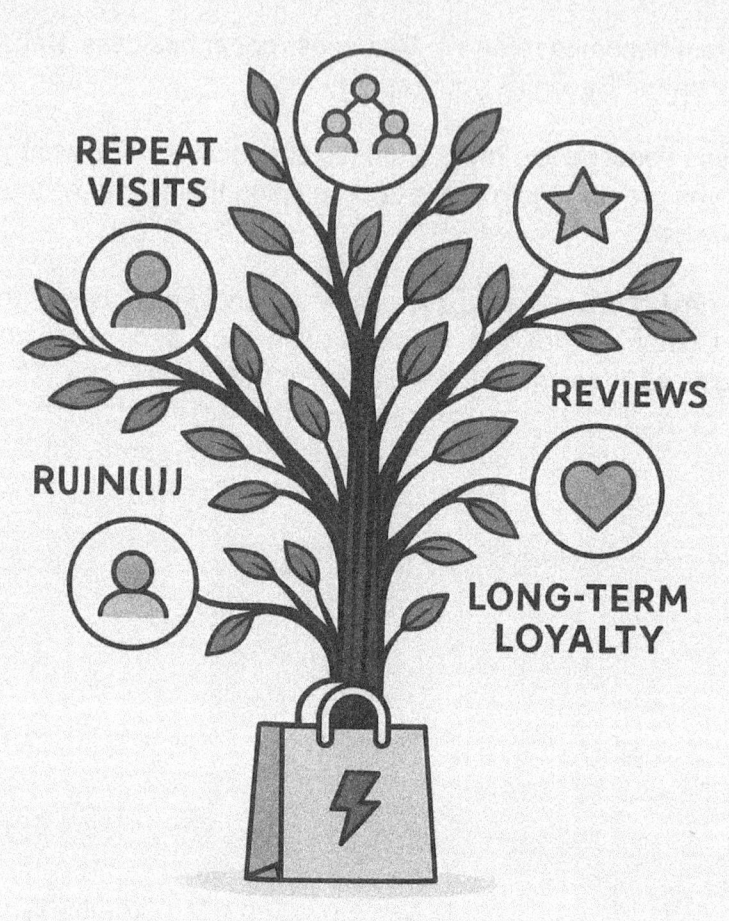

Chapter 11

Handling Objections – When "No" Means "Not Yet"

You've conducted a thorough Interview. You've presented a perfectly customized Solution with clear benefit statements. You've recommended the right multiplication items. The Customer seems engaged and understanding.

Then they say: "I need to think about it."

Or: "That's more than I wanted to spend."

Or: "I saw this cheaper online."

Your stomach drops. The sale you thought was moving smoothly just hit a wall. Now what?

This is the moment many salespeople dread. And here's what usually happens: they either get defensive and pushy, or they give up entirely. Neither works.

Traditional sales training treats objections as enemies to overcome—arguments to win, resistance to break down through clever verbal tricks. This approach makes things worse. It damages trust and usually backfires spectacularly.

WISE Selling views objections completely differently: they're signals that one or both of the Customer's fears is still active. They're questions in disguise.

They're expressions of unmet needs. They're signs that trust isn't complete yet.

Rather than combating objections, you address the underlying concerns using a simple two-step framework: **Soften and Ask**.

This chapter teaches you to handle objections in ways that actually build trust instead of damaging it, surface the real concerns instead of arguing with fake ones, and help Customers move toward confident decisions instead of defensive positions.

Understanding What Objections Really Mean: The Fears Are Still There

Here's what you need to understand first: when a Customer objects, it means you haven't eliminated their fears yet.

Remember from Chapter 8:

Fear of making a mistake → "What if I waste my money? What if this is wrong? What if I regret this?"

Fear of looking stupid → "What if I'm missing something? What if I'm being taken advantage of? What if I should know something I don't?"

Every objection is one or both of these fears showing up in disguise.

"That's too expensive" = Fear of making a mistake ("What if I'm wasting money?")

"I need to think about it" = Both fears ("What if I decide wrong?" + "What if I'm missing something I should know?")

"I'm not sure this will work" = Fear of making a mistake ("What if this fails and I've wasted my money?")

"I saw it cheaper online" = Both fears ("What if I'm overpaying?" + "What if you're taking advantage of my ignorance?")

Your job isn't to argue with the surface statement. Your job is to figure out which fear is still active and address *that*.

The Natural Instinct (That's Wrong)

When someone objects, your natural instinct is to immediately defend your recommendation:

Customer: "That's too expensive."

Your instinct: "But this is actually a great value! When you consider the quality and the warranty and the fact that cheaper options break down quickly, this is really the best investment..."

Why this fails: You just triggered the fear of looking stupid. The Customer is thinking: "Great, now I look cheap and uninformed. This person thinks I'm an idiot who doesn't understand value. My defenses are going up."

The Customer gets more resistant, not less. You're arguing with them, which makes them dig in. Even if your logic is perfect, you've made them feel defensive. Nobody buys from a defensive position.

The WISE Approach: Soften and Ask

When a Customer objects, follow two simple steps:

Step 1: Soften Show compassion, acknowledge their concern is legitimate

Step 2: Ask Demonstrate confidence by calmly uncovering the real concern

This approach works because it addresses both components of trust:

Compassion (softening): "Your concern matters. I respect your perspective. You're not being difficult. This is legitimate."

Confidence (asking): "I'm not defensive because I know I can address real concerns. Let's figure out what's really going on here."

Both fears start to quiet down.

Step 1: Softening

Softening means acknowledging the objection and validating the Customer's right to have concerns.

Good softening phrases:

- "I completely understand..."
- "That's a fair concern..."
- "I appreciate you being honest about that..."
- "A lot of people feel the same way initially..."
- "That makes total sense given..."
- "I can see why that would be concerning..."

Why softening works:

It eliminates the fear of looking stupid. You're saying: "Your concern is legitimate, not ignorant. You're being smart by asking questions, not difficult."

It demonstrates compassion. You're not dismissing their concern or treating it as irrational. You're showing you understand and respect their perspective.

It deactivates defensiveness. When you validate someone's concern instead of arguing with it, they relax. Their guard comes down. They become receptive to conversation.

Without softening, here's what happens in the Customer's mind:

Customer: "That's too expensive."

Salesperson: "But when you consider the quality..." [no softening, jumps straight to defense]

Customer's thoughts: *"This person isn't listening to me. They're just trying to talk me into spending more money. They don't care about my concern. My guard is staying up."*

With softening, here's what happens:

Customer: "That's too expensive."

Salesperson: "I completely understand, after all this is a significant investment and you want to make sure you're spending wisely..." [softening]

Customer's thoughts: *"Okay, they heard me. They're not dismissing my concern. They get that this is real money. I can relax a little and actually listen to what they say next."*

That's the difference. Softening opens the door to real conversation.

Step 2: Asking

After softening, ask a question that uncovers the real concern underneath the surface objection.

Good asking questions:

- "Help me understand what's concerning you specifically..."
- "Is it [specific issue], or is there something else?"
- "What would need to be different for this to feel right?"
- "Can you tell me more about what you mean by that?"
- "Is this the only concern, or are there other factors?"

Why asking works:

It prevents you from solving the wrong problem. The stated objection usually masks the real issue. You need to uncover the real concern before you can address it.

It demonstrates confidence. Weak salespeople fear objections and rush to defend. Confident practitioners explore objections calmly because they know they can address real concerns once identified.

It shows compassion. You're genuinely trying to understand their perspective, not just counter it.

Example of asking uncovering the real issue:

Customer: "This is more expensive than I wanted to spend."

Bad response (no asking): "But look at the quality! This will last ten years while cheaper versions last two years, so actually you're saving money long-term..."

You're addressing value when that might not be the real concern.

Good response (with asking): "I understand completely. Help me understand: is the concern that this total price doesn't fit your budget, or are you not yet seeing why this costs more than less expensive options?"

Now the Customer reveals the real issue:

Option A: "It's just outside my budget. I was thinking more like $800, not $1,200."

Now you know. It's a real budget constraint. You can show options in their range or help them understand whether stretching budget makes sense.

Option B: "I'm just not sure what makes this worth $400 more than the one I saw at the big box store."

Now you know they don't understand the value difference. You can explain specific differences in materials, construction, longevity that justify the price.

Same objection. Two completely different real concerns. Asking uncovers which one you're actually dealing with.

The Complete Soften and Ask in Action

Let's see how this works across different retail scenarios:

Example 1: Jewelry Store - Engagement Ring

Customer: "This ring is more than I wanted to spend."

Bad response (no softening or asking, jumps to defense): "But look at the quality of this diamond! The clarity and color are excellent. This is actually a great value when you consider..."

Customer's internal response: *"This person isn't listening to my concern about price. They're just trying to justify a sale. I don't trust this."*

Good response (Soften and Ask): "I completely understand, an engagement ring is a significant investment, and you want to make sure you're spending wisely. [Soften] Help me understand: is the concern that the total price doesn't fit your budget, or are you not yet seeing why this ring costs more than less expensive options? [Ask]"

Customer reveals real concern: "Honestly, I don't really understand the difference between this $5,000 ring and the $3,000 one."

Now you can address the actual issue: "That's a totally fair question and I'm glad you asked. Let me show you the specific differences in a way that makes sense..."

[Explain clarity, color, cut differences with benefit statements]

"The $3,000 ring has visible inclusions. Look, you can see them with your naked eye in certain light. This $5,000 ring has inclusions that even trained jewelers need magnification to spot. For daily wear, this looks flawless to everyone. That's the value difference - a ring that looks perfect versus one where you'll notice imperfections."

Without Soften and Ask, you'd be explaining value in general terms when their real question was about specific differences between two rings.

Example 2: Running Shoe Store - Price Objection

Customer: "These shoes are $180. I can get running shoes for $60 at the discount store."

Bad response (defensive, no softening): "But these are real running shoes! Those discount shoes aren't designed for actual running. You get what you pay for!"

Customer's internal response: *"Now I feel stupid for mentioning the cheap shoes. This person thinks I'm an idiot. My guard is up."*

Good response (Soften and Ask): "I totally get that—$180 is a real investment in shoes. [Soften] Help me understand: are you looking for the absolute lowest price, or are you wondering what makes these worth three times as much? [Ask]"

If lowest price is the goal: Customer: "Honestly, I just need something cheap for occasional jogging."

Response: "That's fair—if you're truly jogging occasionally, like once or twice a month, those $60 shoes would probably be adequate. But based on what you told me earlier about wanting to run regularly and train for that 5K in the fall, let me explain what happens at different price points.

Those $60 shoes last maybe 100-150 miles maximum and provide minimal support. For someone running 3-4 times per week like you're planning, you'd burn through them in about six weeks. That's $240 per year replacing shoes.

Plus, you'd likely experience knee or shin pain from inadequate support, possibly leading to injury.

These $180 shoes last 400-500 miles which is nearly a year of your training, and provide proper support that prevents injury. We did gait analysis and matched these to your foot strike pattern specifically. Over a year, you actually spend less, and more importantly, you stay healthy enough to keep training."

If they want to understand the value: Customer: "I'm just not sure what makes them worth three times as much."

Response: "Great question. The differences come down to three things that directly affect your running:

First, the cushioning system in these actually absorbs impact properly. Those $60 shoes have basic foam that compresses quickly sometimes as quickly as within a few weeks, you're basically running on flat rubber. These maintain cushioning for 400+ miles.

Second, these are built for your specific gait pattern. We watched you walk and identified that you overpronate. These have stability features that correct that. The discount shoes don't; they're generic. Running in shoes that don't match your gait leads to knee and hip problems.

Third, these are designed for actual running biomechanics. The discount shoes are styled to look like running shoes but aren't engineered for the impact and motion of running. It's like the difference between a hiking boot and a boot that just looks like a hiking boot.

For what you're planning - regular training, building up mileage - these prevent the injury problems that cost way more than $180 in medical bills and lost training time."

Example 3: Electronics Store - "I Need to Think About It"

Customer: "This is a lot of information. I need to think about it."

Bad response (pushy, creates pressure): "But this sale ends today! And we only have two of these left in stock. If you leave, I can't guarantee it'll still be here when you come back..."

Customer's internal response: *"Now I feel pressured and manipulated. This confirms my fear that I'm being pushed into a decision. I'm leaving."*

Good response (Soften and Ask): "That makes complete sense. This is a significant decision, and you want to make sure you get it right. [Soften] Before you go, can I ask: is there something specific you'd like to think through, or a question I haven't fully answered? Maybe I can help clarify so you have what you need to decide. [Ask]"

If they're overwhelmed: Customer: "Honestly, I'm just overwhelmed by all the options and technical details."

Response: "I get that. It is a lot to consider, and I probably gave you more information than you needed. Let me simplify this dramatically.

Based on our conversation, here's what I heard: you need a laptop primarily for working from home, video calls, and some photo editing. That means you need good processing power, a quality webcam, and decent graphics. You don't need gaming features or professional-level specs.

This model checks all those boxes. Everything else is extras that won't affect your daily experience. The three things that matter for your use: it boots up quickly, the webcam is excellent for Zoom calls, and it handles Lightroom smoothly.

Does that simplify things enough to feel manageable?"

If they want to comparison shop: Customer: "I just want to make sure I'm getting the best deal."

Response: "Absolutely fair. You should feel confident. Here's what I'd suggest: take this spec sheet showing exactly what this model includes. If you find this exact model cheaper elsewhere, I want to know—we price-match.

What you won't find elsewhere is what we just spent 30 minutes doing: figuring out exactly what you need versus what you don't. Most stores will try to sell you the most expensive laptop. We matched your actual needs to appropriate equipment.

You're also not just buying a laptop; you're getting free setup, data transfer from your old computer, and someone to call when you have questions. But I respect wanting to verify you're making the right choice. If you decide to shop around, ask other stores these specific questions..." [provides smart shopping guidance]

The Seven Most Common Objections (And What They Really Mean)

While objections come in infinite varieties, seven patterns show up constantly across all retail formats. Let's break down each one:

Objection 1: "That's Too Expensive"

What Customers say:

- "That's more than I wanted to spend"
- "I can't afford that"
- "That seems really expensive"
- "I saw it cheaper online"

What it usually really means (which fear is active):

- "I don't see enough value yet" [Fear of wasting money]
- "This is outside my budget" [Real constraint]
- "I feel guilty spending this much" [Emotional barrier]
- "I think you're overcharging me" [Fear of being taken advantage of]
- "I need to justify this to someone else" [Need backup]

Soften and Ask approach:

Furniture Store Example:

Customer: "This dining table is way more than I wanted to spend."

Response: "I understand completely. A dining table is a significant investment, and you want to spend wisely. [Soften] Let me ask: is the concern that this price doesn't fit your budget at all, or are you not yet seeing why this table costs more than less expensive options? [Ask]"

If budget is a real limitation:

Customer: "It's really outside my budget. I was thinking around $800, not $1,400."

Response: "I appreciate you being straight about that. Based on what you told me—you're looking for something that lasts and you have young kids who'll be hard on furniture—let me show you what's available in your budget range. I'll be honest about what trade-offs you're making at that price point.

At $800, we're looking at veneer over engineered wood rather than solid hardwood. That means it won't last as long - probably 5-7 years before you're replacing it versus 20+ years for solid wood. The veneer can chip with hard use, and the engineered wood can swell if liquid gets in the seams.

If budget is the priority right now, this is a decent option. You'll get years of use from it. But understand you're likely replacing it before your kids are teenagers, whereas solid wood would last until they have kids of their own. Does that trade-off make sense for your situation?"

If value isn't clear yet:

Customer: "I'm just not sure what makes this worth $600 more than what I saw at the big box store."

Response: "That's a completely fair question and I'm glad you asked. The $800 table you saw has veneer over particleboard. It looks good day one, but here's what happens: the veneer chips easily with any impact, the particleboard swells with humidity and spills, and you're replacing it within 5-7 years.

This table is solid oak with mortise and tenon joinery which is the same construction method used in antique furniture that's lasted 100+ years. It handles spills, absorbs dings from daily family use, and actually looks better as it ages because real wood develops character.

The math: $800 every 5-7 years equals $2,400-3,200 over 20 years, plus the hassle of furniture shopping and disposal multiple times. Or $1,400 once for furniture you might eventually pass down to your kids. Long-term, solid wood costs less because you're not buying replacements."

Objection 2: "I Need to Think About It"

What Customers say:

- "I need to think about it"
- "Let me sleep on it"
- "I'm not ready to decide today"

What it usually really means:

- "I'm overwhelmed by information" [Too much, fear of deciding wrong]
- "I don't fully trust your recommendation yet" [Fear of being taken advantage of]
- "I want to comparison shop" [Fear of overpaying]
- "I need permission from someone else" [Real constraint]
- "Something feels off but I can't name it" [Instinct, fear]

Soften and Ask approach:

Camera Store Example:

Customer: "This is a lot to process. I need to think about it."

Response: "That makes complete sense. This is a significant decision, and you want to get it right. [Soften] Before you go, can I ask: is there something specific you'd like to think through, or a question I haven't fully answered? Maybe I can help clarify. [Ask]"

If they're overwhelmed:

Customer: "There are just so many features and options, my brain is full."

Response: "I get that. I probably gave you way too much information. Let me dramatically simplify this.

You mentioned wanting to take better photos of your kids' sports and family events. Three things about this camera matter for that goal:

One: continuous shooting mode captures 10 frames per second. When your daughter is kicking that soccer ball, you get the entire sequence, and you're guaranteed the perfect moment.

Two: autofocus tracks moving subjects automatically. Your son running toward you stays in focus without you doing anything.

Three: performs well in low light. Indoor events like recitals come out clear instead of blurry.

Those three capabilities serve your stated goal. Everything else is bonus. Does that make the decision feel simpler?"

If they want to comparison shop:

Customer: "I want to make sure I'm getting a good deal before I commit."

Response: "Absolutely fair. You should feel confident. Here's what I'd suggest: take this spec sheet with the exact model information. If you find this same camera cheaper elsewhere, we'll match the price.

What you won't find elsewhere is the 30 minutes we spent figuring out exactly what you need. Most stores will try to sell you their most expensive camera. We matched your specific goals to appropriate equipment.

You're also getting free basic training on how to use it, someone to call with questions, and local service if anything goes wrong. But I respect needing to verify. Whatever you decide, make sure whoever you buy from takes time to match the camera to your needs like we did."

If they need spousal approval:

Customer: "I need to talk to my wife before spending this much."

Response: "I completely understand, after all, this is an investment that affects both of you. [Soften] Let me ask: is there anything specific your wife would want to know that I haven't covered? Maybe I can make sure you have all the information for that conversation. [Ask]"

Customer: "She's going to ask if we really need to spend $1,200 on a camera."

Response: "Fair question she'll have. Here's how I'd frame it: You mentioned wanting to capture quality memories of your kids while they're young—these moments don't come back. Phone cameras are fine for snapshots, but for the sports events and family moments you want to document well, you need proper equipment.

This camera will last 8-10 years minimum. That's 75 cents per week over that time to preserve your family's memories. When you think of it as less than a dollar per week for a decade of important moments, the value becomes clear.

Also, here's my card. If your wife has questions or wants to see the camera herself, I'm happy to talk to you both either on the phone or in person. I want you both to feel confident about this."

Objection 3: "I Want to Shop Around"

What Customers say:

- "I need to check other stores"
- "I want to see what else is out there"
- "I'm going to look online"

What it usually really means:

- "I don't trust I'm getting a good deal" [Fear of overpaying]
- "I'm not convinced this is the right product" [Fear of making wrong choice]
- "I'm not ready to commit" [General uncertainty]
- "I want negotiating leverage" [Tactical move]

Soften and Ask approach:

Bike Shop Example:

Customer: "I want to check out a couple other bike shops before deciding."

Response: "That makes total sense. Bikes are personal and you want to be sure. [Soften] Let me ask: is there something about this bike that doesn't feel quite right, or are you wanting to verify this is a good value compared to other options? [Ask]"

If the bike doesn't feel right:

Customer: "I'm not totally sure this is exactly what I want."

Response: "I appreciate you being honest about that rather than buying something you're not excited about. Let's figure out what's not clicking. What specifically doesn't feel right? Is it the fit, the riding position, the components, or something else?"

[Re-enter Interview mode to understand the disconnect, address it]

If they want to verify value:

Customer: "I just want to make sure I'm getting a fair price."

Response: "Absolutely, you should feel confident. Here's what I'd suggest: when you visit other shops, ask them these specific questions about fit and geometry. See if they take the time we took to get your position right.

What I'm confident about is we've matched this bike specifically to your riding style, body measurements, and goals. Most shops won't invest 45 minutes in proper fit unless you specifically demand it. They'll sell you a bike off the floor.

Bike fit matters more than bike brand. A perfectly fitted mid-range bike outperforms a poorly fitted expensive bike every time. Other shops might have similar bikes at similar prices, but whether they take time to ensure proper fit is the real question.

Whatever you decide, make sure whoever you buy from does the fit work we did today. And if you come back here, I'll honor this price and everything we discussed. Fair?"

Objection 4: "I Don't Need All These Features"

What Customers say:

- "This is more than I need"
- "I just want something basic"
- "These features seem like overkill"

What it usually really means:

- "I don't understand why these features matter" [Fear of wasting money on unnecessary things]
- "This seems too complicated" [Fear of looking stupid when I can't use it]
- "I think you're upselling me" [Fear of being taken advantage of]

Soften and Ask approach:

Camera Store Example:

Customer: "This camera has way more features than I'll ever use."

Response: "I hear you. Modern cameras are incredibly capable, and it can feel overwhelming. [Soften] Help me understand: are you concerned you won't use most features and that's wasted money, or are you worried it'll be too complicated to operate? [Ask]"

If concerned about wasted money:

Customer: "Seems like I'm paying for a lot of stuff I'll never touch."

Response: "That's a legitimate concern, and I want to address it directly. You're right that you probably won't use every single feature. But remember what you told me - you want to photograph your kids' soccer games and family events.

Three features on this camera directly serve that goal:

One: continuous shooting captures 10 frames per second. When your daughter kicks that goal, you're capturing the entire sequence - a guaranteed perfect moment.

Two: autofocus tracks moving subjects automatically. When your son's running, the camera keeps him in focus without you doing anything.

Three: low-light capability means indoor events come out clear instead of blurry and grainy.

Those three capabilities aren't available on basic models, and they're exactly what you need for what you described. The other features? You might grow into them, you might not - but you're really paying for those three crucial capabilities that enable your stated goal. Does that clarify the value?"

If worried about complexity:

Customer: "I'm afraid all these buttons and menus will intimidate me."

Response: "Totally fair concern. I don't want you frustrated with something you bought to enjoy. Here's what I'll do: I'll set this camera up in auto mode for you right now. In that mode, it's as simple as a point-and-shoot. You just aim and press the button. All those capabilities I mentioned work automatically.

As you get comfortable over weeks and months, you can explore other features if you want, but you never have to. The camera grows with you without forcing complexity.

Plus, we offer free intro classes every Saturday morning. Come to one and we'll walk you through basics in a relaxed setting with other people learning. You won't feel lost or intimidated, I promise."

Objection 5: "I'm Not Sure This Will Work for My Situation"

What Customers say:

- "I don't think this will fit"
- "I'm not sure this solves my problem"
- "This might not work with what I have"

What it usually really means:

- "You haven't addressed a specific concern I have" [Fear of making mistake]
- "I don't understand how this applies to me" [Need more specific connection]
- "I'm afraid of wasting money on something that doesn't work" [Classic fear of making mistake]

Soften and Ask approach:

Garden Center Example:

Customer: "I'm not convinced these plants will survive in my yard."

Response: "That's a totally fair concern. You don't want to invest in plants that'll die. [Soften] Help me understand what makes you uncertain. Is it your soil conditions, sun exposure, watering situation, or something else? [Ask]"

Customer: "I have heavy clay soil, mostly shade, and I'm worried about keeping things watered consistently."

Response: "Actually, those three concerns are exactly why I recommended these specific plants, not just any plants. Let me show you why these are perfect for your exact situation.

First, all of these are shade-tolerant varieties. See on the tags; they specify 'part-shade to full-shade.' They'll thrive in your lighting.

Second, they're specifically clay-tolerant. Most plants struggle in clay soil, but these varieties actually prefer it to sandy soil. The tags specifically mention 'clay-adaptable.'

Third, once established, say about 6-8 weeks, they're drought-tolerant. If you forget to water or go on vacation, they'll survive.

These aren't generic recommendations I give everyone. I specifically chose plants that match your exact conditions. If I had any doubt they'd thrive, I wouldn't recommend them. My reputation depends on your success!

In fact, if any of these fails within the first year and you followed the planting instructions, I'll replace it free. That's how confident I am these are right for your yard."

Objection 6: "I Saw Bad Reviews Online"

What Customers say:

- "I read negative reviews about this"
- "People online say this breaks easily"
- "The reviews weren't great"

What it usually really means:

- "I'm afraid of making the same mistake others made" [Fear of making mistake]
- "I need reassurance this is reliable" [Fear of wasting money]
- "I'm not sure I can trust you" [Fear of being taken advantage of]

Soften and Ask approach:

Electronics Store Example:

Customer: "I saw reviews saying this TV has connectivity problems."

Response: "I appreciate you doing that research. Reading reviews is smart. [Soften] Let me ask: were the reviews about connectivity problems in general, or were they about specific issues with certain setups? [Ask]"

Customer: "WIFI dropping, apps crashing, HDMI issues."

Response: "Okay, I know exactly what you're referring to, and I'm glad you brought it up because I can explain what happened.

Those connectivity issues affected the first production run that shipped last November. The manufacturer identified the problem. It was a specific firmware version combined with certain router chipsets and they released an update in January.

Current units, including everything we have in stock, come with updated firmware pre-installed. We've sold about 40 of these since January with zero connectivity complaints. I personally set one up for my father-in-law in February, and it's been flawless.

I understand being cautious based on what you read. Those were real problems at the time. Here's what I'll do: we have a 30-day full return policy, no questions asked. If you experience any connectivity issues - WIFI dropping, apps crashing, anything - bring it back for full refund. You can verify for yourself that it works properly in your specific setup. Does that address your concern?"

Objection 7: "I Need to Talk to My Spouse"

What Customers say:

- "I need to check with my husband/wife"
- "My partner needs to see this"
- "We make these decisions together"

What it usually really means:

- "My spouse controls the budget" [Need approval]
- "I need backup to justify this purchase" [Seeking permission/validation]
- "I'm not fully confident in my decision" [Need support]
- Sometimes: Genuine need for joint decision [Legitimate]

Soften and Ask approach:

Furniture Store Example:

Customer: "I love this sofa, but my husband needs to see it before I buy."

Response: "I completely respect that; this does affect both of you and you should both feel good about it. [Soften] Let me ask: is there anything specific your husband would want to know that I haven't covered? Maybe I can make sure you have all the information for that conversation. [Ask]"

If spouse needs to physically see/test it:

Customer: "He wants to sit on it himself. He's really particular about comfort."

Response: "That makes perfect sense because comfort is personal, and he should test it. Here's what I'll do: I'll put this specific sofa on hold for 48 hours. What's the best time for you both to come in together?

I'm here Tuesday through Saturday, 10 AM to 6 PM. I'll walk through everything with both of you, he can test it thoroughly, and you can both ask any questions. Sound good?"

If spouse controls the budget:

Customer: "He's going to ask if we really need to spend this much."

Response: "Fair question he'll have. Here's how I'd frame it: Remember we talked about how your current sofa is already sagging after only three years? That's because it was made with low-density foam over a softwood frame which is not built to last.

This sofa has a hardwood frame warranted for life, and high-density foam that maintains shape for 15-20 years minimum. You're not buying sofas every 3-4 years at $800-1,000 each. You're buying one sofa once at $1,800 that lasts decades. Long-term, you save money by not replacing furniture constantly.

Also, here's my card. If your husband has questions or wants to discuss anything, I'm happy to talk to both of you on the phone or when you visit together. I want you both feeling confident about this."

When Objections Reveal Real Misalignment

Sometimes objections reveal genuine problems. For example, your recommendation truly doesn't fit their needs or budget. In these cases, Soften and Ask leads to honest acknowledgment:

Example:

Customer: "I love this bike, but I really can't justify $2,000 right now."

Salesperson: "I understand that it's a significant investment. [Soften] Help me understand: is the concern that $2,000 is truly outside your budget, or that you're not seeing enough value to justify that price? [Ask]"

Customer: "Honestly, it's just more than I can spend. I'm thinking $800-1,000 maximum."

Salesperson: "I appreciate you being straight about that. Here's my honest assessment: at $800-1,000, we can't give you everything this bike offers. The components at that price point are entry-level. Based on your riding goals - the century rides you mentioned wanting to do - you'd probably outgrow them within a year.

Here are your real options:

One, stretch to $1,500 for a mid-range bike that'll serve you well for years.

Two, buy used. I can point you to where serious cyclists sell quality bikes. You could probably find a good $2,000 bike used for around $1,200.

Three, wait and save until you can get what you really need rather than settling for something that won't serve your goals.

I don't want to sell you something inadequate just to make a sale today. You'll be unhappy in six months, and that doesn't help either of us long-term."

This honesty builds enormous trust. The Customer might stretch budget, might buy used, might wait and come back, but they'll remember you as the honest person who prioritized their success over today's sale.

The Prevention Strategy: Stop Objections Before They Happen

Here's the truth: the best objection handling is objection prevention.

Most objections emerge because earlier WISE phases were incomplete:

Price objections usually mean:

- Interview didn't establish value clearly
- Solution didn't connect benefits to stated needs strongly enough
- You didn't build enough trust (compassion + confidence)

"I need to think about it" usually means:

- Trust wasn't fully built during Welcome and Interview
- Solution presentation was confusing or overwhelming
- Fears weren't eliminated, they're still active

"I'm not sure this will work" usually means:

- Solution didn't address specific concerns from Interview
- You didn't demonstrate enough confidence in your recommendation
- You didn't use benefit statements effectively

Invest thoroughly in Welcome (build initial trust), Interview (understand completely), and Solution (connect specifically to their needs), and objections decrease dramatically.

When objections do arise, Soften and Ask handles them while maintaining trust.

Common Mistakes That Make Objections Worse

Mistake 1: Arguing

Customer: "That's too expensive." Salesperson: "No it's not! When you consider the quality..."

You just made them defensive. They're now committed to their position because you're fighting them.

Mistake 2: Immediately Countering Without Softening

Customer: "I need to think about it." Salesperson: "What's there to think about? I've answered all your questions!" [No softening, jumps to defense]

You just made them feel stupid for needing time. Fear of looking stupid activated.

Mistake 3: Taking It Personally

Objections aren't attacks on you. They're expressions of fear or unmet needs. Stay calm and curious.

Mistake 4: Giving Up Too Easily

One objection doesn't mean "no forever." It means "not yet—I have concerns."

Mistake 5: Using Manipulative Tactics

"This sale ends today!" "We only have one left!" "I can't hold this price if you leave!"

Creating artificial pressure amplifies both fears and destroys trust.

Mistake 6: Not Actually Listening

Going through the motions of Soften and Ask while mentally planning your rebuttal defeats the entire purpose.

Building Your Objection-Handling Skills

Practice 1: Role-play with colleagues

Practice Soften and Ask responses to common objections until they feel natural in your voice.

Practice 2: Analyze past losses

Review sales you lost. What were the objections? What were the real concerns underneath? How could you have responded better?

Practice 3: Develop multiple softening phrases

Find 5 to 6 different softening phrases that feel authentic when you say them. Forced language sounds fake.

Practice 4: Reframe objections mentally

Instead of thinking "Oh no, an objection," think "Good, they're telling me what concern I need to address." Change your emotional response.

Practice 5: Learn from successful colleagues

When someone handles an objection well, analyze what they said and how they said it.

The Big Picture: Objections Are Opportunities

Here's what I want you to remember: objections aren't enemies. They're opportunities.

Every objection is a Customer telling you: "I'm still afraid of making a mistake or looking stupid. Help me feel safe."

When you respond with Soften and Ask, you're saying: "I hear you. Your concern is legitimate. Let's figure out what's really going on and address it together."

That builds trust. That eliminates fear. That moves toward confident decisions.

The goal isn't to win arguments. The goal is to understand and serve Customers better, addressing real concerns rather than combating surface resistance.

Master this, and objections transform from dreaded roadblocks into valuable conversations that strengthen relationships and lead to better outcomes for everyone.

Chapter 12

Experience – Creating Moments That Are Remarkable

The Customer said yes. They've selected the running shoes you recommended, along with the energy gels, Body Glide, and foam roller you suggested for their marathon training. The Interview was thorough, the Solution was customized, and they seem confident about their choices.

For most salespeople, this is the end of the story. Ring up the sale, hand over the bag, say "Have a nice day," and move on to the next Customer.

For WISE practitioners, this is where the Experience phase truly begins.

The Experience phase - the E in WISE - encompasses everything from the purchase decision through checkout, initial product use, and the ongoing relationship that determines whether this Customer returns and refers others or disappears forever.

Traditional retail training barely mentions what happens after the sale, focusing almost exclusively on closing techniques. This is exactly backward. Your reputation, your income, and your long-term success are determined far more by what happens after the purchase than by the moment of purchase itself.

This chapter teaches you to create experiences Customers remember, value, and talk about. You'll learn how to lock in purchase decisions, handle those critical last two minutes, follow up effectively, and, most importantly, handle problems in ways that actually strengthen trust rather than destroy it.

The Problem You Don't See: Buyer's Remorse

Jennifer just purchased a $2,400 elliptical machine for her home gym. You conducted an excellent Interview, presented a perfectly matched Solution, and Jennifer felt completely confident about her decision at the moment of purchase.

Three days later, she's lying awake at 2 AM thinking:

"Did I really need to spend that much?"
"What if I don't actually use it?"
"My husband is going to think I'm crazy."
"Maybe I should have researched more."
"I could have gotten something cheaper online."

By morning, she's decided to return it.

This is buyer's remorse—the post-purchase anxiety and second-guessing that follows significant purchases. It's predictable, it's preventable, and it costs you sales you thought you'd already made.

Here's what's really happening: Remember those two fears from Chapter 8?

Fear of making a mistake: "What if I waste my money? What if this doesn't work?"

Fear of looking stupid: "What if I made a dumb decision? What if I got taken advantage of?"

You eliminated both fears during the sale. She trusted you. She bought.

But now she's alone. You're not there reassuring her. And those fears come creeping back in.

Her husband asks: "How much did that cost?" [Fear of making a mistake activated]

Her friend says: "Why didn't you just join a gym?" [Fear of looking stupid activated]

She sees a different model online for less money. [Both fears activated]

Without you there to maintain the trust you built, doubt grows. The fears you worked so hard to eliminate come roaring back.

Your job in the Experience phase is to prevent this. You need to lock in the decision so strongly that when those fears try to return, she has the confidence to push them away herself.

Locking in the Sale: Reinforcing Their Confidence

Locking in means actively reinforcing that the Customer made a wise decision. It happens immediately after the purchase decision, typically while you're processing payment or writing up the order.

Bad lock-in (generic, meaningless):
"Great choice! You're going to love it!"

Every salesperson says this. It means nothing. It provides no substance she can lean on when doubt creeps in.

Good lock-in (specific, based on Interview, substantial):

"Jennifer, I have to tell you; you made a really smart decision here. Let me explain why I'm so confident about that.

Remember you mentioned you've struggled to stay consistent with gym memberships because of the commute and time constraints? This elliptical solves that completely. Your workout is literally ten feet from your bedroom. No excuses about traffic or finding parking or the gym being closed.

You also said you have knee issues that make treadmill running uncomfortable. The elliptical's motion is zero-impact so your knees will thank you. You're getting cardio benefits without the joint stress that's been stopping you.

And you were concerned about durability, whether this would hold up. This model is commercial-grade. It's the same one used in hotels and apartment fitness centers where it gets pounded by dozens of people every single day. For one-person home use, this will literally outlast you. You'll be passing this down to your kids.

Based on everything you told me about your fitness goals, your schedule constraints, and your need for something that lasts, this is exactly what you need. When that credit card statement arrives next month, you'll feel good about this decision because you know it's serving your health goals every single day."

See the difference?

This lock-in accomplishes several critical things:

It reminds them of the careful process: They didn't impulse-buy. They went through a thorough consultation and made a thoughtful decision based on their specific needs.

It references specific things they said: By citing details from the Interview, you prove the recommendation was customized for them, not a generic pitch you give everyone.

It preempts the doubts that will come: By addressing concerns they mentioned like cost, durability, convenience, knee issues, etc., you're preparing her for when those doubts resurface. She'll remember: "Oh right, he explained that. This does make sense."

It gives her language to defend her decision: When her husband asks "Why did you spend $2,400?", she has your reasoning. "Because it's commercial-grade and will last forever, and it solves my knee problems, and I'll actually use it because it's right here at home."

It demonstrates you genuinely care: Your detailed reasoning shows you're invested in her success, not just your commission. This reinforces the trust you built.

More Lock-in Examples

Furniture Store:

"Michael, you made an excellent choice with this sofa. Here's why:

You mentioned you have three kids under ten, and your current furniture has taken a beating. This sofa has a kiln-dried hardwood frame. That's the same construction technique used in furniture that lasts 50+ years. Your kids can jump on this, spill on this, beat it up, and it'll handle it.

The fabric is performance-grade, specifically designed for families like yours. Spills wipe clean with a damp cloth so no panic when the juice box explodes. And it won't show wear patterns like lighter fabrics that start looking shabby after a few years.

You also said you wanted something that didn't look like 'kid furniture' - something you'd still love when the kids are grown. This style is classic enough it won't look dated in ten years, but not so formal you're constantly worried about the kids damaging it.

And remember your concern about the price? This is the kind of investment that saves money because you're not replacing it every five years like cheaper furniture. You're buying one sofa that serves you for the next 20 years.

This decision balances your current needs with your long-term goals perfectly. You're going to be really happy you invested in quality."

Camera Store:

"Sarah, this camera is exactly right for what you're trying to accomplish. Here's why I'm so confident:

You mentioned wanting to photograph your kids' sports - soccer, basketball, fast action. This camera's continuous shooting captures 10 frames per second. When your daughter kicks that goal, you're getting the whole sequence. You're virtually guaranteed that perfect moment instead of hoping you pressed the shutter at exactly the right time.

The autofocus system tracks moving subjects automatically. Your son running toward you stays in sharp focus without you doing anything. That's technology that didn't exist in consumer cameras even five years ago.

And you were concerned about complexity, whether you'd be overwhelmed. We set this up in auto mode that way it's as simple as point-and-shoot right now. As you get comfortable over the next few months, you can explore other features, but you never have to. It grows with you.

For the sports photography goal you described, at the budget you had, this gives you capabilities you literally cannot get anywhere else at this price point. When you're looking at photos of your kids ten years from now, you'll be really glad you invested in capturing those moments properly."

The Pattern: Every good lock-in references specific Interview details, connects to their stated needs, addresses concerns they mentioned, and explains why this specific solution matches their specific situation.

Why Lock-in Works: The Psychology

When you lock in effectively, several psychological mechanisms work in your favor:

Cognitive reinforcement: You're providing rational justification they can recall when doubt arises. "Oh right, he explained why this costs more due to its commercial-grade construction."

Emotional reassurance: After making a significant purchase, people crave reassurance. Your confidence reduces their anxiety. But this only works if you built real trust first.

Authority bias: Humans naturally defer to experts. When an expert confidently says, "you made the right choice," we feel relieved. But you have to have earned that expert status through the earlier WISE phases.

Inoculation effect: By mentioning potential concerns explicitly – "You were worried about durability" - you inoculate them against those concerns becoming problems later. When doubt surfaces, they think: "Oh, we talked about that. He addressed it."

The key: Lock-in must be genuine and specific. Generic reassurance doesn't work. It has to be based on real Interview details and demonstrate you actually understand their situation.

The Last Two Minutes: Your Lasting Impression

Here's something psychological research has proven: people disproportionately remember the end of experiences. The "peak-end rule" states that memories are formed primarily by the most intense moment and the final moment.

The last two minutes of a Customer's visit create their lasting impression of the entire experience. Don't waste this crucial window.

What NOT to Do in the Last Two Minutes:

- Become distracted by other Customers while finalizing their transaction
- Rush them out the door because you're busy
- Seem relieved they're leaving
- Turn your attention to your phone or computer
- Hand them their bag with a generic "Have a nice day" while already looking past them

I see this constantly. The salesperson spends 30 minutes helping someone, then completely checks out during checkout. The Customer leaves feeling like they just became a burden.

What TO DO in the Last Two Minutes:

Action 1: Provide Specific Post-Purchase Guidance

Don't just hand over products. Give them specific next steps that ensure success:

Camera Store:
"Before you leave, one important thing: charge this battery for at least three hours before you use it. The partial charge from the factory isn't enough. Once it's charged, the menu has a 'first-time setup' option that only takes ten minutes to walk through before your daughter's recital so you're not figuring it out in the moment. You want to be ready when she takes the stage."

Garden Center:
"These plants look small now, but they'll spread significantly. Space them 18 inches apart. I know that looks like too much space, but by mid-summer you'll see why. And water deeply twice a week rather than shallow watering daily. Deep watering encourages root growth; shallow watering keeps roots near the surface where they're vulnerable."

Home Improvement Store:
"When you get home, read the instructions on this paint before you start. It needs to go on in thin coats. A lot of people try to cover in one thick coat and end up with drips and runs. Two thin coats take the same time and look 100% better. Use a quality brush for cutting in the edges—it makes a huge difference."

Why this matters: Specific guidance demonstrates continued investment in their success. It prevents problems that could lead to dissatisfaction or returns. And it gives them one more piece of evidence that you actually care.

Action 2: One Final Confidence Boost

Right before they leave, reinforce the lock-in one more time:

"I'm really confident this is going to solve the problems you've been having. Based on everything you told me, this is exactly right for your situation. You made a smart decision."

Short. Direct. Confident.

Action 3: Give Them Your Direct Contact

Hand them your business card with a personal touch:

"Here's my card with my direct number. I'm here Tuesdays, Thursdays, and Saturdays, 10 to 6. If you have any questions as you're getting started with this, call me directly. Please don't call the main store number and get whoever answers. Call me. I want to make sure this works perfectly for you."

This does several things:

- Makes you accessible for questions
- Shows continued commitment to their success
- Differentiates you from generic store service
- Creates a personal connection that builds loyalty

Action 4: The Two-Card Technique

Here's a particularly effective tactic: Give them TWO of your business cards.

"Here are two of my cards. One is for you. Keep it with your paperwork or in your wallet. If you have questions or need anything related to your marathon training, call me directly.

The second is for a friend. When someone asks about your training or compliments your results, you can give them my card. I'll take just as good care of them as I did you today."

This accomplishes multiple things:

- Ensures they have your contact info readily available
- Plants the referral seed explicitly
- Flatters them (assumes their project will succeed enough that people will ask)
- Makes referring easy since they have a card to hand someone

Most Customers put one card in their wallet and keep the second. When referral opportunities arise, they remember they have your card to share.

Action 5: Walk Them Out

If you can, walk them partway to their car or at least to the door while continuing conversation:

"Are you heading straight home to set this up, or do you have other errands? ...Well, safe drive, and let me know how that first workout goes!"

This extra 30 seconds makes a disproportionate impact. They remember that you walked them out. It feels like service you'd get from a high-end establishment, not typical retail.

Action 6: The Explicit Referral Request

The absolute last thing before they leave:

"Thanks so much for coming in today. If you're happy with how this works out, tell your friends. I'd love to help them too."

This explicit request plants a seed. When someone compliments their purchase, they'll remember you asked and they'll mention your name.

Post-Purchase Follow-Up: Maintaining Connection

The experience doesn't end when they leave. What you do after the sale determines whether they return, refer others, and become long-term Customers.

Follow-Up 1: Thank You (That Evening or Next Day)

Send a quick text or email:

"Jennifer, thanks for coming in today. I'm confident that elliptical is going to serve you well for your marathon training. If any questions come up as you're getting started, don't hesitate to reach out. - Michael"

Short. Personal. Demonstrates you're still thinking about their success.

Follow-Up 2: Check-In (1-2 Weeks Later)

Call or text to see how things are going:

"Hi Jennifer, Michael from [Store]. Wanted to check in and see how the elliptical is working out. Are you finding it comfortable on your knees? Any questions about the programs or settings?"

This accomplishes several goals:

- Catches problems early (before they become returns or negative reviews)
- Demonstrates ongoing commitment to their success
- Provides opportunity to address any concerns
- Builds the relationship foundation
- Opens door for additional sales if they're realizing they need accessories

Follow-Up 3: Milestone Contact

Based on their project or goal timeline, reach out at meaningful moments:

"Jennifer, your marathon is coming up in three weeks, right? How's the training going? Are you feeling ready? How have the knees been holding up with the increased mileage?"

For home renovation: "You should be wrapping up that bathroom project by now. How did it turn out? Did you run into any challenges with the tile?"

For new hobby: "You should have a few weeks of experience with the camera now. How are you enjoying it? What questions have come up?"

These milestone contacts show you remember them as individuals and care about outcomes, not just transactions. This is what builds loyalty.

The Reality of Follow-Up

I know what you're thinking: "This sounds great, but I don't have time to follow up with everyone."

Fair point. Here's the reality: You can't follow up with everyone equally. Prioritize:

Tier 1 - Always follow up:

- Large purchases (over $500)
- First-time Customers
- Customers who seemed uncertain but bought anyway
- Any purchase where you spent significant time

Tier 2 - Follow up when possible:

- Regular Customers making normal purchases
- Smaller purchases to new Customers

Tier 3 - Minimal follow-up:

- Quick, small purchases to repeat Customers

Even if you only follow up with Tier 1 Customers, you're ahead of 90% of salespeople who never follow up at all.

How to Make Follow-Up Manageable:

- Set phone reminders when you make the sale: "Follow up with Jennifer next Tuesday"
- Keep a simple notebook with Customer names and follow-up dates
- Spend 15 minutes at the start of each shift checking who you need to follow up with
- Use your phone's camera to photograph business cards or receipts as reminders

It doesn't require fancy systems. It requires commitment.

When Things Go Wrong: The Problem Is NOT the Problem

Here's where most salespeople completely fail the Customer—and destroy all the trust they built.

The elliptical arrives damaged. Or the camera has a defective button. Or the order was wrong. Or delivery was delayed. Problems happen.

Most salespeople focus on fixing the problem: "Let me call the warehouse." "I'll process a return." "We'll get you a replacement."

They're solving the wrong problem.

Understanding the Real Problem

Remember what happened when Jennifer bought that elliptical?

She had two active fears:

- Fear of making a mistake
- Fear of looking stupid

You eliminated both fears through the WISE process. She trusted you. She believed your recommendation. She took a risk. She spent $2,400 based on your guidance.

Now the product has failed.

The problem isn't the broken elliptical. The problem is broken trust.

She overcame her fears and trusted you. And now she's thinking:

"Maybe I DID make a mistake. Maybe I SHOULD have researched more. Maybe I WAS stupid to trust this salesperson. Maybe I got taken advantage of."

Both fears are back at maximum intensity. Worse than before, because now they're confirmed by reality.

If you only focus on fixing the product by processing the return, arranging replacement, etc. you are not addressing what's really wrong. You're treating the symptom, not the disease.

The Real Problem to Solve: Their Emotions and Trust

When a Customer contacts you with a problem, your job is to:

1. Restore their faith in their decision
2. Rebuild the trust that was damaged
3. Show them they were RIGHT to trust you
4. THEN fix the product

Here's what this looks like in practice:

Bad Response (focuses only on logistics):

Customer: "The elliptical arrived damaged. The console is cracked and one of the pedals is bent."

Salesperson: "Oh no. Okay, let me pull up your order. I'll process a return and we'll get a replacement out to you. It'll be about a week for delivery."

What the Customer hears: "You have a problem. I'll fix it eventually. Good luck with that."

What the Customer feels: "My fears were justified. This was a mistake. I knew I shouldn't have trusted this person. I'm returning this and buying elsewhere."

Now watch the WISE response:

Good Response (addresses emotions first, then logistics):

Customer: "The elliptical arrived damaged. The console is cracked and one of the pedals is bent."

Salesperson: "Oh man, Jennifer, I'm so sorry. That's incredibly frustrating, especially when you're excited to start training and this was supposed to be the beginning of your marathon journey. I know you trusted my recommendation, and this isn't what you deserved to receive. This isn't acceptable, and I'm going to make this right for you personally.

Here's what's going to happen: First, I'm calling the warehouse right now to arrange expedited replacement. Not standard delivery, expedited. You're going to have a perfect elliptical within 72 hours, not the normal seven days.

Second, I'm arranging pickup of the damaged unit, so you don't have to deal with hauling it anywhere or figuring out return logistics. They'll come get it when they deliver the new one.

Third, once the new one arrives and you verify it's perfect, I'm crediting your account $100 because this delayed your training plan and you shouldn't have to deal with this hassle. That's on me.

Here's what I need from you: When the new one arrives, text me a photo so I know it arrived in perfect condition. If there's ANY issue - I mean anything - you call me directly and I'll handle it. I'm personally making sure this gets resolved right.

You made a good decision on this elliptical for your marathon training. The product is exactly right for your needs and your knees. This was a delivery problem, not a product problem, and I'm making sure you get what you paid for. You trusted me, and I'm going to prove that trust was well-placed. Deal?"

Breaking Down Why This Works

It acknowledges their emotions first: "That's incredibly frustrating" validates how they feel. You're not minimizing their experience.

It validates their trust: "I know you trusted my recommendation" explicitly acknowledges the risk they took and that you understand it.

It takes personal responsibility: "I'm going to make this right for you personally" shows this isn't just a corporate problem because *you* own it.

It provides specific action with timeline: Expedited delivery within 72 hours is concrete, not vague.

It removes their burden: They don't have to figure out logistics or deal with return hassles.

It over-corrects: The $100 credit isn't required, but it demonstrates you value their time and trust more than $100.

It separates product quality from delivery problem: "This was a delivery problem, not a product problem" protects the original recommendation. Their decision was still right.

It reaffirms the original decision: "The product is exactly right for your needs and your knees" reminds them why they bought it in the first place.

It creates partnership: "I'm personally making sure this gets resolved" makes you allies, not adversary and victim.

It rebuilds confidence: "You trusted me, and I'm going to prove that trust was well-placed" directly addresses the broken trust.

The Outcome Difference

Bad response outcome: Customer gets replacement eventually. They feel like they dealt with a problem alone. When it's time to buy something else, they remember the hassle and shop elsewhere. They don't refer anyone. They might leave a negative review.

Good response outcome: Customer gets replacement quickly with compensation. They feel like you protected them and took personal responsibility. When it's time to buy something else, they come back to you specifically because you proved you'll take care of them. They tell this story to friends: "Something went wrong, but the salesperson bent over backward to make it right—that's where you should shop." They leave a positive review mentioning your name.

The Principle: Fix Emotions First, Product Second

This is the critical mindset shift: **The problem is not the problem. The broken trust is the problem.**

Every time a Customer contacts you with a problem, follow this sequence:

Step 1: Acknowledge the emotion
"I'm so sorry. That's frustrating/disappointing/unacceptable."

Step 2: Validate their trust
"You trusted my recommendation and this isn't what you deserved."

Step 3: Take personal ownership
"I'm going to fix this personally for you."

Step 4: Provide specific action plan
Tell them exactly what's going to happen and when.

Step 5: Remove their burden
Handle logistics so they don't have to.

Step 6: Over-correct when appropriate
For significant problems, go beyond just fixing—compensate for the hassle.

Step 7: Reaffirm the original decision
Separate the problem from the product quality or your recommendation.

Step 8: Rebuild confidence explicitly
"You made the right choice trusting me. I'm proving it by making this right."

This sequence addresses the real problem which is their emotional state and broken trust while also solving the logistics.

More Problem-Handling Examples

Camera Store - Defective Product:

Customer: "The camera has a sticky shutter button. Sometimes it doesn't fire when I press it."

Bad response: "Bring it in and we'll send it for repair. Should take about two weeks."

Good response: "I'm really sorry about this. That's exactly the opposite of what should be happening, especially with your daughter's recital coming up next month. You trusted my recommendation that this would capture those important moments, and a sticky shutter defeats that completely.

Here's what we're doing: I'm giving you a loaner camera to use immediately while we handle the repair. You won't miss any photo opportunities waiting for service. Bring yours in anytime this week and walk out with the loaner.

I'm also expediting the repair. I'll mark it priority service, so you get yours back in one week instead of two. And if for any reason the repair takes longer than one week, I'm upgrading your order to the next model at no additional cost. I want you to have perfect working equipment for that recital.

This is a defect in this individual unit, not the model itself. I've sold dozens of these with zero issues. This is exactly the right camera for sports photography like you're doing. We just got a lemon unit, which rarely happens. I'm making sure you get a perfect one and that you don't miss any important moments waiting for service. Okay?"

Furniture Store - Delivery Delay:

Customer: "My sofa was supposed to be delivered yesterday. Now they're saying it'll be another two weeks."

Bad response: "Yeah, the warehouse has been really backed up. I'll see if I can get an update for you."

Good response: "That's completely unacceptable, and I'm sorry. You planned around that delivery date, your current furniture is probably already gone or unusable, and now you're in limbo. You trusted me when I gave you that delivery date, and we failed you.

Here's what I'm doing right now: I'm calling my manager to see if we have any floor models we can deliver to you today as a temporary solution until your ordered sofa arrives. If we don't have this exact one, we'll find something comparable you can use.

I'm also calling the warehouse directly while you're on the phone to get a firm commitment on when your actual sofa will arrive. Not 'about two weeks,' a specific date.

And because this delay disrupted your plans and caused this hassle, I'm taking 10% off your total order. This isn't how we do business, and you shouldn't have to pay full price after being let down on timing.

You picked the perfect sofa for your family's needs. The product itself is exactly what you need. This is a warehouse logistics problem that I'm fixing. You didn't make a mistake trusting me. I'm going to prove that right now. Can you hold while I make these calls?"

The Pattern: Every response acknowledges emotions, validates trust, takes ownership, provides specific action, over-corrects, and reaffirms the original decision.

When You Can't Fix It Immediately

Sometimes you genuinely can't fix a problem immediately. Maybe the warehouse doesn't have stock. Maybe the manufacturer is slow. Maybe it's beyond your control.

Don't hide this. Don't make promises you can't keep. Be honest while still addressing emotions:

"Jennifer, I'm going to be straight with you. The warehouse doesn't have this model in stock right now, and we're looking at a three-week wait for the next shipment. I know that's not what you want to hear, and it doesn't solve your training timeline.

Here's what I can do: Option one, we can switch you to a different model that's in stock. This one has similar features and would work for your needs. I'll discount it to match what you paid for the original.

Option two, I can put you first in line for the next shipment and give you a $200 credit to compensate for the wait and the impact on your training schedule.

Option three, if neither of those works, I'll process a full refund immediately, and I'll personally help you find a comparable machine at another store. I'll even call ahead to tell them what you need so you don't have to start from scratch.

The decision is yours. What matters to me is that you end up with the right equipment for your marathon training, even if it's not from us. What would work best for you?"

This response:

- Is honest about the situation
- Provides multiple solutions
- Gives the Customer control
- Prioritizes their success over your sale
- Shows integrity by offering to help them buy elsewhere if needed

This kind of honesty and customer-first attitude builds trust even in failure. Customers remember that you put their needs first.

The Recovery Paradox

Here's something fascinating that research has proven: Customers whose problems are handled exceptionally well often become MORE loyal than Customers who never experienced problems.

Why? Because problems reveal character. Anyone can provide good service when everything's working. How you handle failures shows what you're really about.

When you handle a problem brilliantly by addressing emotions, taking ownership, over-correcting, and following up you demonstrate:

- Your competence under pressure
- Your genuine commitment to their success
- Your integrity
- That you have their back when things go wrong

This creates deep trust. These Customers become your most loyal advocates because you proved yourself when it mattered most.

So don't fear problems. Handle them brilliantly, and you turn disasters into opportunities to build unshakeable loyalty.

The Compound Effect of Remarkable Experiences

One remarkable experience creates a multiplier effect:

Multiplication 1: They return for future needs instead of price-shopping elsewhere.

Multiplication 2: They buy more when they return because they trust your recommendations.

Multiplication 3: They refer friends and family, which is the most effective marketing that exists.

Multiplication 4: They leave positive reviews mentioning your name, which influences dozens of future Customers.

Multiplication 5: They give you grace when problems occur because the relationship foundation is strong.

Each remarkable experience doesn't just create one sale; it creates years of value.

And the inverse is true: One poor experience, particularly poor problem handling, creates negative multiplication. They never return. They tell people to avoid you. They leave negative reviews. The damage spreads.

Your Sustainable Competitive Advantage

Here's the bottom line: Anyone can sell products. Anyone can quote prices. Anyone can process transactions.

Not everyone can create remarkable experiences that eliminate fear, build trust, and handle problems in ways that strengthen relationships.

This is your competitive advantage. Amazon can match prices. Online retailers can match selection. Big box stores can match convenience.

None of them can match the human relationship, the personal trust, the expert guidance, and the caring follow-through that you provide through WISE Selling.

Your income, your reputation, and your career success don't come from transactions. They come from relationships built through consistently remarkable experiences.

The Welcome phase builds initial trust. The Interview phase deepens understanding. The Solution phase demonstrates competence. But the Experience phase is where you prove everything you've claimed. It's where trust either solidifies into loyalty or crumbles into disappointment.

Master the Experience phase - the lock-in, the last two minutes, the follow-up, and especially the problem handling - and you create customers for life who become your most effective marketing and your most reliable income stream.

This is how you build a career instead of just doing a job. This is how you become someone Customers ask for by name. This is how you create sustainable success that doesn't depend on foot traffic or economic conditions or competition.

One remarkable experience at a time.

Chapter 13

Building Your Sales Culture – The Foundation for Remarkable Experiences

On Monday morning, a Customer walks into your store and has an exceptional experience. She works with Michael, who executes WISE Selling flawlessly. He welcomes her warmly, conducts a thorough Interview, presents a customized Solution with clear benefit statements, handles her objections with Soften and Ask, and ensures she leaves confident about her complete solution. She feels heard, valued, and genuinely helped. It's a Remarkable Experience.

On Wednesday, the same Customer returns with a question about her purchase. Michael has the day off. She works with Sarah instead.

Sarah seems distracted. She gives minimal attention to the question. Her answers are vague and unhelpful. She makes the Customer feel like an interruption. The interaction takes five frustrating minutes that leave the Customer wondering if she made a mistake buying from this store.

By Friday, the Customer has left a negative review online. Not about her purchase - that's working perfectly. Not about Michael - she mentions he was excellent. About the inconsistent experience: "One salesperson was incredible; another couldn't care less. Can't trust what you'll get here."

This scenario plays out in retail stores everywhere, every single day.

Individual excellence doesn't create Remarkable Experiences when it's surrounded by mediocrity or indifference. You need cultural excellence - a shared commitment to WISE principles that ensures every Customer, every time, receives the same high-quality experience regardless of who's working that day.

This chapter teaches you how culture multiplies individual excellence into organizational excellence. You'll learn the fundamentals of building WISE culture but understand this: we're only scratching the surface. For the comprehensive deep dive on culture building - the complete methodology, frameworks, and implementation tools - see my book *Culturrific!:* That book provides the full architecture. This chapter gives you the essential foundation.

What Is Sales Culture? (And Why Most Stores Get It Wrong)

Culture is the "how we do things around here" idea. It's the shared beliefs, values, behaviors, and norms that define how a group operates.

Sales culture specifically refers to:

- How team members view their role (order-takers or consultants?)
- What behaviors get rewarded and recognized
- Whether knowledge is shared or hoarded
- Whether collaboration or competition dominates
- How Customers are discussed when they're not present
- What standards actually exist and get maintained
- How mistakes and learning are handled
- Whether excellence is expected or optional

Strong sales cultures have:

- Shared language: Everyone speaks the same language
- Consistent standards: Quality doesn't depend on which employee helps
- Mutual support: Team members help each other succeed
- Customer focus: Decisions prioritize Customer success, not convenience
- Continuous improvement: The team constantly gets better
- Accountability: Standards are maintained, not just stated
- Pride: Team members are proud to work here

Weak sales cultures have:

- Wild inconsistency: Quality depends entirely on who helps you
- Internal competition: Team members undermine each other for sales
- Shortcuts everywhere: Standards exist on paper but aren't maintained
- Transaction focus: Numbers matter more than Customer outcomes
- Stagnation: No one improves because there's no expectation of excellence
- Blame and excuses: Problems are never anyone's responsibility
- Apathy: Team members don't care about the work or each other

Here's what most retail operators get wrong: they think culture is about ping-pong tables, casual Fridays, and employee appreciation pizza parties.

That's not culture. That's perks.

Culture is about what happens when nobody's watching. It's about whether your team maintains Interview thoroughness during a Saturday rush. It's about whether they follow up with Customers even when it's inconvenient. It's about whether they help each other or compete with each other.

Culture is revealed under pressure. When the store is slammed, when employees are tired, when the manager isn't watching what behaviors show up? That's your real culture.

Why Culture Is the Multiplier of Everything

You can have the most talented salesperson in the world executing WISE Selling perfectly. But if that person is surrounded by colleagues who don't care, don't try, and resent excellence, three things happen:

First: Customers experience inconsistency. They work with your star employee once, then get someone mediocre the next time. They can't trust the experience, so they don't return.

Second: Your star employee gets demoralized. Excellence surrounded by mediocrity is exhausting. They either lower their standards to fit in or leave for a better environment.

Third: The culture pulls everyone toward the lowest common denominator. It's easier to lower standards than maintain high ones when nobody else cares.

Conversely, when you build strong culture, the opposite happens:

First: Customers experience consistency. Every interaction meets high standards. They trust the experience and return repeatedly.

Second: Good employees get better. Excellence surrounded by excellence is energizing. Team members push each other to improve.

Third: The culture pulls everyone toward higher standards. It's easier to maintain high standards when everyone else does too.

This is why culture is the multiplier. Individual skill × weak culture = wasted potential. Individual skill × strong culture = organizational excellence.

The Culture Equation (That Most Managers Miss)

Here's the equation that determines whether you deliver Remarkable Experiences consistently:

Remarkable Experience = Individual Skill × Cultural Foundation × Organizational Systems

All three elements must be present.

Individual Skill is what the earlier chapters in this book teach: Welcome, Interview, Solution, Experience, and all the techniques within each phase.

Cultural Foundation is the shared commitment to WISE principles across the entire team. (Which is what this chapter addresses.)

Organizational Systems are the structures, processes, and policies that enable excellence like technology, scheduling, training programs, compensation structures, operational procedures.

You can't have one without the others:

Excellent individuals in toxic culture = Inconsistent experiences, high turnover, wasted talent

Strong culture without skilled individuals = Consistently mediocre experiences, good intentions without capability

Skills and culture without supporting systems = Frustrated team fighting unnecessary obstacles, burnout

You need all three. But most managers focus only on individual skill development while ignoring culture and systems. That's why training doesn't stick and improvement doesn't last.

The Five Cultural Foundations

In *Culturrific!*, I detail the complete architecture of culture building. Here, I'm going to give you the five essential foundations specifically for building WISE sales culture. These are your starting point.

Foundation 1: Shared Purpose

Teams need common understanding of why the work matters beyond paychecks. Purpose answers: "What are we really doing here?"

Weak purpose statements:

- "We're here to sell products"
- "We're here to hit our numbers"
- "We're here to make money"

These aren't wrong, but they're uninspiring. They don't create meaning. They don't differentiate you from any other store. They don't make anyone care about excellence.

Strong purpose statements:

- "We help people achieve their fitness goals through expert guidance and complete solutions"
- "We transform houses into homes by helping families find furniture that serves their life beautifully for decades"
- "We preserve life's precious moments by ensuring people have the right photography equipment and knowledge to capture what matters"
- "We make home improvement projects successful for people who lack confidence in their abilities"
- "We're a community hub where cyclists of all levels find equipment, knowledge, and connection"

See the difference? Strong purpose statements focus on Customer outcomes, create meaning beyond transactions, and inspire team members to care about doing the work well.

How to build shared purpose:

Step 1: Define it clearly with your team. Don't impose it from above. Ask: "What do we really do for Customers beyond selling products? When we're at our best, what impact do we have?"

Write it down. Make it visible. Put signs in the break room, behind the register, on team materials and more.

Step 2: Reference it constantly. In team meetings, during coaching, in daily interactions, connect activities to purpose:

"The reason we spend time doing thorough Interviews is because our purpose is helping people achieve fitness goals and we can't do that without understanding what they're trying to accomplish."

"When you spent 45 minutes with that Customer who only bought $30 of supplies, you were living our purpose by making their project successful regardless of transaction size. That's who we are."

Step 3: Celebrate purpose-driven actions. When team members demonstrate purpose-driven behavior, recognize it publicly:

"Sarah spent an hour helping a nervous first-time homeowner understand exactly what they needed for their bathroom. The sale was $200, but she treated it like a $2,000 project because our purpose is making projects successful, not maximizing transaction size. That's what we're about."

Step 4: Hire for purpose alignment. During interviews, assess whether candidates naturally care about helping people succeed. Skills can be taught; genuine care is harder to instill.

Ask: "Tell me about a time you helped someone solve a problem where their success mattered more to you than any benefit you got."

Listen for whether they focus on helping others or personal gain.

Foundation 2: Shared Language

WISE Selling works best when everyone uses the same framework and terminology.

Shared language creates:

- **Consistency**: Customers hear similar approaches from different team members
- **Collaboration**: Team members can discuss Customer situations efficiently using common vocabulary
- **Training efficiency**: New employees learn one system, not six different personal approaches
- **Quality standards**: Everyone knows what "good Interview" or "complete Solution" means
- **Rapid communication**: Complex information gets communicated quickly

How to build shared language:

Step 1: Adopt WISE terminology organization-wide. Everyone uses Welcome, Interview, Solution, Experience. Everyone understands "Soften and Ask," "benefit statements," "multiplication," "Customer types," "lock-in."

Step 2: Create reference materials:

- Laminated cards with key Interview questions for each Customer type
- Benefit statement examples for your top products
- Common objections with Soften and Ask responses
- Welcome phase approaches adapted to your store
- Lock-in templates for major product categories

Step 3: Practice together regularly. Weekly 30-minute role-plays where team members practice WISE phases using shared language. Provide specific feedback:

"Good Interview on past experience and expectations. You missed conditions of use so let's practice incorporating that."

"Your Solution had strong benefit statements, but you didn't attempt multiplication. Let's work on integrating that naturally."

Step 4: Coach using shared language. When providing feedback, reference the framework:

"Your Welcome was warm and you got their name, but you skipped Points of Pride. That builds confidence early. Let's work on including that."

"Excellent Soften and Ask on that price objection. You uncovered the real concern instead of just defending the price."

Example showing the difference:

Without shared language:

Team member A: "So I just helped a Customer and we're getting them the tent."

Team member B: "Cool, which one?"

Team member A: "The REI Quarter Dome."

Team member B: "Nice."

Zero useful information exchanged. No collaboration. No quality verification.

With shared language:

Team member A: "I just completed Interview with a Customer who was a novice type, first-time backpacker. They're primarily doing weekend trips in established campgrounds, occasional backcountry. Based on conditions of use and experience level, I'm recommending the Quarter Dome for ease of setup and appropriate weight."

Team member B: "Good call for a newby. Did you multiply with sleeping pad and stakes? The standard stakes won't work in the rocky terrain they mentioned planning to camp in."

Team member A: "Got the pad and ground cloth. Good catch on stakes. I'll add those before checkout."

See the difference? The second conversation shows team members speaking the same language, which enables actual collaboration and better Customer outcomes.

Foundation 3: Shared Standards

Standards define "good enough." Without clear standards, quality becomes subjective and varies wildly across team members.

Key standards to establish:

Interview thoroughness: "Every Customer receives Interview covering past experience, expectations, and conditions of use before Solution is presented. Minimum 5 open-ended questions for purchases over $100."

Benefit statement usage: "Every Solution includes at least 3 benefit statements using 'This has, that means' structure connecting to specific Interview information."

Multiplication: "Every transaction includes recommendations for complete solutions with 2-4 multiplication items from appropriate categories."

Lock-in execution: "Every purchase over $100 receives lock-in reinforcement referencing at least 3 specific Interview points explaining why this solution matches their situation."

Data capture: "Every transaction is linked to Customer profile with complete contact information and meaningful notes about their project/goal, not just products purchased."

Follow-up: "Every purchase over $200 receives thank-you contact within 24 hours, and check-in contact within 7-14 days."

Welcome execution: "Every Customer is greeted within 60 seconds using gratitude opening and name exchange within first 2 minutes."

Objection handling: "All objections are addressed using Soften and Ask before providing solutions. No defensive immediate countering."

How to build and maintain standards:

Step 1: Document them clearly. Write down exactly what behaviors meet standards. Make them specific and observable:

Weak: "Provide excellent Customer service"

Strong: "Greet every Customer within 60 seconds, conduct Interview with minimum 5 questions per area, present Solution with minimum 3 benefit statements connected to Interview, execute lock-in for purchases over $100"

Step 2: Train everyone on standards. Every team member must understand what's expected and why. Dedicate training time to each standard: why it matters, how to execute it, what good execution looks like, common mistakes, practice opportunities.

Step 3: Monitor adherence consistently. Observe interactions regularly. Track metrics that reflect standards: average Interview duration, multiplication rate, Customer information capture rate, follow-up completion rate.

Step 4: Address violations promptly. When team members consistently fail to meet standards despite coaching, address it directly:

"I've noticed your Interviews are consistently 2-3 minutes instead of the 5-10 minutes we need for thorough understanding. This means you're missing information that would help you recommend better solutions. Let's work on improving this."

Step 5: Evolve standards based on results. If standards aren't producing Remarkable Experiences, adjust them. Review quarterly: Are they still serving Customer success? Do they need refinement?

Foundation 4: Collaborative Culture

Traditional retail often creates internal competition: salespeople competing for Customers, hoarding knowledge, protecting "their" clients, undercutting each other.

This destroys Remarkable Experiences and makes everyone miserable.

WISE culture is collaborative. Team members:

- Share Customer context when handing off
- Help each other with difficult situations
- Share knowledge about products and techniques freely
- Celebrate each other's successes genuinely
- Cover for each other during busy times
- View Customer success as shared responsibility
- See themselves as a team, not competitors

How to build collaborative culture:

Practice 1: Structured handoffs. When one team member hands a Customer to another, provide complete context:

"Sarah, this is Jennifer. We had a conversation about her training for her first marathon. She's a Novice runner, neutral gait, budget around $150. Previous IT band issues concern her. I showed her three options. I need to help another Customer so can you continue with the best Solution for her, please?"

This maintains continuity and serves the Customer. The alternative - "Sarah, can you help this Customer?" with no context - forces starting over, frustrating everyone.

Practice 2: Knowledge sharing sessions. Weekly 15-minute sessions where team members share:

- Products they've learned about
- Successful Interview questions or techniques
- Benefit statements that resonated
- Challenging situations and how they handled them
- Customer feedback received
- Objections encountered and Soften and Ask approaches

This distributes knowledge across the team rather than keeping it siloed.

Practice 3: Team problem-solving. When a team member faces difficulty, others help rather than watching them struggle:

"Hey Michael, you look stuck. What's going on? ...Okay, they want X but need Y based on what you're describing. Let me show you how to present that."

Or: "I'll cover your other Customers for ten minutes so you can focus on solving this."

Practice 4: Recognition of collaborative behavior. Publicly celebrate when team members help each other:

"Thanks to Michael for jumping in during Saturday's rush and helping everyone's Customers while we were all slammed. That teamwork makes this place work."

Practice 5: Eliminate territorial behavior. Some retail creates "my Customer" mentality where salespeople guard their clients. Eliminate this.

Instead: "We serve Customers together. They're not 'your' Customers or 'my' Customers, they're our Customers. We all take care of them."

Here are some examples showing the difference.

Non-collaborative culture:

Customer is working with Tom on selecting an engagement ring. Tom steps away to get something from the back room. Sarah sees the Customer standing alone but doesn't approach because "that's Tom's Customer." Customer stands awkwardly waiting, feeling ignored.

Tom returns: "Sorry about that wait."

Later, Tom discovers Sarah was available: "Why didn't you engage with my Customer?"

Sarah: "They're your sale. I didn't want to step on your toes."

Collaborative culture:

Tom steps away. Sarah immediately approaches: "Hi, I'm Sarah. Tom mentioned you're looking at engagement rings - exciting! While he's grabbing those other options, is there anything I can answer?"

Customer: "Actually, I'm trying to decide between round and cushion cut. What's your opinion?"

Sarah: "Great question. Let me show you the difference side by side..." [Helps Customer narrow choices, takes notes on preferences]

Tom returns.

Sarah: "Tom, while you were getting those, your Customer and I looked at round versus cushion. He's leaning toward cushion because he likes how the facets catch light. I took notes on what appealed to him about each."

Tom: "Perfect, thanks Sarah. Sir, let's talk through cushion options with what Sarah learned..."

In the collaborative culture, both employees prioritize Customer experience over territorial concerns. Tom appreciates Sarah's help. The Customer receives seamless service.

Foundation 5: Learning Culture

Remarkable Experiences require continuous improvement. What works today needs refinement tomorrow as Customer expectations evolve, products change, and team members discover better techniques.

Learning culture characteristics:

Characteristic 1: Mistakes are learning opportunities, not punishments. Team members aren't punished for honest mistakes made while trying to serve Customers well.

Example: Team member recommends a product that turns out wrong for the Customer's situation. Customer returns it dissatisfied.

Weak response: "You should have asked better questions. That was bad. Be more careful."

Team member feels defensive, learns to avoid risks, doesn't understand what to do differently.

Strong response: "Okay, let's talk through what happened so we learn from it. Walk me through your Interview. What did you learn that led to that recommendation?"

[Team member explains]

"I see. Here's what you missed: you didn't explore conditions of use thoroughly. They mentioned outdoor use, but you didn't ask about weather conditions, temperature ranges, or frequency. They needed [different product] because they're using it in freezing temperatures weekly. What you recommended works great for occasional indoor use, which is what you assumed.

Let's role-play similar situations. The key Interview question you need is: 'Tell me specifically about the conditions where you'll use this? Items like temperature, weather, frequency, environment.' That would have revealed what you needed."

The strong response turns the mistake into learning without shame.

Characteristic 2: Regular skill development. Teams practice together consistently, not just during initial training.

Weekly or biweekly 30-minute practice sessions:

- Role-play difficult Customer scenarios
- Practice new product benefit statements
- Review and refine Interview questions
- Share successful techniques
- Practice objection handling
- Practice lock-in for new products
- Role-play handoffs and collaboration

These should be psychologically safe spaces where people can try things, fail, get feedback, and improve without Customer consequences or ridicule.

Characteristic 3: Customer feedback is welcomed and analyzed, not hidden or blamed on Customers.

"We got a negative review about feeling rushed. Let's read it and talk about what happened. This was Saturday afternoon around 2 PM. Who worked with this Customer?"

[Team member identifies themselves]

"Okay, no judgment, just learning. What was going on that made them feel rushed?"

[Team member explains it was during a rush with multiple Customers waiting]

"I get it. Saturdays can get crazy. So, the question: how do we maintain Welcome and Interview quality even during rushes? What could we do differently? This isn't about blame; it's about improving our system."

[Team discusses solutions]

Characteristic 4: Expertise is developed and shared. Team members develop deep expertise in specific areas and share it:

- One person becomes the marathon training expert
- Another masters technical fabrics
- Another specializes in helping Novices
- Another becomes the bike fitting specialist

This creates a knowledge network where team members refer Customers to each other for specialized needs while maintaining generalist capabilities in WISE fundamentals.

Characteristic 5: External learning is incorporated. Team members attend workshops, read industry publications, visit trade shows, take courses, and bring back learning to share.

Budget for and encourage external learning. Expect people to share what they learn.

The Manager's Role: Chief Culture Officer

If you're a manager or owner, understand this: building culture is your primary job, not something you do when you have time.

You are the chief culture officer. Culture rises or falls based on your commitment.

Manager responsibilities:

Responsibility 1: Model excellence personally. You can't ask team members to execute WISE Selling if you don't do it yourself. When you work the floor, demonstrate the behaviors you expect.

Actions speak infinitely louder than words. A manager who rushes through Interviews while demanding team members be thorough creates cynicism and resentment.

Responsibility 2: Coach consistently. Regular feedback and coaching, not just annual reviews. Observe interactions daily, provide specific feedback referencing WISE framework and standards.

"I watched your interaction. Your Interview was excellent. You uncovered needs well beyond what they initially stated. Your Solution connected benefits directly to Interview points beautifully. Where we can improve: you didn't attempt multiplication. That Customer mentioned marathon training, camping, getting their kids into hiking - multiple multiplication opportunities. Let's talk about recognizing and integrating those more naturally."

Responsibility 3: Remove obstacles. When team members face systematic obstacles to executing WISE Selling, remove them:

- Inadequate product knowledge? Provide better training
- Not enough time during rushes? Adjust staffing
- Questions beyond team's expertise? Arrange specialist training
- POS system too slow? Invest in better technology
- Products frequently out of stock? Improve inventory management

Don't blame team members for systematic problems. Fix systems.

Responsibility 4: Celebrate and recognize excellence. Publicly recognize team members who exemplify WISE Selling:

- Highlight specific behaviors: "Michael's Interview was textbook. He uncovered needs they didn't realize they had"
- Create visible recognition: "Remarkable Experience Champion" award
- Celebrate learning and improvement: "Sarah has strengthened her multiplication. Her transaction value is up 40% because she's consistently recommending complete solutions"

Responsibility 5: Address performance issues. When team members consistently fail to meet standards despite coaching, address it directly through progressive performance management.

Allowing poor performance to continue sends the message that standards don't matter. It demoralizes high performers.

Responsibility 6: Protect culture from toxicity. One toxic team member destroys culture faster than ten good employees can build it.

Toxic behaviors spread. Negativity is contagious. High performers leave toxic environments.

Address toxic behavior quickly and directly: clear feedback about problematic behaviors, expectations for immediate change, support for change if they're willing, removal if change doesn't occur.

Responsibility 7: Invest in cultural development. Culture requires time, resources, and attention:

- Schedule regular team practice sessions (paid time)
- Provide training materials and resources
- Invest in supporting tools (POS, CRM)
- Allow time for follow-up during work hours
- Budget for team development
- Create physical environment supporting culture

Managers who say "we value culture" but won't invest resources are lying to themselves and their teams.

Individual Contributors: What You Can Do Without Authority

If you're reading this as a salesperson without management authority, you might wonder what you can do to influence culture.

More than you think.

Individual culture building:

Action 1: Model excellence personally. Execute WISE Selling flawlessly yourself. Be the example others observe and hopefully emulate.

Action 2: Share knowledge generously. When you learn something valuable, share it with colleagues. Don't hoard knowledge.

Action 3: Collaborate actively. Help colleagues with their Customers. Provide context when handing off. Ask for help when needed.

Action 4: Speak WISE language. Use framework terminology consistently. This spreads shared language naturally.

Action 5: Recognize peers. When colleagues do excellent work, acknowledge it: "That was a masterful Interview. How did you uncover all that information?"

Action 6: Be positive about culture. If management is trying to build WISE culture, be supportive rather than cynical or resistant.

Action 7: Advocate constructively. If you see cultural problems, raise them constructively: "I've noticed we're struggling with follow-up completion. Can we discuss systems to make it easier?"

Action 8: Mentor newcomers. Help new team members learn WISE principles. Your peer mentoring is often more effective than management training.

You can't build culture alone, but you significantly influence it. Your choices matter.

Measuring Cultural Health

How do you know if your culture is strong or weak? Track these indicators:

Indicator 1: Consistency across team members. Mystery shop repeatedly with different employees. Do you get Remarkable Experiences consistently, or does quality vary wildly?

Strong culture: Minimal variation
Weak culture: Massive inconsistency

Indicator 2: Customer feedback patterns. What do reviews say?

Strong culture reviews mention: feeling heard, expert guidance, complete solutions, exceptional service, consistency ("every time I come here"), team quality ("everyone here is helpful")

Weak culture reviews mention: feeling rushed or ignored, generic advice, inconsistent experience ("depends on who you get"), lack of follow-through, indifferent employees

Indicator 3: Team member satisfaction and tenure. In strong cultures, people enjoy work because they're part of something meaningful.

Strong culture: High satisfaction, low turnover, team members refer friends for employment

Weak culture: Low satisfaction, high turnover, difficulty attracting quality candidates

Indicator 4: Standards adherence through observation. Observe 20 Customer interactions. Track how many include proper Welcome, thorough Interview, benefit statements, multiplication, lock-in, data capture.

Strong culture: 90%+ adherence
Weak culture: Under 70% adherence

Indicator 5: Customer return rate. What percentage return for second, third purchases?

Strong culture: 60%+ make second purchase
Weak culture: Most are one-time buyers

Indicator 6: Referral rate. What percentage of new Customers come from referrals?

Strong culture: 40%+ from referrals
Weak culture: Under 20% from referrals

Monitor these quarterly. Improving trends indicate strengthening culture. Declining trends require intervention.

Culture as Your Sustainable Competitive Advantage

In retail where products and prices are increasingly similar, culture becomes the differentiator creating sustainable competitive advantage.

What competitors can easily copy:

- Your products (same brands available everywhere)
- Your prices (price matching is instant)
- Your physical space (with capital investment)
- Your stated policies (returns, warranties)

What competitors cannot easily copy:

- Your culture and the behaviors it produces
- The relationships your team builds with Customers
- The expertise developed and shared within your team
- The systems and processes refined over years
- The Customer trust earned through consistent excellence
- The community connection created through Remarkable Experiences

These advantages only exist if your culture enables them consistently.

The store with strong WISE culture doesn't compete primarily on price or selection. It competes on the Remarkable Experience that comes from consistent excellence enabled by cultural foundations ensuring every team member delivers high-quality interactions every time.

Why culture is sustainable advantage:

It takes years to build. You can't create strong culture quickly. Competitors can't replicate overnight.

It's invisible from outside. Competitors see results (high satisfaction, loyal Customers, strong sales) but can't see the cultural foundations producing them.

It requires authentic commitment. You can't fake culture. Competitors who try without authentic commitment fail.

It compounds over time. Culture gets stronger as practices become habits, habits become norms, and norms become "how we do things."

It retains talent. Strong culture attracts and retains excellent people who become increasingly excellent through the culture.

The Deep Dive: *Culturrific!*

This chapter has given you the essential foundations for building WISE sales culture. But we've only scratched the surface.

For the complete methodology on culture building - the comprehensive frameworks, detailed implementation strategies, specific tools, step-by-step processes, and real-world case studies - I encourage you to read my book *Culturrific!* Sorry, I know that the third time I have said that.

Culturrific! provides:

- The complete architecture of culture building
- Detailed frameworks for each cultural element
- Implementation tools and templates
- Troubleshooting guides for common cultural problems
- Methods for measuring and evolving culture
- Case studies showing culture transformation
- Leadership strategies for sustaining culture over time

This chapter gives you the foundation. *Culturrific!* gives you the complete blueprint.

The Long-Term Cultural Journey

Building WISE culture doesn't happen in weeks or months. It takes sustained commitment over years.

Year 1: Foundation establishment. Define purpose, adopt WISE framework, establish shared language and standards, begin consistent practice and coaching, start measuring, see initial improvements.

Year 2: Refinement and deepening. Refine execution based on Year 1 learning, deepen expertise through continued practice, strengthen collaboration, improve supporting systems, see measurable metric improvements.

Year 3: Cultural maturity. Culture becomes more self-sustaining as team members coach each other naturally, new hires absorb culture through immersion, standards are maintained without constant oversight, team takes pride in cultural identity.

Year 5+: Cultural embedding. Culture is deeply embedded in organizational DNA, team members can't imagine working any other way, competitive advantage solidifies, Customer loyalty is extraordinarily high, culture becomes recruiting advantage.

The investment pays compounding returns: Customer lifetime value increases dramatically, referral rates grow exponentially, team member retention improves, reputation strengthens, competitive position solidifies, premium pricing becomes sustainable.

Starting Your Cultural Journey

If you're a manager or owner feeling overwhelmed by the scope, here's where to start:

Step 1: Commit personally. Believe in and commit to WISE principles. Apply them yourself first.

Step 2: Define your purpose. Work with your team to articulate why your store exists beyond selling products.

Step 3: Introduce WISE framework. Teach Welcome, Interview, Solution, Experience to your entire team.

Step 4: Establish initial standards. Pick 3-5 most important standards first. Focus on Interview thoroughness, benefit statements, Customer information capture. Master these before adding more.

Step 5: Begin regular practice. Schedule weekly 30-minute practice sessions. Make them mandatory and paid time.

Step 6: Measure and monitor. Start tracking Customer satisfaction, return rates, transaction value, follow-up completion. Review monthly.

Step 7: Recognize and celebrate. When you see WISE behaviors, recognize them publicly.

Step 8: Address gaps promptly. When standards aren't met, coach immediately.

Step 9: Expand gradually. As initial standards become habitual, add more.

Step 10: Maintain patience and persistence. Culture building is a marathon. Commit to the multi-year journey.

The Cultural Imperative

Here's the bottom line: **You cannot consistently deliver Remarkable Experiences without a strong culture.**

Individual excellence produces occasional excellence. Cultural excellence produces consistent excellence.

Occasional excellence doesn't build sustainable business. Customers can't trust inconsistency. They don't return. They don't refer. They don't pay premiums.

Consistent excellence builds sustainable business. Customers trust consistency. They return repeatedly. They refer enthusiastically. They pay premium prices for reliable value.

WISE Selling techniques are powerful. A skilled individual using them creates wonderful experiences for Customers they personally serve.

WISE culture is transformational. An entire team using WISE Selling creates Remarkable Experiences for every Customer, every time thus building business success that compounds over decades.

The choice is yours: Remain a collection of individuals with varying approaches and results, or become a unified team delivering consistent Remarkable Experiences through shared culture.

Choose culture. Choose WISE. Choose Remarkable Experiences.

Your Customers (and your career) deserve nothing less.

Your Journey Begins

You've reached the end of this book, but you stand at the beginning of something far more important: your journey toward mastery of WISE Selling and the creation of Remarkable Experiences.

Everything you've read - the frameworks, techniques, examples, and principles - exists only as potential until you apply it. Knowledge without application is merely entertainment. Application transforms knowledge into skill, skill into habit, and habit into mastery.

What You Now Know

Let's review the essential framework you've learned:

You understand the fundamental truth about retail today: The old transactional model no longer works. Customers have infinite information and access to any product at competitive prices online. Your value now comes from consultation, expertise, relationship, and experience—things Amazon can't replicate.

You understand the 50/50 Principle that changes everything:

When you merely MEET Customer expectations, there's only a 50% chance they'll return. Think about that – half of Customers you serve adequately will never come back. You can't build a sustainable business on 50/50 odds.

But when you EXCEED expectations - when you deliver Remarkable Experiences - 98% of Customers return. That's the difference between hoping for survival and building thriving business.

Here's the eye-opener most salespeople miss: **salespeople who meet expectations think they're doing a great job.** The Customer came in for shoes, left with shoes, seemed happy. Success, right?

Wrong.

That's 50/50 territory. That Customer is just as likely to buy from a competitor next time as return to you.

This is why WISE Selling represents a fundamental shift in how you measure success:

Success is not based on selling something to the Customer.

Success is based on HOW you sell something to the Customer.

The WHAT (the product sold) creates 50/50 odds.

The HOW (the experience of buying) creates 98% odds.

WISE Selling focuses on the HOW. It focuses on you being the guide who eliminates fears and builds trust, not the hero who just pushes products.

You've learned the WISE framework—four phases that structure every interaction that exceeds expectations:

Welcome establishes first impressions and builds initial trust through genuine warmth (compassion) and professional competence (confidence). You set the stage for everything that follows.

Interview uncovers what Customers really need through systematic exploration of past experience, expectations, and conditions of use. This is where you gather the intelligence that makes everything else possible. This is where you become their guide, not just an order-taker.

Solution presents customized recommendations with clear benefit statements connecting features to Customer outcomes. It includes multiplication the art of ensuring Customers leave with complete solutions that lead to success, not partial solutions that lead to failure.

Experience transforms transactions into relationships through lock-in, follow-up, and especially problem resolution that actually strengthens trust rather than destroying it. This is where 50/50 odds become 98% odds.

You've learned about the two fundamental fears every Customer walks in with:

The **fear of making a mistake**: "What if I waste my money? What if this doesn't work? What if I regret this?"

The **fear of looking stupid**: "What if I ask dumb questions? What if I'm being taken advantage of? What if everyone else knows something I don't?"

These fears create that defensive wall Customers build. They're why Customers hesitate, research obsessively, ask for time to think, and comparison-shop endlessly.

These fears are why merely meeting expectations isn't enough. When you just meet expectations, you haven't eliminated the fears—you've just temporarily satisfied them. The fears return the moment they leave your store. That's why they might not come back.

You've learned the trust equation that eliminates both fears and exceeds expectations:

Trust = Compassion + Confidence

Compassion eliminates the fear of looking stupid by making Customers feel safe asking questions, admitting what they don't know, and revealing their true concerns without judgment. They feel heard and valued.

Confidence eliminates the fear of making a mistake by demonstrating your competence to guide them correctly; that following your recommendations will lead to success, not regret. They feel certain about their decision.

Both are necessary. Neither alone is sufficient. This is the psychological foundation that separates meeting expectations (50/50) from exceeding them (98%).

You've learned about personality types - Analytical, Driver, Practical, and Trendsetter - and how to adapt your approach because each type builds trust differently and processes decisions differently. Exceeding expectations means serving them the way THEY need to be served, not the way you're most comfortable serving.

You've mastered the language of value through benefit statements that translate technical features into outcomes Customers understand: "This has [feature]. That means [benefit for you]." This is how you demonstrate confidence while making Customers feel informed (compassion).

You understand objection handling through Soften and Ask. How to validate concerns (compassion) before demonstrating you can address them (confidence). Objections are fears showing up in disguise. Handle them correctly and you exceed expectations. Handle them poorly and you confirm their fears.

You've learned that when problems occur, the product failure isn't the real problem. The broken trust is the problem. Customers overcame their fears and trusted you, and now that trust is damaged. Your job is to restore their faith first, fix the product second. This is where you can actually exceed expectations during failure—turning 50/50 odds into 98% odds even when things go wrong.

You understand culture building. That individual excellence creates occasional Remarkable Experiences, but cultural excellence creates consistent Remarkable Experiences. Every Customer, every time. You can't build a business on 98% return rates if only one employee delivers Remarkable Experiences and everyone else delivers 50/50 experiences.

Most importantly, you understand that **your role isn't being the hero who sells products**. Your role is being the guide who eliminates fears and builds trust so you can help Customers succeed at things they care about.

Heroes have egos. Heroes focus on the sale.

Heroes get 50/50 odds.

Guides have humility. Guides focus on Customer success.

Guides get 98% odds.

The Gap Between Knowing and Doing

There's a gap, sometimes a chasm, between knowing what to do and actually doing it consistently.

Reading this book took hours. Mastering WISE Selling takes years.

You might feel overwhelmed. That's natural. You're not expected to implement everything immediately. Mastery is built incrementally.

You might feel skeptical. "Will this really work?" "Is it worth the investment?" "Can I actually change how I work?"

Let me address these doubts directly:

Does WISE Selling Work?

Yes, profoundly.

Not because I say so, but because it's built on timeless truths about human psychology, trust, and decision-making.

Here's why it works: **People don't change. The two fears are universal and permanent.** Every Customer who's ever walked into a retail store has been afraid of making a mistake and afraid of looking stupid. This was true 50 years ago. It's true today. It will be true 50 years from now.

WISE Selling works because it systematically addresses these permanent human realities. It works because it focuses on exceeding expectations by eliminating fears and building trust and not just completing transactions.

The 50/50 Principle isn't theory. It's reality. You've seen it yourself even if you didn't have the language for it. Customers who seemed happy never return. Customers who got what they came for buy elsewhere next time.

Now you understand why: You met expectations. You didn't exceed them. You sold them something but didn't eliminate their fears or build deep trust.

WISE Selling gives you the framework to exceed expectations systematically. Every Customer, every time.

Is It Worth the Investment?

Consider the alternative: continuing to deliver 50/50 experiences.

In a retail environment where Customers have infinite alternatives and can buy anything online at competitive prices, what happens to stores and salespeople operating at 50/50 odds?

They're constantly churning through new Customers because only half come back. They're competing on price because they haven't built loyalty. They're fighting for survival instead of thriving.

Salespeople and stores that consistently exceed expectations that deliver 98% return rates operate in a completely different reality. They have loyal Customer bases that return repeatedly. They generate referrals. They command premium prices because Customers trust them. They build sustainable businesses.

The math is simple:

50/50 approach: You need constant new Customer acquisition. You're replacing half your Customer base continuously. You're on a treadmill.

98% approach: Your Customer base compounds. Repeat Customers buy more over time. They refer others. You build sustainable growth.

The investment is time and effort to learn and apply WISE principles consistently.

The return is moving from 50/50 odds to 98% odds.

The ROI is extraordinary.

Can You Actually Change?

Yes, if you choose to.

Change is difficult. Your current habits - meeting expectations, being the hero, focusing on the sale - feel comfortable and familiar.

But here's the truth: If you keep doing what you're doing, you'll keep getting 50/50 results. Half of people you serve won't return. Is that acceptable to you?

You've changed before. You learned to read. You learned to drive. You learned your current job. You've developed countless skills through deliberate effort and practice.

This is no different.

The question isn't "Can you change?" It's "Will you commit to moving from 50/50 to 98%?"

That's a choice only you can make.

Your Implementation Path: From 50/50 to 98%

Don't try to implement everything simultaneously. That guarantees overwhelm and failure.

Instead, follow this progression by building one element at a time until exceeding expectations becomes natural:

Month 1: Master the Interview (The Foundation of Exceeding Expectations)

The Interview is where you separate yourself from 50/50 salespeople. Most salespeople ask the minimum questions needed to identify a product. You're going to become the guide who truly understands.

Week 1: Review Chapter 4 multiple times. Memorize the core question categories: past experience, expectations, conditions of use.

Week 2: Practice asking these questions in every Customer interaction. Don't worry about perfection. Just ask more questions and listen more carefully than you have before.

Notice what happens: You're uncovering information you never knew before. You're understanding their situation deeply. You're becoming their guide, not just an order-taker.

Week 3: Add the summarize-and-confirm technique. After gathering information, summarize what you learned and confirm accuracy: "Let me make sure I understand correctly…"

This shows compassion (you listened) and builds confidence (you understood).

Week 4: Begin adapting Interview depth to personality types. Practice identifying Analytical vs. Driver vs. Practical vs. Trendsetter and adjust your approach.

Track your progress: Are your Interviews getting longer? Are you uncovering information you wouldn't have discovered before? Are Customers responding positively, sharing more, seeming more engaged?

What success looks like: By the end of Month 1, your average Interview for purchases over $100 should be 5-10 minutes. Customers should be volunteering information. You should have detailed understanding of their specific needs.

This is what separates 50/50 from 98%. You've invested time understanding them. They feel heard. They're already thinking: "This person actually cares and gets what I need."

Month 2: Add Benefit Statements (Making Value Clear)

Continue strong Interview practice while adding benefit statements to Solution presentations.

Week 1: Review Chapter 9. Write benefit statements for your ten most frequently sold products using "This has, that means" formula.

Week 2: Practice these benefit statements in every Solution presentation. Say them out loud until they flow naturally.

Week 3: Begin connecting benefit statements to Interview findings using "Remember you mentioned" structure. This shows you listened and connects features to their specific situation.

Week 4: Expand benefit statements to more products. Practice translating any feature into a benefit on demand.

Track your progress: Are you using at least three benefit statements per Solution? Are Customers showing better understanding? Are objections decreasing?

What success looks like: Customers are nodding in understanding. They're not confused about why products matter. They're saying "That makes sense" and "I didn't realize that."

This is exceeding expectations. You're not just showing products—you're educating them on why products serve their specific needs. They leave informed and confident, not confused and uncertain.

Month 3: Integrate Multiplication (Complete Solutions)

Continue Interview and benefit statement excellence while adding multiplication.

Week 1: Review Chapter 10. List the essential accessories, performance enhancers, problem preventers, and complementary products for your main categories.

Week 2: Practice recommending 2-4 multiplication items with every transaction, connecting each to Interview findings.

Week 3: Refine your multiplication language. Stop saying "Would you like..." Start saying "To make sure you're completely set up for success, you'll also need..."

Week 4: Track multiplication rate and average transaction value.

Track your progress: What percentage of transactions now include multiplication items? Has average transaction value increased?

What success looks like: By the end of Month 3, 70%+ of your transactions include multiplication items. Average transaction value has increased 30-40%.

More importantly: Customers aren't returning frustrated because you forgot to tell them about something essential. They're succeeding because you gave them complete solutions.

This is exceeding expectations. They came for one thing, you ensured they had everything needed to succeed. That's being a guide, not a hero.

Month 4: Add Experience Phase Elements (Building the Relationship)

Continue everything from Months 1-3 while adding Experience components.

Week 1: Master lock-in. After every purchase decision, provide specific reinforcement referencing at least three Interview findings that explain why this solution is right for them.

Week 2: Ensure complete data capture. Every transaction gets a Customer profile with meaningful notes about their project, goals, and concerns.

Week 3: Implement thank-you follow-up. Every purchase gets 24-hour thank-you contact.

Week 4: Add check-in follow-up. Purchases over $200 get 1-2 week check-in: "How's it working? Any questions?"

Track your progress: Are you consistently locking in purchases? Is Customer information capture 100%? What percentage are getting follow-up?

What success looks like: Customers are leaving visibly confident. Follow-up completion rate is 90%+. Customers are responding positively: "Thanks for checking in—everything's working great!"

This is exceeding expectations. You didn't just sell them something and forget about them. You're invested in their success beyond the transaction.

This is what turns 50/50 into 98%.

Month 5: Strengthen Objection Handling

By now you're executing basic WISE framework reasonably well. Time to strengthen objection handling.

Week 1: Review Chapter 11. Memorize Soften and Ask structure. Remember: objections mean one or both fears are still active.

Week 2: Practice softening every objection before responding. Get comfortable with compassion phrases: "I completely understand..." "That's a fair concern..."

Week 3: Practice asking questions to uncover real objections: "Help me understand what's concerning you specifically..."

Week 4: Combine Soften and Ask fluidly. Address the real fear rather than the surface objection.

Track your progress: Are you resolving objections more successfully? Are conversion rates improving?

What success looks like: Objections feel like conversations instead of confrontations. You're hearing "That makes sense" after Soften and Ask.

This is exceeding expectations. Instead of getting defensive or pushy, you validated their concern (compassion) and addressed the real issue (confidence).

Month 6: Master Problem Resolution (Where 50/50 Becomes 98%)

You're now competent in all WISE phases. Time to master the most trust-building skill: problem resolution.

Week 1-2: Review the problem handling section in Chapter 12. Internalize this: The problem is NOT the problem. The broken trust is the problem.

Week 3: When problems occur (and they will), consciously apply the framework. Address emotions before logistics. Restore trust before fixing the product.

Week 4: Follow up after problem resolution to ensure satisfaction and rebuilt trust.

Track your progress: When problems occur, do Customers feel heard and taken care of? Are you retaining Customers who experience problems?

What success looks like: Problems that could have destroyed relationships actually strengthen them. Customers tell others: "Something went wrong, but they bent over backward to make it right. That's where you should shop."

This is where you prove the difference between 50/50 and 98%. Anyone can deliver when things go perfectly. Exceeding expectations means turning failures into loyalty-building moments.

Months 7-12: Build Consistent Mastery

Continue practicing all elements. Focus on:

Making it natural: WISE Selling should feel conversational, not scripted.

Adapting seamlessly: Quickly identify personality types and adjust your entire approach.

Handling complexity: Multiple decision-makers, unusual applications, challenging situations.

Coaching others: Teaching deepens your own mastery.

Continuous refinement: Every interaction is practice. Every month, focus intensive effort on your weakest area.

Mastery isn't perfection. It's consistently exceeding expectations and moving from 50/50 to 98%.

Measuring Your Progress: From 50/50 to 98%

How do you know if you're moving from 50/50 to 98%? Track these metrics:

Leading Indicators (immediate feedback):

- Average Interview duration for major purchases (should reach 5-10+ minutes)
- Number of benefit statements per Solution (should reach 3-5)
- Multiplication rate (should reach 70%+)
- Customer information capture completeness (should be 100%)
- Follow-up completion rate (should reach 90%+)

Lagging Indicators (results over time - this is where you see 50/50 becoming 98%):

- **Repeat purchase rate** (the ultimate measure is truly they coming back?)
- **Referral rate** (are they telling others?)
- Customer satisfaction scores
- Return rate (should decrease)
- Average transaction value (should increase 30-50%)
- Personal sales volume
- Customer reviews mentioning you by name
- Customers asking for you specifically

The most important metric: What percentage of Customers you serve return for their next purchase?

If it's around 50%, you're meeting expectations but not exceeding them.

If it's approaching 90%+, you're exceeding expectations and mastering WISE Selling.

Review these monthly. Improving trends confirm you're moving from 50/50 to 98%.

Overcoming Obstacles (Because They Will Come)

You will encounter obstacles. Anticipate and prepare for them:

Obstacle 1: "Meeting Expectations Should Be Good Enough"

This is the most dangerous obstacle because it feels reasonable.

"The Customer got what they came for. They seemed happy. That's good enough, right?"

Wrong.

That's 50/50 thinking. That's hero thinking. "I sold them shoes. I'm the hero."

Remember: 50/50 odds means you'll never see half of those "happy" Customers again. Can you build a career on 50/50?

Guide thinking says: "Did I eliminate their fears? Did I build trust? Did I exceed their expectations, so they'll definitely return?"

That's 98% thinking.

Obstacle 2: Time Pressure

"I don't have time for 10-minute Interviews when it's busy."

Reality: This is 50/50 thinking. Rush through shallow Interviews, get 50/50 results.

Thorough Interview creates 98% results. Those Customers return. They buy more. They refer others. They're worth the investment.

Better to serve three Customers excellently (98% return) than ten Customers adequately (50% return). Do the math on lifetime value.

Obstacle 3: "But I'm Already Successful"

Maybe you are. Maybe you're hitting your numbers, making decent money, doing fine.

But ask yourself honestly: What percentage of Customers you serve return for their next purchase?

If it's around 50%, you're operating on 50/50 odds even if you feel successful. You're constantly replacing half your Customer base. You're on a treadmill.

98% odds means your success compounds. Your Customer base grows. Your referrals multiply. Your income increases without working harder.

Fine is the enemy of great. 50/50 is the enemy of 98%.

Obstacle 4: Personal Discouragement

"I tried this and it didn't work" or "I'm not getting better fast enough."

Reality: Moving from 50/50 to 98% takes time. Skill development isn't linear. You'll have breakthroughs and plateaus.

What matters is the trend over months. Are more Customers returning? Are referrals increasing? Is average transaction value growing?

If yes, you're moving from 50/50 to 98%. Keep going.

Trust the process. Keep practicing. The compound effect of exceeding expectations builds over time.

The Power of 98%: What Changes When You Exceed Expectations

Here's what happens when you consistently exceed expectations:

You eliminate *both* fears for every Customer.

The Analytical leaves confident they made an informed decision. No fear of mistakes. No fear of looking stupid.

The Driver leaves confident they made a fast, correct decision. No fear of mistakes. No fear of looking stupid.

The Practical leaves confident they got exactly what they needed. No fear of mistakes. No fear of looking stupid.

The Trendsetter leaves confident they got something innovative and impressive. No fear of mistakes. No fear of looking stupid.

Every Customer, every time, regardless of personality type—both fears eliminated through compassion and confidence. Expectations exceeded.

That's what creates 98% return rates.

And here's the multiplication effect:

One Customer receiving a Remarkable Experience (98% category):

- Returns for their next purchase instead of shopping around
- Buys more because they trust your complete solution recommendations
- Refers friends and family
- Writes positive reviews
- Forgives problems because the relationship foundation is strong
- Becomes a source of sustainable income for years

One Customer receiving an adequate experience (50/50 category):

- Might return, might not (literal coin flip)
- Shops around for better prices
- Tells no one about you
- Leaves no reviews
- Blames you when problems occur
- Provides no sustainable value

This is why mastery matters. This is why moving from 50/50 to 98% changes everything.

Beyond Individual Mastery: Building 98% Culture

If you're a manager or owner, here's the truth: You can't build a business on 98% return rates if only one employee delivers Remarkable Experiences while everyone else delivers 50/50 experiences.

Cultural excellence means every team member, every Customer, every time achieves 98% odds.

Review Chapter 13 regularly. Your job is building a culture that makes exceeding expectations the standard, not the exception.

Your team will only sustain WISE Selling if you:

- Model it personally (you can't ask them for 98% while delivering 50/50 yourself)
- Establish clear standards (define what exceeding expectations is)
- Provide regular practice and coaching (weekly skill development)
- Measure what matters (track repeat purchase rates, not just sales volume)
- Celebrate excellence (recognize people who exceed expectations)
- Address 50/50 performance (coach those who just meet expectations)
- Protect culture (remove people who resist exceeding expectations)
- Invest resources (time, training, tools for 98% performance)

Individual excellence creates occasional 98% experiences.

Cultural excellence creates consistent 98% experiences.

Every Customer, every time. That only happens through culture, not individual heroics.

The Deeper Why: Beyond the Numbers

Let me close with something deeper than business metrics.

I spent years being the hero. I loved selling. I loved closing deals. I loved hitting numbers.

And I operated at 50/50 odds without realizing it.

It took me a long time to realize that being the guide meaning focusing on Customer success, eliminating fears, building trust, wasn't just better for business. It was better for me.

Being the hero is exhausting. You're constantly chasing new Customers to replace the ones who don't return. You're fighting for every sale. You're on a treadmill.

Being the guide is sustainable. Your Customers return. They refer others. You build relationships, not just transactions. You help people succeed at things they care about.

That's meaningful work.

When you eliminate fears and build trust, you're not just selling products. You're enabling success.

The marathon runner who finishes because you ensured they had complete solutions.

The family whose home renovation succeeds because you guided them through confident decisions.

The nervous novice who gains confidence because you made them feel safe.

These are real impacts on real lives.

WISE Selling transforms retail from transaction processing to value creation. From being the hero who sells stuff to being the guide who helps people succeed.

One perspective leads to 50/50 odds, burnout, and mediocrity.

The other leads to 98% odds, sustainability, and meaningful work.

Your choice matters.

Final Thoughts: From 50/50 to 98%

The gap between 50/50 and 98% is bridged by consistent practice over time.

Start tomorrow. Not "someday." Tomorrow.

Choose one element - probably Interview - and practice it deliberately for thirty days. Then add another element. Then another.

Six months from now, you'll see the numbers changing. More Customers returning. More referrals. Higher transaction values. Your work becoming more satisfying.

A year from now, WISE Selling will feel natural. You'll be operating consistently at 98% odds.

Five years from now, you'll have built a sustainable career based on Customers who trust you deeply, return reliably, and refer enthusiastically.

But only if you start. Only if you persist. Only if you choose 98% over 50/50.

Remember:

Every Customer walks in with two fears—fear of making a mistake and fear of looking stupid.

Your job is to eliminate both fears through compassion and confidence.

Your goal is to exceed expectations so consistently that 98% return.

That's what WISE Selling makes possible.

That's what separates being the hero (50/50) from being the guide (98%).

I believe you can achieve it.

The question is: Do you?

Your journey begins now.

Go be the guide. Eliminate fears. Build trust. Exceed expectations.

Every Customer, every time.

Welcome to the 98%.

Acknowledgments

No book is written alone, despite a single name appearing on the cover.

To the thousands of retail professionals I've worked with over decades – you taught me far more than I taught you. Your challenges, questions, successes, and struggles shaped every concept in this book. Your Customers' stories illustrate every principle. You are the real experts; I simply organized what you demonstrated.

To my mentors in retail and sales – particularly those who showed me that selling could be service, that consultation could be commerce, and that excellence could be systematic rather than accidental. Ron, Rich, Carter, Coleman.

To the researchers whose work forms the foundation of WISE Selling – psychologists studying trust and decision-making, behavioral economists revealing how people choose, communication scholars teaching us how to listen and persuade effectively. Your academic work has practical application, even if you never set foot in a retail store.

To my family – for tolerating the countless hours I spent writing, rewriting, editing, and refining. For understanding when I disappeared into my office for weekends and evenings. For believing this book mattered enough to justify the sacrifice. Catherine, Madeline, Alexa, Lily, Mindy.

To early readers who provided feedback on drafts – you caught errors, challenged assumptions, and asked questions that strengthened every chapter. I won't name you here in case people hate the book and want to blame you.

To retail business owners and managers willing to implement WISE principles and share results – you proved these concepts work across every category and context.

To Customers everywhere – though you'll never read this acknowledgment – thank you for the privilege of serving you. You make retail meaningful. You're why any of this matters.

And finally, **to you, the reader** – for investing time and mental energy in these pages. For caring enough about your craft to study it. For believing retail can be more than transactions. Your commitment to excellence will create Remarkable Experiences that ripple through communities and change lives in ways you may never fully know.

Thank you.

About the Author

Matthew Hudson has spent over three decades studying, practicing, and teaching retail excellence. His career spans frontline sales positions, store management, corporate training development, and retail consulting across dozens of industries.

He's trained over 10,000 retail professionals in specialty stores ranging from outdoor gear to jewelry, home improvement to photography, fitness equipment to furniture. He's consulted with independent retailers and major chains, luxury brands and value retailers, brick-and-mortar stores and omnichannel operations.

But his real education came from watching thousands of Customer interactions – some brilliant, some disastrous, most mediocre – and asking why some salespeople consistently create Remarkable Experiences while others struggle.

The WISE framework emerged from decades of observation, experimentation, and refinement. It synthesizes psychological research, sales best practices, and hard-won real-world experience into a systematic approach anyone can learn.

Throughout his career, Matthew has guided startups through their critical evolution into stable corporations, accumulating over 10,000 hours of sales training and more than 1,000 coaching sessions. His proven methodology has helped architect successful sales processes for numerous U.S. corporations and associations, consistently driving revenue growth while fostering positive cultural transformation.

Matthew has had the privilege of working with industry leaders including Dell, New Balance, Absolute Software, and Disney, bringing his expertise in sales process design, corporate culture transformation, and scalable growth infrastructure to organizations of all sizes. As an author, he has written nine books covering sales methodology, signage optimization, and corporate culture transformation, plus two children's books that showcase his creative versatility.

Beyond his corporate work, Dr. Hudson demonstrates his commitment to community impact through his founding of six non-profit organizations. He currently serves as President of the Layla Rose Ranch Horse Rescue in Texas, embodying the same leadership principles and passion for positive transformation that drive his professional endeavors.

You can reach him at matt@hudsonhead.com

Sources and Further Reading/ Development

WISE Selling synthesizes decades of research and practice. While this book presents concepts in accessible language for retail practitioners, the foundations come from rigorous academic and professional research.

Trust and Relationship Building

Miller, Donald R *Building a StoryBrand 2.0,* HarperEnfoque, 2025.

- Teaches you how to connect to Customers the way they want.

Covey, Stephen M.R. *The Speed of Trust: The One Thing That Changes Everything.* Free Press, 2006.

- Explores trust as competitive advantage and how to build it systematically

Maister, David H., Charles H. Green, and Robert M. Galford. *The Trusted Advisor.* Free Press, 2000.

- Foundation for trust equation: Credibility + Reliability + Intimacy / Self-Orientation

Zak, Paul J. *Trust Factor: The Science of Creating High-Performance Companies.* AMACOM, 2017.

- Neuroscience of trust and how organizational culture affects trust-building

Customer Psychology and Decision Making

Ariely, Dan. *Predictably Irrational: The Hidden Forces That Shape Our Decisions.* Harper, 2008.

- Behavioral economics revealing how people make decisions (vs how we think they do)

Cialdini, Robert B. *Influence: The Psychology of Persuasion.* Harper Business, 2006.

- Classic work on six principles of influence and persuasion

Kahneman, Daniel. *Thinking, Fast and Slow.* Farrar, Straus and Giroux, 2011.

- How people think and decide: System 1 (fast, emotional) vs System 2 (slow, rational)

Thaler, Richard H. and Cass R. Sunstein. *Nudge: Improving Decisions About Health, Wealth, and Happiness.* Yale University Press, 2008.

- How choice architecture influences decisions

Communication and Listening

Goulston, Mark. *Just Listen: Discover the Secret to Getting Through to Absolutely Anyone.* AMACOM, 2009.

- Techniques for deep listening and connecting with difficult people

Pink, Daniel H. *To Sell Is Human: The Surprising Truth About Moving Others.* Riverhead Books, 2012.

- Modern understanding of sales as service, clarifying questions, and attunement

Stone, Douglas, Bruce Patton, and Sheila Heen. *Difficult Conversations: How to Discuss What Matters Most.* Penguin Books, 2010.

- Framework for handling objections and difficult conversations

Retail-Specific Research and Practice

Berry, Leonard L. *Discovering the Soul of Service: The Nine Drivers of Sustainable Business Success.* Free Press, 1999.

- Service excellence principles applicable to retail

Paco Underhill. *Why We Buy: The Science of Shopping.* Simon & Schuster, 1999.

- Customer behavior in retail environments

Pine, B. Joseph II and James H. Gilmore. *The Experience Economy.* Harvard Business Review Press, 1999.

- Foundation for understanding experience as economic value

Sales Methodology

Rackham, Neil. *SPIN Selling.* McGraw-Hill, 1988.

- Research-based questioning methodology for consultative sales

Richardson, Linda. *Perfect Selling.* McGraw-Hill, 1997.

- Relationship-based selling emphasizing needs discovery

Ziglar, Zig. *Secrets of Closing the Sale.* Berkley, 1984.

- Classic sales techniques adapted for relationship selling

Organizational Culture

Collins, Jim. *Good to Great.* Harper Business, 2001.

- What separates great organizations from merely good ones

Groysberg, Boris, Jeremiah Lee, Jesse Price, and J. Yo-Jud Cheng. "The Leader's Guide to Corporate Culture." *Harvard Business Review*, January-February 2018.

- Framework for understanding and shaping culture

Hudson, Matthew. *Culturrific!* 2014

- How to build a terrific Experience Culture in your business

Kotter, John P. *Leading Change.* Harvard Business Review Press, 2012.

- Process for creating organizational change

Lencioni, Patrick. *The Advantage: Why Organizational Health Trumps Everything Else in Business.* Jossey-Bass, 2012.

- Building healthy organizational culture

Customer Experience

Dixon, Matthew, Karen Freeman, and Nicholas Toman. "Stop Trying to Delight Your Customers." *Harvard Business Review*, July-August 2010.

- Research showing that reducing Customer effort matters more than delight

Reichheld, Fred. *The Ultimate Question 2.0: How Net Promoter Companies Thrive in a Customer-Driven World.* Harvard Business Review Press, 2011.

- Net Promoter Score and Customer loyalty measurement

Schmitt, Bernd. *Experiential Marketing: How to Get Customers to Sense, Feel, Think, Act, Relate.* Free Press, 1999.

- Framework for creating experiences beyond functional benefits

Additional Resources

While the above books provide theoretical foundation, much of WISE Selling comes from:

- **Observing thousands of Customer interactions** across dozens of retail categories
- **Testing techniques** with real Customers and measuring results
- **Training feedback** from thousands of retail professionals sharing what works in practice
- **Customer feedback** revealing what creates remarkable experiences
- **Business metrics** showing correlation between practices and outcomes

The academic research validates and explains why WISE principles work. The real-world practice proves they work and refines how to apply them effectively.

For Continued Learning

Retail excellence is a journey, not a destination. Continue learning through:

- **Industry publications** specific to your retail category
- **Manufacturer training** on products you sell
- **Professional associations** connecting retail professionals
- **Customer feedback** as continuous source of learning
- **Peer learning** from colleagues executing WISE exceptionally
- **Practice and reflection** on your own interactions

Mastery requires continuous learning. Never stop studying your craft.

Matthew Hudson. PhD Author

WISE Selling The Art of Creating Remarkable Experiences Every Customer Every Time

www.ingramcontent.com/pod-product-compliance
Lightning Source LLC
Chambersburg PA
CBHW051034160426
43193CB00010B/937